WIELAND WAGNER:

THE POSITIVE SCEPTIC

Wieland Wagner in 1965

WIELAND WAGNER:
THE POSITIVE SCEPTIC

by

GEOFFREY SKELTON

ST MARTIN'S PRESS
NEW YORK

AFFILIATED PUBLISHERS: Macmillan & Company Limited, London,
also at Bombay, Calcutta, Madras and Melbourne
The Macmillan Company of Canada Limited, Toronto

Every new production is a step on the way to an unknown goal—WIELAND WAGNER

The art of the theatre is the same in one respect as any other art. It is the work of one man. Unlike most other arts it can only be seen and heard during the life of the man who creates it. It cannot be copied for future generations by future theatrical artists. It is necessary, then, that it must be accepted whilst the artist is still living—GORDON CRAIG

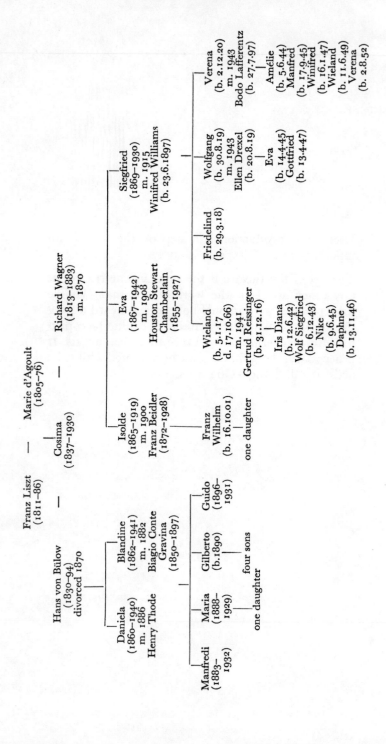

Franz Liszt (1811–86) — Marie d'Agoult (1805–76)

Richard Wagner (1813–1883) — Cosima (1837–1930), m. 1870

Hans von Bülow (1830–94), divorced 1870

Daniela (1860–1940), m. 1886, Henry Thode

Blandine (1862–1941), m. 1882, Biagio Conte Gravina (1850–1897)

Isolde (1865–1919), m. 1900, Franz Beidler (1872–1928)

Eva (1867–1942), m. 1908, Houston Stewart Chamberlain (1855–1927)

Siegfried (1869–1930), m. 1915, Winifred Williams (b. 23.6.1897)

Manfredi (1883–1932)

Maria (1888–1929), one daughter

Gilberto (b.1890), four sons

Guido (1896–1931)

Franz Wilhelm (b. 16.10.01), one daughter

Wieland (b. 5.1.17, d. 17.10.66), m. 1941, Gertrud Reissinger (b. 31.12.16)

Iris Diana (b. 12.6.42)
Wolf Siegfried (b. 6.12.43)
Nike (b. 9.6.45)
Daphne (b. 13.11.46)

Friedelind (b. 29.3.18)

Wolfgang (b. 30.8.19), m. 1943, Ellen Drexel (b. 20.8.19)

Eva (b. 14.4.45)
Gottfried (b. 13.4.47)

Verena (b. 2.12.20), m. 1943, Bodo Lafferentz (b. 27.7.97)

Amélie (b. 5.6.44)
Manfred (b. 17.9.45)
Winifred (b. 16.1.47)
Wieland (b. 11.6.49)
Verena (b. 2.8.52)

CONTENTS

Chapter

Introduction   11

1 Hitler and Bayreuth   19

2 Creation of a Dynasty   26

3 1917–30: Childhood Years   33

4 1930–6: Changing Influences   39

5 1936–8: First Stage Designs   49

6 1938–42: Study in Munich   58

7 1943–4: Producing in Altenburg and Nuremberg   64

8 1944–5: End of an Illusion   78

9 1945–8: The Creative Black Years   81

10 1949–51: Preparations in Bayreuth   92

11 1951–2: First Bayreuth Productions   104

12 1953: Repercussions   113

13 1954: Editing Masterpieces   121

14 1955–6: The Theatrical Idea   130

15 1957–9: Completing the Canon   138

16 1960: Desire for Change   148

17 1961–2: Signs and Symbols   154

18 1962–5: High Pressure   165

19 1965: Second Production of the Ring   176

20 1966: The Final Year   187

21 Conclusion   193

    Appendices
    Stage Settings and Productions by Wieland
       Wagner   203

    Bibliography   215

    Index   217

LIST OF ILLUSTRATIONS

Wieland Wagner in 1965 (*S. Lauterwasser*)   *Frontispiece*

Facing page

Wieland, aged one, with his grandmother Cosima, aged eighty-one (*Richard Wagner Archiv, Bayreuth*)   30

Wieland, aged five, with his father and mother, brother and sisters (*Richard Wagner Archiv*)   30

Wieland, aged twenty-one, as a soldier (*Richard Wagner Archiv*)   31

Wieland, aged twenty-seven, with his wife Gertrud and their children Iris and Wolf Siegfried (*Richard Wagner Archiv*)   31

Wieland, aged twenty-nine: self-portrait (*Richard Wagner Archiv*)   40

Oil painting by Wieland, 1939: *Im Atelier* (*Richard-Wagner-Gedenkstätte Bayreuth*)   40

Wieland, aged thirty-five, at rehearsals in the *Festspielhaus* (*S. Lauterwasser*)   41

Wieland, aged forty-eight, rehearsing Brünnhilde with Birgit Nilsson in Bayreuth (*S. Lauterwasser*)   56

Wieland, aged forty-nine, rehearsing Berg's *Lulu* with Anja Silja and Carlos Alexander in Stuttgart (*S. Lauterwasser*)   57

Reception hall in Wahnfried in Cosima's days (*Richard Wagner Archiv*)   64

The same after post-war conversion (*S. Lauterwasser*)   64

Wahnfried (*S. Lauterwasser*)   65

The *Festspielhaus*, Bayreuth (*Festspiele Bayreuth: Heinz Eysell*)   65

Parsifal, 1937: The Temple of the Grail (*Richard-Wagner-Gedenkstätte*)   96

Parsifal, 1951: The Temple of the Grail (*Festspiele Bayreuth: Wilhelm Rauh*)   96

Rheingold, Scene Two: first Bayreuth production (*Festspiele Bayreuth: S. Lauterwasser*)   97

Rheingold, Scene Two: second Bayreuth production (*Festspiele Bayreuth: Wilhelm Rauh*)   97

Die Walküre, Act One: first Bayreuth production (*Festspiele Bayreuth: Adolf Falk*)   108

Die Walküre, Act One: second Bayreuth production (*Festspiele Bayreuth: Wilhelm Rauh*)   108

Tristan und Isolde, Act Three: first Bayreuth production (*Festspiele Bayreuth: Schwennicke*)   109

Tristan und Isolde, Act Three: second Bayreuth production (*Festspiele Bayreuth: Wilhelm Rauh*)   109

Tannhäuser, Act Two: first Bayreuth production (*Festspiele Bayreuth: S. Lauterwasser*)   116

Tannhäuser, Act Two: second Bayreuth production (*Festspiele Bayreuth: S. Lauterwasser*)   116

Fidelio at Stuttgart, 1954 (*Werner Schloske, Stuttgart*)   117

Die Meistersinger, The Festival Meadow: first Bayreuth production (*Festspiele Bayreuth: S. Lauterwasser*)   128

Die Meistersinger, The Festival Meadow: second Bayreuth production (*Festspiele Bayreuth: S. Lauterwasser*)   129

Lohengrin at Bayreuth: Act Two (*Festspiele Bayreuth: Wilhelm Rauh*)   160

Lohengrin at the Metropolitan, New York: Act One (*Louis Mélancon, New York*)   160

Der Fliegende Holländer at Bayreuth: Scene One (*Festspiele Bayreuth: Ilse Buhs*)   161

Carmen in Hamburg, 1958: final scene (*Peyer, Hamburg*)   168

Salome in Stuttgart, 1962 (*Werner Schloske, Stuttgart*)   169

Aida in Berlin, 1961: Amneris's room (*Ilse Buhs, Berlin*)   184

Otello at Frankfurt, 1965: Act One (*Günter Englert, Frankfurt-am-Main*)   184

The grave in the Bayreuth town cemetery (*Richard Wagner Archiv*)   185

Wieland's handwriting (Letter to Overhoff, 15 September 1944)   76

Parsifal's Cross: a psychological pattern by Wieland Wagner   106

INTRODUCTION

LIKE PALLAS ATHENE, Wieland Wagner appeared to spring fully formed and fully armed on a surprised world. His production of *Parsifal*, which reopened the Bayreuth Festival after the Second World War in 1951, proclaimed in unmistakable terms a new approach to the works of Richard Wagner which was in the following years to influence opera production throughout the world. At that time he was thirty-four years old and known only to a handful of people—inside Germany as well as outside—and that alone on the strength of being Richard Wagner's grandson. It was certainly not enough in itself to gain the world's attention.

There was of course some interest in what Wieland and his younger brother Wolfgang, now succeeding their mother, would do in an attempt to rehabilitate their grandfather on his own home ground after Hitler had so disastrously compromised him, and no doubt whatever they did would have attracted publicity at the time. The fact that they chose to throw all tradition overboard would not in itself, however, have aroused permanent interest unless it had been, first, convincing and, second, sustained.

In the following fifteen years, until his death in 1966 at the age of forty-nine, Wieland proved beyond all doubt that he possessed a real and important talent and an original outlook on operatic production that was applicable not only to the works of his grandfather, but to those of composers as diverse as Gluck, Beethoven, Verdi, Bizet, Richard Strauss, Alban Berg and Carl Orff. He was not always successful, but certainly he was always invigorating and controversial. Everything he did was as fiercely attacked as it was defended. This was as he wished it to be. He was not a man of compromises. He had three favourite sayings. One was Richard Wagner's *Kinder, schafft Neues* (Do something new); another was Franz Liszt's *Der Buchstabe tötet den Geist* (The letter kills the spirit); and the third Gustav Mahler's *Tradition heisst Schlamperei* (Tradition means not bothering). To these he added a fourth of his own: *Mittellinie bedeutet Mittelmass* (Compromise equals mediocrity).

Wieland Wagner was a truly revolutionary spirit, and it is in the nature of revolutionaries that they do not care to acknowledge indebtedness to anybody but themselves. Wieland certainly possessed this characteristic. When asked about the people who had influenced him, he might grudgingly mention a few names such as Adolphe Appia, Gordon Craig or Bertolt Brecht, but always with a critical reference to their limitations as far as he himself was concerned. He acknowledged no living teachers, preferring to describe himself as self-taught. And he was reluctant to talk at all about his life before 1951. If he mentioned such inescapable factors as his parents, his home surroundings or the Nazi times in which he grew up, it would always be in a disparaging way. He did not speak of "my grandfather", but always of "Richard Wagner" or at most *der Alte* (the old man).

This is a sign of the psychological process of disassociation. Wieland evidently found it necessary to put a deliberate distance between himself and his grandfather in order to win the freedom to regard him as "one of the greatest composers in history, a universal figure like Aeschylus, Shakespeare and Calderon". These words, quoted from the Foreword which Wieland wrote for my book *Wagner at Bayreuth: Experiment and Tradition*, provide a convincing answer to those detractors who suggest that Wieland's method of presenting Richard Wagner's works was a deliberate attempt to destroy them, an act of revenge against an overpowering ancestor who, by building a shrine for himself at Bayreuth and putting his own family in charge of it, had restricted his grandson's freedom to develop in his own way as an individual.

There was certainly an element of personal rebellion in Wieland's approach, but it was directed less against Richard Wagner than against the composer's family—in particular against Cosima, his own grandmother, who had sought to lay down eternal rules for the production of Wagner's works, based on the composer's own methods of dealing with them. This had been a perfectly legitimate act in its own time, as Wieland freely admitted, but he blamed Cosima (he called her

"Cosima", never "my grandmother") for her priestess-like attitude, which made any questioning of her doctrine seem like blasphemy. In his own mind his divergences from accepted practice in presenting the music dramas were acts of rebellion against Cosima, not against the composer.

It was a necessary act of self-preservation that impelled Wieland and his brother Wolfgang, when they gained control of the Bayreuth Festival, to play down the "German supremacy" angle of Wagner's works, which had naturally been exploited in the Nazi era. But the huge and enduring impact of the new Bayreuth style, as Wieland's work in the *Festspielhaus* came to be called, cannot be explained in terms of negatives. It was a matter of positive achievement, of genuine talent.

There is a sort of talent—the sort we call genius—which can be regarded as truly inborn. No one can really explain what it is that produces from otherwise undistinguished parental combinations such towering geniuses as Richard Wagner. Wieland had no obvious inborn talent—except perhaps, in a very modest way, in the field of painting, where his genuine if unexciting ability sprang from no easily seen inherited source. In the field of theatrical production his talent was clearly the result of heredity, opportunity and character.

Anybody who knew Wieland personally during his lifetime, even as superficially as I did, would have no difficulty in recognising the character qualities he inherited from his grandfather Richard Wagner, whom he clearly resembled outwardly: that mixture of aggression and vulnerability that, for those living close to him, could make life very difficult. Less easily seen were the qualities he inherited from his great-grandfather Franz Liszt: possibly because Liszt did not leave so much evidence of them lying about. But Wagner's son Siegfried once defined them. In Liszt, he said, there were elements of St Francis, Dionysos and Wotan—not so much combined as in contrast to one another. In Wieland these qualities were perhaps more closely combined, and in consequence mutually inhibiting. But they were there.

From his father, Siegfried, Wieland inherited certainly his left-handedness, perhaps the quiet voice and the outward stillness, but not the humour and sociability which endeared Siegfried to so many. Winifred Wagner, his mother, is British by birth, and that to the German mind presupposes practicality and pragmatism. We in this country know better, and in any case do not fall into the error, common to all foreigners, of labelling everyone English who comes from the British Isles. Winifred Williams, as she was named before her marriage, was born in Hastings, but her father was Welsh and her mother half Danish. All the same, Winifred Wagner is by nature a practical person, and it is fairly clear that *that* side of the heritage went to Wolfgang rather than to Wieland. In fact, I could never see anything at all "English" in Wieland Wagner. He certainly could not speak the language, though he had studied it at school for a few years.

The only true German in Wieland's pedigree was Richard Wagner himself. It might have been a way out of the post-Nazi dilemma to have played up his polyglot heritage, but Wieland claimed no exoneration on his own behalf. He strove, quite rightly, to stress the universality (in an artistic sense) of his grandfather, but he never attempted to deny that he himself was in every sense a German of the generation that, if not guilty of bringing Hitler to power, had supported him blindly in the final holocaust. Inwardly he accepted his share of the collective guilt, and his active years after the war could be seen as his way of trying to atone and make good the terrible damage his nation had done to the world.

It is true that he publicly acknowledged no personal guilt, and there is no reason to suppose that there *was* any personal guilt to acknowledge. But in fact he had been very close to Hitler in his childhood and youth. It was a part of his life that he preferred not to dwell on. Hence the impression, which he himself helped to foster, that life began for him after the war, when all that was over and done with.

His attitude was understandable. The Bayreuth Festival is, after all, a business as well as an artistic enterprise. Having worked so hard and so successfully to re-establish it in a post-Hitlerian world, Wieland was obviously reluctant to see old suspicions and resentments aroused by an examination of its Nazi past, however small a role he might himself have played in it. The dangers were all the greater since his mother was still alive and openly unrepentant. Though playing no active part in the running of the festival, she enjoyed great popularity in the town of Bayreuth—even among those who had no sympathy with her political views—for her honesty in standing up for her beliefs, when practically all others in Germany were busy pretending that their allegiance to Hitler had been on the surface only.

The grandsons felt it was safest to put a blanket of silence over Bayreuth's past, trusting to time to bring forgetfulness. But, paradoxically, they themselves created the conditions which made it impossible for this policy to succeed. Their new Bayreuth was far too original and startling to be accepted without question. One was bound to ask why and how it came about.

Such questions cannot be answered by silence. Why indeed should they be? Bayreuth has nothing really to hide. And, if it had, it would not be the fault of the grandsons, both of whom were children when Hitler came to power, and neither of whom were allowed any say in the running of the festival while their mother was in charge of it. If things happened then of which they disapproved (and many things did), they seized their chance when their own time came to put them right. Consequently it can do no harm to Wieland and his brother, at this distance of time, to identify these things and consider the part they played in Wieland's artistic development. On the contrary, it can only show how thoroughly Wieland repudiated the tyranny of his past and how genuinely he strove to create something more worthy to replace it.

Possibly Wieland would not thank me for my efforts, however good their intentions and however firmly based on my admiration and respect for his achievements. His brother Wolfgang certainly has his doubts, and he sought to discourage me from writing a complete biography of Wieland. As he pointed out, there is so much that is obscure and insufficiently substantiated that such a book at this stage would lack a scientific basis. It is a valid argument as far as it goes, but against it I put up the counter-argument that Wieland's achievement is by its very nature ephemeral: already most of his revolutionary productions have been withdrawn from the stage, and those that can still be seen (at Bayreuth and elsewhere) are only second-hand, as it were—kept alive by former associates who, however devoted, are nevertheless not Wieland himself. To do justice to his work, it is therefore essential that both he and it should be written about in as much detail as possible while memories are still strong. Such writings, if too personally motivated to be regarded as fully authoritative, will at the very least keep the subject alive until such time as a "scientifically based" biography can be produced by others who, having got all the facts indisputably right, might nevertheless have difficulty in breathing life into the all-but-forgotten subject. (What would we not give nowadays for some contemporary accounts of William Shakespeare and Henry Purcell?)

Anyway, the reader has now been warned not to regard this book as an authoritative biography, though he can be assured that I have done my best to get the facts right. This has not always been easy. Wieland's own reticence about his personal life is still observed by some of his close associates, who for various reasons preferred not to speak to me about him. Others, friends as well as enemies, though willing to speak, obviously spoke from their own point of view, so that I was faced at times with downright contradictory evidence. In such cases I have had to draw my own conclusions. There are inevitably some matters about which I have been unable to write openly out of consideration for persons still living.

Among those with whom I did speak or correspond were Wieland's widow Gertrud, his son Wolf Siegfried and his youngest daughter Daphne, his mother, his sister Verena and her husband Bodo Lafferentz, his cousin Count Gilbert Gravina and the following friends and associates (in alphabetical order): Dr Joachim Bergfeld, Professor Ernst Bloch, Dr Helmut Danzer, Paul Eberhardt, Professor Rudolf Hartmann, Professor Adolf Hopf, Siegfried Lauterwasser, Walter Legge, Ernst Lüsenhop, Erich Maschat, Professor Carl Orff, Professor Kurt Overhoff, Curt Palm, Professor Wolfgang Sawallisch, Professor Wolfgang Schadewaldt, Walter Erich Schäfer, Hildegard Sievert, Anja Silja and Gertrud Strobel.

I have drawn on material gathered from Wieland Wagner himself and other associates in connection with my previous book and the series of broadcasts about the Bayreuth Festival and the Wagner family which I made at various times for the British Broadcasting Corporation.

I have also made use of Wieland's own writings (of which

there are unfortunately very few) and the various accounts of him and his work that have been published either as books or in newspapers and periodicals. These are acknowledged either in the bibliography at the end of my book or within the text itself.

HITLER AND BAYREUTH

I HAD THE feeling when I set out to write this book that I was embarking on something more than just an account of the life of a very eminent man in a rather restricted field of artistic activity—that of operatic production. In a wider sense Wieland Wagner stands as representative of the Germany of his generation. This was the generation that came to maturity in the Hitler period. Innocent victims of it in the sense that they were imbued with its ideas at an age at which they could have had no judgment to resist them, they were the ones who had in the end to take up weapons to fight the war into which Hitler's ideas inevitably led them. Those who emerged alive after the defeat had to pay the cost. Politically discredited, they were looked on with suspicion by a world that was slow in sorting out the good from the bad (and made many mistakes in the process). And even then they were not wholeheartedly accepted. It was only the succeeding generation—their children—who were given the ordinary courtesy of being considered innocent until they were proved guilty. Their parents had to live under the strain, which most of us escape, of having to show their good faith by active deeds, liable always to be confronted with their past by others envious of their occasional success.

In this situation Wieland Wagner occupied an unenviably exposed position. Richard Wagner had founded a dynasty in Bayreuth, and one in which his own brand of German fanaticism, formed in a very different context, was cultivated and expanded by his disciples and successors until it merged with the far more dangerous nationalism of Hitler. Very possibly Siegfried and his wife and sisters, Houston Stewart Chamberlain and Hans von Wolzogen, indulging in their dream of the restoration of national pride squandered by Kaiser Wilhelm in the First World War, did not immediately recognise Hitler for the ruthless militant he was. They first got to know him just before the Munich *Putsch* of 1924, when his failure and subsequent imprisonment could not have raised alarm in their breasts at his efficiency so much as sympathy for his ineffectuality. By the time they (or such of them as were still alive) had grounds for recognising him as what he was, it was already too late.

In any case, as far as Bayreuth was concerned, fate played right into Hitler's hands. In 1930, just before he came to power, both Cosima Wagner and her son Siegfried died. At the age of thirty-three Winifred Wagner found herself in charge of the festival, appointed by the terms of her husband's will to look after it until their four children, equal inheritors, were old enough and able enough to take over. Her position was a weak one. Young, inexperienced and of non-German birth, she was vulnerable to intrigues and jealousies on all sides. First, there were her sisters-in-law, two of whom (Daniela and Eva) had been an integral part of Cosima's and Siegfried's Bayreuth. They had known the master in the flesh and considered themselves better guardians of his decrees than their brother's young wife. Second, there were the artists, who thought they could take advantage of Winifred's lack of formal training as a musician and producer to seize more power for themselves. And, third, there were the Nazi party officials, who saw no reason why Bayreuth should be excluded from their reforming zeal.

Winifred, justifiably anxious for her little realm, saw her salvation in a direct appeal to Hitler's friendship. He responded eagerly. Not only did he make it clear to the party that Winifred enjoyed his personal protection, but he demonstrated his confidence in her by doing something that no German head of state since Wagner's patron, King Ludwig II of Bavaria, had ever done: he attended the festivals in person. Winifred had beaten down her enemies, and at that time felt no need to count the cost. Indeed, she probably did not see it in that light at all, since she was in sympathy with Hitler's political aims. The immediate benefit, after a shaky start, was clear in terms of improving box-office receipts.

Why did Hitler give Bayreuth this special position in his heart? There were several reasons, of which only a few might have been political. Among those were the need to demonstrate to his party officials that he was the boss, and what better way than by insisting on his right—in relatively minor matters—to make his own decisions? He was also astute enough to realise that a small dash of inconsistency in his personal behaviour might do more good than harm to his public image: it would make him appear more human, thereby comforting his friends while disconcerting his enemies. Yet another political reason was that Winifred was British by birth, and Hitler never abandoned his dream of winning the British to his side: he used her more than once as a go-between at state receptions and ambassadorial meetings.

But there were certainly more personal feelings involved, chief among them his immense and genuine veneration for the music of Wagner. Like the young Ludwig, he succumbed first of all to *Lohengrin*, which he first heard at Linz while still a child. Wieland had a theory that it was from *Lohengrin* that he later took the title of *Führer* for himself—basing it on Lohengrin's call to the people at the end of the opera: *Zum Führer sei er euch ernannt!*

Hitler knew all the music dramas thoroughly by the time he found himself in Bayreuth for the first time. He was there in October 1923 for a political rally, and he seized the opportunity to call at Wahnfried. The friendly reception that this still obscure young politician received in Richard Wagner's house must have aroused in him a deep sense of gratitude which was never forgotten. He had been accepted on equal terms by Richard Wagner's son and his young wife, who had thus recognised him as worthy of the god whose shrine they guarded. He came again in the following year, when he was allowed to visit the innermost recesses of the *Festspielhaus*, and then several times more, when he got to know the four young children and was called by them "Onkel Wolf". He was a popular uncle. Wieland in fact in very young years is reported to have thrown his arms round Hitler and cried, "You should be our daddy, and daddy should be our uncle."

It was a childish remark, not to be taken seriously, but it does throw some psychological light on both the persons concerned. It shows, on Wieland's side, a sense of remoteness from his own father and, on Hitler's side, that capacity,

inexplicable to all (like myself) who did not know him personally,
to inspire affection. Hitler had no family of his own, and here
was a ready-made family prepared to accept him and, what is
more, a family of young Wagners.

Siegfried's death cemented the relationship. The young
children were in need of a father, and Hitler was ready to fill
the gap, as far as his increasing political responsibilities
allowed him. Any complications that might have arisen in his
relationship with their mother were neatly resolved by the
clause in Siegfried's will that Winifred should remain in charge
of the festival only so long as she did not remarry. In that case
the direction of the festival would pass into the hands of the
Bayreuth town authorities. Winifred had no intention of
allowing this to happen. So Hitler had the advantage of a
family without the added complication of a wife.

He also had the advantage that he was in no way legally
responsible for the children and their mother. The relationship was based entirely on mutual regard, with no sense of
obligation on either side. Hitler helped when he was asked, but
he never pressed his attentions on the family. Their personal
meetings were rare. Sometimes Winifred, and the children too
as they grew older, would visit him in Berlin and occasionally,
when he was in the neighbourhood, he would drop into
Wahnfried incognito and enjoy a few hours as Onkel Wolf in
the family circle.

Hitler was particularly interested in Wieland, who was the
eldest Wagner grandson and therefore in Hitler's mind the
predestined heir to Bayreuth and Wahnfried. When the time
came he expressed this feeling by exempting Wieland from
military service on the grounds that his duty was to preserve
and perpetuate the family name. Wieland was consequently
one of the few young Germans who did not serve as a soldier
during the Second World War, but for reasons that were to
be of no help to him afterwards. He was in fact by that decree
more identified with Hitler than his own brother Wolfgang,
who was called up as a soldier at the very beginning of the
war and served in the Polish campaign, where he was severely
wounded.

This was one of the ironies in Wieland's life that must have
done much to influence his subsequent development as a

revolutionary. Hitler, the beloved uncle of his childhood and his main protector in later years, was in the end unmasked as an ogre. It had taken Wieland a very long time to recognise the fact. It always seems incredible to outsiders that Germans claim not to have known anything of the brutalities in the concentration camps until the Nazi régime had been wiped out. But this is to ignore both the patriotic emotions of the time and the efficiency of the Nazi machine in covering up its tracks. A family as close to Hitler as the Wagners were might have been expected to know more than most, yet it could easily have worked the other way. There is the ordinary human tendency not to believe the worst of people of whom one is personally fond, coupled (in this case) with the sense of being at one with Hitler against his own party. More than once, and not only on her own behalf, Winifred had brought cases of injustice and inhumanity on the part of Nazi officials to Hitler's notice, and Hitler had apparently put matters right. It was with his approval that she continued to engage Jewish or Jewish-connected artists for the festival long after they had been driven out of German opera houses elsewhere. Thus the tendency inside Wahnfried was to believe in Hitler personally and to despise the party, which appeared to the privileged Wagner circle sorely to abuse his trust.

The sort of anti-Semitism prevailing in Wahnfried was the sort defined by Richard Wagner himself: the Jews were an alien race with no roots in the Germanic culture which, through their genius for management and their clannishness, they attempted to monopolise. Though, according to this doctrine, it was right to resist their efforts in general, one could still remain on terms of personal friendship with individual Jews, if it was advantageous to do so. Though Winifred did not go so far as Richard Wagner, who engaged a Jewish conductor, Hermann Levi, to direct the first performances of *Parsifal*, she did retain Franz von Hoesslin, who had a Jewish wife, as one of her principal conductors right up to 1940. This, in the circumstances of the time, was even more provocative an act than Richard Wagner's engagement of Levi, yet it cannot and should not be taken as a deliberate demonstration of disapproval against a policy of anti-Semitism. It was rather the tendency, common to most human beings, to except themselves from the implications of a policy in which they might theoretically even believe.

However, Hitler, who preferred to leave the unsavoury details of his anti-Semitic policy to people like Himmler and Streicher who enjoyed carrying them out, would in any case have been unlikely to spend his few hours with his "family" in Bayreuth discussing atrocities against the Jews. He would have been far more ready to talk about singers, production plans and the children's progress at school. He was also interested in Wieland's paintings, having once had ambitions in that direction himself.

Hitler's recognition of Wieland as the direct heir to Bayreuth was not entirely shared by the family itself. This was another of the ironies which had a significant influence on Wieland's character. His father Siegfried can be excused for not having realised his artistic qualities as a child. Keen on drawing as Wieland was from a very early age, he showed no outstanding talent for it. A chalk drawing which Wieland made at the age of twelve for his father's fifty-ninth birthday, preserved in the archives at Wahnfried, is in no way different from what any child of that age would have done. About this time (1928) Siegfried made his will, which was to come into effect not much more than two years later. No doubt memories of his own difficulties, when as a young man he had to decide whether to do the expected thing and accept his Bayreuth inheritance or follow his own inclinations to become an architect, made him resolve not to tie down his own elder son in the same way. In leaving Bayreuth to his four children equally, he left it to time to decide which of them had the inclination and talent to take it on, thus freeing the others from any sense of obligation.

However sensible and liberal the theory, the practice subsequently proved the danger of good intentions. Not only did Siegfried tie down his own wife to perpetual widowhood from the age of thirty-three, but he also failed to foresee the consequences if all or at any rate more than one of his children should show interest in assuming the inheritance. This is in fact what happened—providing, in an already quarrel-prone family, opportunities enough for further disputes.

The main sufferer, at least in his own mind, was Wieland. On top of the usual psychological difficulties of an eldest child, arising from the traumatic experience of no longer possessing exclusively its mother's love, he was now deprived of the traditional material compensation for them: the undisputed heritage. He had to compete with his own brother and sisters for the right to take over from his mother.

But, before entering into the details of the struggle, it will be necessary to describe more of the family background against which it was waged.

2

CREATION OF A DYNASTY

THE LITTLE TOWN of Bayreuth, set among low, pine-covered hills in the province of Franconia, had lost all its former glory at the time Richard Wagner decided to settle there and build a theatre for the performance of his own works. Once a principality, it had reached its peak in the eighteenth century, when the moving spirit was the Markgravine Wilhelmine, a sister of Frederick the Great. She had succeeded in introducing a note of royal dignity into it, building a large residence in classical style in the town itself, a summer residence a few miles outside and a magnificent baroque opera house which possessed the largest stage in Germany.

These three buildings—*Schloss*, *Erimitage* and *Markgräfliches Theater*—were hardly more than museum pieces when in 1871 Wagner arrived in Bayreuth on a tour of inspection. His hopes of putting the great stage of the *Markgräfliches Theater* to use in the production of his works proved impracticable: it was the wrong shape, and the auditorium was too small. But in the town itself he saw exciting possibilities. There was plenty of room to build a theatre of his own according to his own specifications. King Ludwig II could occupy the royal residence, which in any case now belonged to the Bavarian crown, and thus escape from the Munich they both hated. And Wagner could build himself a house nearby. Now at last they could realise their dream of a temple of German art in a lovely setting, free from all other distractions, social or political.

Only part of this plan was realised. The town authorities, seeing a chance of recovering some of its former glory, gladly gave Wagner a plot of land on which to build his *Festspielhaus*. And to one side of the park surrounding the royal residence Wagner acquired a site for the erection of a house of his own. King Ludwig, however, had no intention of settling in Bayreuth. He had already begun to build romantic castles in remote corners of the Alps, and the classical splendours of the Markgravine's residence had no attractions for him. The palace remained empty, while beside it Wahnfried arose and—on top of a hill at the other end of the town—the *Festspielhaus*.

From then on these two buildings, and the activity that arose from them, dominated the town. Bayreuth had indeed been given new life, but it had not become, as it might have done, the artistic centre of the Bavarian monarchy: it was the centre of an exclusively Wagnerian society, and life in the town revolved around the festival. The hotels and restaurants were filled with singers and musicians, and at festival times even the private houses made a little extra money by letting rooms to visitors. Houses were built or taken over permanently by Wagner's associates and assistants, such men as Baron Hans von Wolzogen, Houston Stewart Chamberlain and the conductor Hans Richter.

Wahnfried, into which Richard Wagner and his family moved on 28 April 1874, is a large house, though by royal standards modest enough. A square building, it is set in the centre of a large garden screened from the road at the front by a blank stone wall. A straight drive leads between trees and lawns to the front door, before which stands a bronze bust of the young King Ludwig II. The flat front of the house is adorned with a *sgraffito* panel depicting the Art Work of the Future. Hope for the future is represented by the figure of a boy with the features of Wagner's own son Siegfried. With him are personifications of the German myth (represented by Wagner's first Tristan, Ludwig Schnorr von Carolsfeld); antique tragedy (Wilhelmine Schröder-Devrient, his first Senta); and music (Cosima).

Here, in the house he named Wahnfried since he hoped to find in it peace (*Frieden*) from the delusions (*Wahn*) of his past life, Wagner lived and wrote *Götterdämmerung* and *Parsifal* and held court to his friends and associates during the remaining nine years of his life, leaving it only during the cold raw winters for the milder climate of Italy. After his death in Venice on 13 February 1883 his body was brought back to Bayreuth by rail and, after a procession through the town reminiscent of a royal funeral, laid to rest at the point where the garden of Wahnfried merges into the palace park.

The presence of that grave at the bottom of the garden was to have a lasting effect on the remaining members of the family and their successors. The dynastic implication was obvious. Only one of Cosima's daughters had left Wahnfried in Wagner's lifetime: Blandine (Hans von Bülow's daughter), who had married Count Gravina of Palermo in 1882. The rest of the children, with the exception of Isolde, remained in or near Wahnfried for almost the whole of their lives. Von Bülow's elder daughter Daniela married an art historian, Henry Thode, in 1887, but she continued to put Wahnfried at the centre of her life, with the inevitable result that the marriage broke down and ended in 1915 in divorce. Eva, the second of Wagner's daughters, was already forty-one when she married Houston Stewart Chamberlain, who was twelve years older, in 1908. They continued virtually to live in Wahnfried for some years, although Chamberlain had a house of his own just beside it.

Isolde too had kept within the Wahnfried circle in marrying Franz Beidler, who had been a musical assistant at the festival since 1896 and in 1904 and 1906 conducted some performances of the *Ring* and *Parsifal*. But when Siegfried took over the management of the festival after 1906, he decided to dispense with Beidler's services. His professed reason was that Beidler took his work too lightly, but it seems more likely that he felt Beidler might regard Cosima's retirement as an opportunity to increase his own influence on festival affairs. The dynastic danger was all the greater in that Beidler and Isolde had a son: at that time Wagner's only true grandson. Isolde, a loyal wife, went into exile with her husband. A few years later, for the sake of her son, she attempted to establish by law her right to be regarded as a daughter of Richard Wagner. The defendant was her own mother, who was at that time too ill to know what was going on, and the case was fought on her behalf by Houston Stewart Chamberlain and his wife, who stoutly maintained that Eva was Wagner's only true daughter. Isolde lost her case (which does not say much for the justice of the law). It is an excellent example of the sort of savagery that dynastic considerations lead to. The victims were Cosima, whose breakdown in health was certainly to some extent due to the quarrel with her favourite daughter; Siegfried, who was forced by his fears into an uncharacteristic act of ruthlessness; and most of all Isolde, whose name was no longer spoken in the family until her death in 1921. Siegfried's wife Winifred, who entered the family in 1915, never even met her.

The villains in this particular story were undoubtedly Chamberlain and his wife Eva, whose resistance to Isolde was built, as they well knew, on lies. But, having no children of their own, they cannot be accused of acting selfishly on their own behalf. Their main consideration was the continuation of the Wagner line, which it was Siegfried's duty to perpetuate and not to delegate to a disloyal sister. In 1915, when Siegfried was about to set out on his annual visit to Berlin, Eva wrote him what she called a sisterly letter, reminding him in truly Wagnerian language that he was now forty-five years old, and it was high time that he ceased to lavish his love solely on his pet dogs and looked around for "the maid whom you, Wahnfried and our cause so sorely need". She went on to suggest a few names which might fulfil the requirements as she saw them.

Siegfried was prompt in giving Eva her satisfaction, even if he ignored all her suggestions and made a choice of his own. Eva could in fact have included Winifred Williams in her list, for she had met her the previous summer at the festival, which Winifred had attended in the company of her adoptive father, the eighty-four-year-old Karl Klindworth. Klindworth, a pupil of Liszt and friend of Wagner since their meeting in London in 1855, had taken the ten-year-old orphan (who was distantly related to his wife) into his home and brought her up with loving care. He supervised her musical education and introduced her slowly to Wagner's works, though not allowing her to see them on the stage until he judged her ripe for them. That time came in 1914, when Cosima invited Klindworth to Bayreuth and graciously granted his request to bring his young protegée with him.

In an interview I made for the BBC in 1969, Winifred Wagner recalled her first meeting with Siegfried during the interval of a *Ring* rehearsal. "For me this meeting with Siegfried meant love at first sight," she said. "It was his kind, warm voice that impressed me most—but his whole appearance, his wonderful large blue eyes enchanted me, and I left Bayreuth in a trance."

Winifred had attended rehearsals not only of the *Ring*, but of *Der Fliegende Holländer* as well, which Siegfried was producing anew for the 1914 festival. She immediately resolved to rename herself Senta. Siegfried, arriving in Berlin, lost no time in visiting the Klindworths and found, on their side as well as Winifred's, full encouragement. The only difficulty was her nationality. Germany was now at war with Britain, and Winifred was still legally a British subject. Klindworth, on the outbreak of war, had at once applied to adopt her formally in order to prevent her internment or eviction from Germany. The adoption was approved, but Winifred was not granted German nationality. Only marriage to a German could give her this protection, and Siegfried lost no time in making sure of his Senta. The marriage took place in Wahnfried on 22 September 1915, barely two months after his proposal. And Winifred Williams, after a short period as Senta Klindworth, became Winifred Wagner. Siegfried liked her English name better.

In his biography of Siegfried Wagner, Zdenko von Kraft describes the wedding. "The hall at Wahnfried was festively arrayed. On a high chair in the middle sat Frau Cosima like a Druid priestess, dressed in a long grey silk robe. The bride, in a simple white dress beneath a huge veil, stood beside her. . . . It was an intimate family gathering. Otherwise only the witnesses, a few invited guests and, in true patriarchal style, the family servants were present."

Cosima was delighted to see her son married at last, and equally delighted with her daughter-in-law, sixty years younger than herself. Winifred's strict, sequestered upbringing at Klindworth's hands, she wrote to a friend, met with her full approval, and she added, "The fact that the eighteen-year-old girl is good-looking and charming in manner does not seem to me a disadvantage."

Fortunately Winifred possessed, beside these qualities, a healthy sense of humour, which enabled her to fit into the rigid pattern of life in Wahnfried without great difficulty. She worshipped—the word is her own—Cosima, who, for all her aristocratic ways, was warm-hearted and who quickly put her at her ease. She devised a time-table for Winifred to occupy

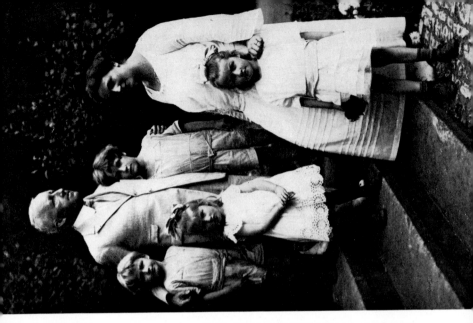

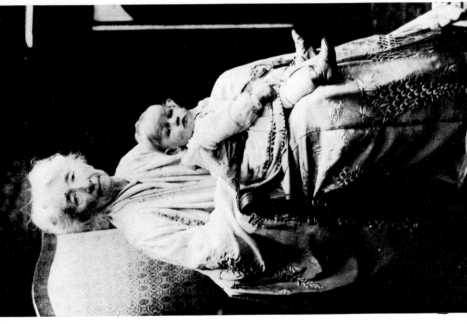

Right: Wieland, aged one, with his grandmother Cosima, aged eighty-one

Far right: Wieland, aged five, with his father and mother, brother and sisters

Wieland, aged twenty-one,
as a soldier

Wieland, aged twenty-seven,
with his wife Gertrud and
their children Iris and
Wolf Siegfried

her during the mornings when Siegfried disappeared into the study he had had built beside Wahnfried to work on the composition of his own operas. First, Winifred had to dust the large hall in which Cosima used to receive visitors. At about ten o'clock Cosima would come downstairs and, after an inspection, would ask Winifred to read to her or to write letters for her in French. After an hour of that, Winifred would do some practice on the piano. If Daniela happened to be present, this might take the form of duets, in which Daniela, playing the bass part, was liable to hog more than her own half of the piano. This brought Winifred up to lunch-time, when Siegfried would emerge from his study and join the family. Afterwards he and Winifred would accompany Cosima on a drive into the country in a horse-drawn carriage, interrupting it for a short walk. Then home to tea, at which the family would be joined by a few close friends. After that, Winifred was at last able to be alone with her husband. She would go with him to his study, where he would play over the music he had written during the morning. She would write letters at his dictation or read to him. Very soon she was able to write letters for him without supervision and help him with research for the librettos of his operas, which (like his father) he wrote himself.

With Eva Chamberlain, Winifred had some difficulties. Eva was in fact in charge of the running of the household, and in the first year of Winifred's marriage there were constant little disputes between them. After eight months of uneasy strife, Eva moved with her husband into their house next door.

But Winifred was not to become the complete mistress of Wahnfried for some years yet. Cosima may have handed over the running of the festival to her son, but at Wahnfried she was still the centre. Her health was not good, and she needed constant attention. She suffered from severe headaches and nervous tensions, and would periodically lose consciousness for days at a stretch, or imagine she was hearing non-existent music. Even after moving into her own house, Eva continued as her constant companion.

Though growing increasingly frail, Cosima still retained an interest in affairs, and she continued to receive distinguished guests right up to the end of her long life. Perhaps she was no longer quite aware that times had changed, and the old aristocratic order to which she was so devoted was no longer as unquestioned as it once had been. Winifred recalled in our radio conversation the visit of some royal personages, whom the aged Cosima received in the presence of her daughter Daniela, now nearing seventy, and Siegfried in his late fifties. "She was sitting on her chair and bowing the whole time—always deeper, deeper, so that her children would copy her. But they didn't."

That was the dynastic Wahnfried into which, on 5 January 1917, Wieland was born. He was christened Adolf Wieland Gottfried—the first of life's ironies as far as he was concerned: the Adolf was not in honour of Hitler, who was at that time an obscure soldier serving in the Austrian army, but in memory of Richard Wagner's literary uncle.

3

CHILDHOOD YEARS

1917–1930

WIELAND'S ARRIVAL, MORE than a century after the birth
of his grandfather, was greeted with great delight by the
family. When Winifred returned from the hospital to place
him ceremoniously in Cosima's arms in the great hall of
Wahnfried, Siegfried's friend Carl Gianicelli sat at the piano
playing the G major melody from the second act of *Lohengrin:
Es gibt ein Glück, das ohne Reu'*. . . .

Wieland did not long remain the only child. Fourteen
months later, on 29 March 1918, his sister Friedelind was born,
followed on 30 August 1919 by Wolfgang and on 2 December
1920 by Verena. In spite of four uninterrupted years of pregnancy and nursing, Winifred continued to work as her husband's secretary, and the babies were handed over to the care
of a nanny, Emma Baer, who at the time of Wieland's death
was still in service at Wahnfried. Winifred had very definite
ideas on the duties of a wife. "My device was: nobody can look
after Siegfried as well as I can, but somebody else *can* look after
the children."

This remained the pattern until Siegfried's death in 1930.
While the children were being born the festival was still in
abeyance. There was even a period at the end of the war when
shortage of fuel forced the whole family with the exception of
Cosima, whose room could be kept heated, to move to Siegfried's small house in the garden. Siegfried could not afford to
remain idle: no festival also meant no income, and so it was all
the more important at this period for him to write his own
operas and get them performed and to accept conducting
engagements outside Bayreuth. It was a difficult and depressing
time. After plans for the production of one of his operas had

B

fallen through in 1920, he wrote, "God grant that my children will be spared the wish to become artists! They would do better to become town clerks than to suffer the disappointments which I have to endure."

An unsettled political background, coupled with rapidly increasing inflation, added to Siegfried's financial difficulties. He undertook a conducting tour of the United States early in 1924 in the hope of earning some solid currency with which to reopen the festival. With Winifred he visited Detroit, Baltimore, St Louis, New York and other towns, and she gave lectures at various clubs along the way to contribute her share. The children remained at home in the care of Emma. Siegfried and Winifred returned to Germany via Rome, where in May 1924 Siegfried met Mussolini. He wrote in his diary: "A depressing contrast for us. He is all will, strength, almost brutality. Fanatic expression in the eyes, but without the light of love as in Hitler and Ludendorff. Romans and Germans! We spoke mainly about ancient Rome. He bears some resemblance to Napoleon. Splendid race of people! A man like that rules Italy, and Bernhardchen rules us! It is really pitiful to see Germany sunk so low."

The profit from Siegfried's American tour was only thirty thousand marks—a small sum with which to renovate the *Festspielhaus* after an interval of ten years and repair or replace damaged scenery and costumes. But at least the social climate had not changed so radically as it did after the Second World War, and Siegfried could do what was later an impossibility for his sons: reopen the festival with performances of *Parsifal* and the *Ring* identical with the productions of 1914, though with mainly new singers. The production of *Die Meistersinger* which was also played, had not in fact been done since 1912. However, the festival was a success and could be repeated in the following year.

For the four young children, who had been running wild in the garden at Wahnfried, the reopening of the festival provided a new field of interest. During rehearsals they had the run of the *Festspielhaus*, where all sorts of fascinating new toys were discovered, such as the Rhine Maidens' swimming machine and the imposing dragon Fafner. No restrictions were placed on them, and they did just as they pleased. There was nothing precocious about their behaviour: they had no great interest in the music or the drama. Daniela, their Aunt Lulu, who was in charge of the wardrobe, had some costumes made for them, representing characters out of the *Ring*. Dressed in these, they devised performances of their own for their friends. They knew the story of the *Ring*, for in yet younger days their father had given them a model theatre in which he performed the work for them, though without music. As they grew older, they took over the presentation themselves.

That was, however, the full extent of their formal education as far as Wagner was concerned. It was not lack of interest on the part of their parents, but rather a deliberate policy. Both of them having been strictly brought up, Siegfried among older sisters in the rarified atmosphere of Wahnfried, and Winifred solitarily by the very elderly Klindworths in Berlin, they were anxious that their own children should enjoy the complete freedom they themselves had missed. Siegfried, being easygoing by nature, was no disciplinarian. With his reserved and moody elder son he had in any case little real contact. He might join him for a short while in kicking a football in the garden or give him some encouragement in his drawing, but on the whole he preferred the company of his elder daughter Friedelind, who was cheerful and outspoken and joined him without waiting to be asked. Wieland was emotionally more attached to his mother, and he was probably at this stage jealous of his father, who kept her so occupied that she had little time for her children. Before the festival reopened, there were occasions when Siegfried went away alone, and then Wieland momentarily came into his own. "Huschele [i.e. Wieland] and I are leading an idyllic existence," Winifred wrote to Siegfried. "He is touchingly concerned about me. At mealtimes he comes and sits very close to me, though there is plenty of room at the big table. And at nights he sleeps beside me." But the relationship was not always idyllic. On another occasion she wrote, "This morning there was a terrible scene with an enraged Huschele, who could not forgive me for going to the station without him."

Left to their own devices, the children were inventive and fully alive to the advantages of living at Wahnfried. At festival times there were always visitors anxious to see the house and

Wagner's grave at the bottom of the garden. The children found a useful source of income in wheeling customers around the Wahnfried sights in a handcart. (One of their customers, they later discovered, had been Himmler.) Such escapades were of course possible only when their parents were out of the house, and they knew better than to go too near Cosima's window.

In the autumn of 1923, when he was six, Wieland was sent to school. His first report from the junior school of the local teachers' training college (*Seminarschule, Lehrerbildungs-Anstalt Bayreuth*) shows him to have been rather weak in singing, but in this and subsequent reports, all preserved in the Wahnfried archives, he was particularly praised for his application and good behaviour. He was a rather solitary child, slow to make friends.

Two years later he began to have piano lessons, and in December 1926 he made his first public appearance as a pianist, playing a duet at a school concert with his teacher, Fräulein Anna Mann. It was an arrangement of Luther's hymn *Vom Himmel hoch* and, according to his sister Friedelind, Wieland's part consisted of the melody played with one finger of each hand. However simple it may have been, the first public appearance of Richard Wagner's grandson rated a report in the local paper. This did not go beyond the facts, but the report was picked up by other papers, even foreign ones, and improved on until Wieland was being hailed far from home as an infant prodigy.

Siegfried, now more than ever occupied with festival affairs, was content to leave the musical education of his children to the school and to Fräulein Mann. His approval of their progress was no more committed than that of any average music-loving father. In 1927 he wrote to a friend: "Christmas was very delightful. The children provided the music. Wieland is nicely musical. Mausi [i.e. Friedelind] gets occasional attacks of tempo diarrhoea and rushes off with the crotchets. Verena sings prettily, and Wolf wants to learn the flute."

To some performances of his own operas in nearby towns Siegfried took Wieland and Friedelind. *Der Bärenhäuter* (his first opera, produced in 1899 in Munich) was performed in Weimar in 1926 and in Augsburg in 1928; *Sternengebot* (1908) in Weimar at the same time and at Karlsruhe in 1929; *Banadiet-*

rich (1910) in Weimar, also in 1929. Grateful as he was for these and a few other performances of his works, Siegfried knew by now that he would never make his mark as a composer. In January 1928 he wrote to his friend Ludwig Karpath in Vienna, "So things go on at a snail's pace, as befits one who, to quote Dr Becker, 'does not belong to these times.' An unintended compliment! Wagner's son and Liszt's grandson would scarcely be proud of being identified with times in which people gloat over severed heads and Jonny strikes up."

Siegfried wrote this letter just after completing the composition of *Die heilige Linde*, which was to be his last finished work. He continued to compose in a desultory way, but the capitulation was evident. From now on his energies were devoted mainly to the service of Bayreuth and his father's works. There was much to be done. Uncomfortable as he felt in the world of Richard Strauss and Ernst Křenek, however unworthy he found the Weimar Republic as successor to the betrayed monarchy, he recognised that Bayreuth could not live for ever on old traditions. Cosima, now past her ninetieth year, was withdrawn, except at rare intervals, into a mental world of her own. Houston Stewart Chamberlain, after years of growing paralysis, had died in 1927. Adolf von Gross and Hans von Wolzogen, the last of Richard Wagner's direct assistants, were eighty-four and seventy-eight respectively. Between them and his own wife and children was a vast age gap. Siegfried himself formed the bridge and, whatever his personal inclinations, he felt the responsibility he owed to the younger generation to which he would one day have to hand over his heritage.

Financial difficulties still plagued him. He had set his heart on proclaiming his new style for Bayreuth with a production of *Tannhäuser*, which had not been done at the festival since 1904. In 1927 there was not enough money available, and he had to content himself with a new production of *Tristan und Isolde*, which was cheaper to mount. It was not until 1930 that Siegfried could present *Tannhäuser*, and he owed the opportunity to a number of friends who organised a subscription fund for his sixtieth birthday in 1929.

Wieland himself, in one of the few references to his father which he made in later life, regarded that *Tannhäuser* as marking the first real break with Cosima's outworn tradition. What was

really new about it, apart from the use of solid sets to replace
the traditional backcloths, is difficult to establish after all these
years. The scenery (designed by Siegfried himself), while very
beautiful, was in the traditional realistic style. Contemporary
accounts suggest that it was the naturalness of movement,
through which the drama simply seemed to "happen", that
made the greatest effect. This was certainly in striking contrast
to the artificial, pre-ordained gestures of Cosima's classic
Bayreuth style.

The year 1930, in which Wieland had his thirteenth birthday, began for Siegfried with a conducting tour in England,
with concerts in Bristol and Bournemouth. In Bristol he had a
slight heart attack, which he ignored. A fortnight later he was
off again to Milan to stage and conduct the *Ring*. On both
journeys Winifred accompanied him. They were still in Milan
when Cosima fell seriously ill. She died on 1 April, before her
son's return from Italy, and her ashes were laid beside her husband in the garden at Wahnfried.

In view of her age Cosima's death could not have been
entirely unexpected, but nevertheless it was a severe shock to
Siegfried, who had always been very close to her. A short
holiday in Italy appeared, however, to restore him, and he
started rehearsals for the coming festival, including the new
Tannhäuser, with his customary vigour. On 16 July, during a
rehearsal of *Götterdämmerung*, he collapsed. He was taken to
hospital, where he appeared to be making a slow recovery,
though he was not well enough to attend the opening of the
festival with his new *Tannhäuser* production on 22 July. Shortly
afterwards he had a further heart attack and on 4 August,
while the festival was still running, he died. He was buried in
the municipal cemetery in Bayreuth, where his grandfather
Liszt also lies.

4

CHANGING INFLUENCES

1930–1936

FRIEDELIND WAGNER HAS written in her book *The Royal Family of Bayreuth* of the agonies she felt at the death of her father. Wieland, who was thirteen years old at the time, was less personally affected. Unlike Friedelind, he had developed no close contacts with Siegfried. The death of his grandmother Cosima meant even less. He, together with his brother and sisters, had in their younger days enjoyed quite an affectionate relationship with her. Though in her last years she had been practically confined to her room, the four children were often with her. Particularly in helping her through her attacks of nervous tension, which, though decreasing in severity, increased in frequency as she grew older, their cheerful presence proved helpful.

But the children were never integrated into the family life at Wahnfried to the extent that Siegfried and his sisters had been in their younger years. In Richard Wagner's day the house had been the constant meeting place of eminent musicians and writers. Music and literature, contemporary and past, were continually heard and discussed. Siegfried and his sisters, even if only watching from the side lines, nevertheless had the opportunity to absorb a rich store of knowledge and experience. Siegfried's children, in line with their parents' policy of allowing them to grow up in unrestricted freedom, were not exposed to the same extent to this intellectual contact with their elders. The tradition of musical soirées and readings may have continued in Wahnfried, but Siegfried, so much out of touch with his own times, displayed little interest in new artistic trends. These gatherings, increasingly confined to the family and a few close friends, were more concerned with the past than the future. Goethe, Rousseau, Dickens, Schopenhauer, Aeschylus, Balzac: these were some of the favourite authors, and occasionally Houston Stewart Chamberlain would read something from his own works.

Such elderly fare could not make much impression on young minds, and consequently the children tended to follow their own interests outside Wahnfried rather than in it. In 1927 Wieland had moved on from the *Seminarschule* to the *Humanistisches Gymnasium* in Bayreuth, and here he came into contact with two class-mates who were to remain close to him for the rest of his life. One was Gertrud Reissinger, the daughter of a scientist, who subsequently became his wife. Gertrud was not impressed by Wieland at first sight. He was a fat and rather rough boy, and he seemed to take pleasure in terrifying the girls in his class. He was always kicking a football about, and the girls were in constant fear of receiving it in their faces. But, perhaps because in the class-room he shared a desk with her, Wieland's attitude towards Gertrud was tempered, and she became a frequent visitor to Wahnfried.

His other friend was Helmut Danzer, who later became a doctor (and in the light of his medical knowledge diagnosed the cause of Wieland's boyhood tubbiness as glandular). Danzer met Wieland on more equal terms than Gertrud, since he was himself an expert footballer. But their true point of contact was drawing, at which Danzer was, in his own opinion, at that time more accomplished than Wieland. To escape from his brother and sisters (who, however close basically, tended to squabble), Wieland would cycle off into the country with Danzer, both armed with drawing materials.

*

The deaths of Cosima and Siegfried led inevitably to changes in the life at Wahnfried. Winifred, now in sole charge of the festival, did some internal decorations, replacing curtains that had hung there since Richard Wagner's day and refurnishing rooms in which she could work and receive visitors in her own way. But any hopes the children might have had that their mother might have more time for them than before were disappointed. She had in fact much less. The difficulties of her

Wieland, aged twenty-nine: self-portrait

Oil painting by Wieland, 1939: *Im Atelier*

Wieland, aged thirty-five, at rehearsals in the *Festspielhaus*

position in relation to the festival, as a young woman of foreign birth, with no artistic qualifications beyond those she had acquired in assisting her husband, were intensified by family and professional jealousies, and it required all her considerable energies to ensure that the festival should be kept going at all.

The nanny, Emma Baer, was still there to look after the children's material comforts, but Winifred decided that they needed more help on the intellectual side. In January 1931 Lieselotte Schmidt, a young woman from Stuttgart who had spent some weeks in the summer of 1929 helping the children with their school work, received from Winifred a letter headed "SOS from Wahnfried's nursery". It read: "The children all claim that they cannot get on at school without your help. Wieland wants Greek and mathematics explained, Mausi [Friedelind] is stuck in arithmetic, Wolfi needs coaching in Latin, etc." Winifred went on: "We were in Spinabad near Davos from 25.12 to 5.1. for a ski course. Wieland won the *Schlusslauf*, and we were all bursting with pride."

Lieselotte responded to the call and went at once to Wahn-fried, where she remained, apart from short absences, until her death in 1938 following a car accident. She worked not only with the children, but increasingly with Winifred as well, becoming her secretary. During these years Lieselotte wrote frequent letters to her parents in Stuttgart, relating in much detail what was going on in Bayreuth. Her letters, now in the archives at Wahnfried, give a graphic picture of the surround-ings in which Wieland spent his formative years between the ages of fourteen and twenty-one.

Her first account of him sounds slightly disenchanted: "19.7.29.: From six o'clock onwards I am with Wieland: one hour Latin (going very well) and half an hour piano. He is in a bad mood today. He misses Maus, who wrote for the first time today (from her new boarding-school). At meals he is also moody, and won't eat." "20.7.29.: Studied and practised with Wieland, who is still very grumpy." "23.7.29.: From Mausi came three miserable cards and one mournful letter for Mama. All the children and Emma were in tears, and Wieland went back to bed till lunchtime. Afterwards again until tea." But as time went on, her impression of him changed, and she was full of praise for his quiet resolution and devotion to his work.

Lieselotte's letters reveal a home into which National Socialism had penetrated to the furthest corners. She herself was a fanatic supporter of Hitler, and the nanny Emma was a party member of long standing, as was Winifred herself. Even Hans von Wolzogen, once Wagner's personal assistant, who was now well into his eighties, made his contribution to the children's Nazi education by writing a play for their puppet theatre in which Kasperle slaps a Jew for trying to force his attentions on a girl. The aunts Daniela and Eva too, though at odds with Winifred on her methods of running the festival, had no quarrel with her friendship with Hitler, who, at the time of Siegfried's death, had progressed from being just a promising young politician to a political force on the point of breaking through. In fact, a year before Siegfried's death Eva had accompanied Winifred and the children as privileged guests to a spectacular Nazi party rally in Nuremberg, while Daniela regularly attended Nazi meetings in Bayreuth.

For the festival of 1931, the first under her own management, Winifred was faced with the need to find a musical director to replace Karl Muck, who had decided to take Siegfried's death as an excuse to retire from the Bayreuth scene after an uninterrupted association of thirty years. Her choice fell on Wilhelm Furtwängler who, though a highly successful Wagner conductor in Berlin, had not yet appeared in Bayreuth. He came to Wahnfried in March 1931 with his secretary, Berta Geissmar, to discuss the appointment, and on 17 March Lieselotte wrote to her parents: "We have had two very busy Furtwängler days. He is very simple and natural, without any side or conceit (he could take lessons in that from the horrible Geissmar, a very clever and intelligent, hundred per cent Jewess). . . . Yesterday he was paraded before the aunts at lunch. . . . The children were banned from all meals to save a lot of unnecessary noise— and for fear they might tell the Geissmar woman too openly to her face how ugly she is. That's the only point about him we can't understand, but somewhere the artist's unpredictability must come out, I suppose—even in him. But he speaks quite openly about Jews—and in a pretty disparaging way. So, incidentally, does she, but in her case it's just hypocrisy . . . . Yesterday evening there was a Nazi demonstration in the town. The children went and were very enthusiastic."

Lieselotte was young of course and was writing uninhibitedly to her parents, not for publication. Though it would be unfair to take this passage as an accurate summary of what occurred in Wahnfried on that occasion, it can be assumed that such sickening talk—by no means uncommon even among otherwise intelligent people in the Germany of those days—would often enough have reached the children's ears.

Busy as he was with his own affairs, Hitler found little time to visit Wahnfried, and so Heinz Tietjen was the first man in the children's eyes to break into the exclusively feminine domination of Wahnfried. During the festival of 1931 Arturo Toscanini, who had been brought to Bayreuth in 1930 by Siegfried to conduct *Tannhäuser*, had endeared himself to them, but his visits to Bayreuth were brief, and were soon to end entirely. Tietjen, the director of the Berlin *Staatsoper*, was appointed by Winifred in 1932 to take over the artistic direction of the festival, and she also invited him to supervise the education of her children, particularly on the musical side.

Tietjen, fifty-one years of age at that time, was a distinguished conductor and producer as well as a clever and resourceful administrator. The fact that he had an English mother was an added recommendation in Winifred's eyes, but her main reason for choosing him was that he had made a production of *Lohengrin* in Berlin which Siegfried had greatly admired. It was an admirable choice from the artistic point of view, and in the difficult times of Nazi dominance Tietjen's diplomatic cunning was to prove a great help to Winifred in her efforts to preserve some measure of independence in the running of the festival. His human qualities were less evident: Tietjen inspired respect among his associates, but seldom affection.

However, his relationship with the children at Wahnfried started promisingly. Wieland confided to Gertrud that it was pleasant to have a man in the house again to whom he could talk, and Lieselotte Schmidt wrote on 16 February 1932 that the children all liked him—"and quite rightly: he is a kind and sensitive person, and for Wieland in particular a friend and adviser in artistic and human problems." Later in the same year Tietjen listened to the children playing the piano. "He was very touched by Wieland's diligence and persistence, but deplored his rhythmic slackness."

It was a very small (and no doubt entirely justified) piece of criticism, but evidence that Tietjen was not going to treat the children with indulgence just because they bore the Wagner name. They would be expected to prove their ability. Winifred took the same view. The old family atmosphere that had prevailed during the festival in Siegfried's time began to disappear. Hitherto the children had remained at Wahnfried in festival time. Now at the conclusion of rehearsals, which they were allowed to attend, they were sent off to the family summer house at Nussdorf on the Lake of Constance, which Winifred had bought in 1931. The children's natural pleasure in this lakeside paradise was thus tempered somewhat by a sense of banishment.

*

In January 1933 Hitler became German chancellor, and in the flag-waving celebrations that followed, the Wagner family, adult and juvenile, joined in happily. To mark the occasion Wahnfried was thrown open to the public on Wagner's death anniversary (13 February), and Lieselotte recorded that all day the pilgrimage through the house to the grave in the garden continued unbroken. On the same day Winifred, Daniela and Eva were presented with the freedom of Bayreuth.

A similar honour was accorded Arturo Toscanini, who was expected to return to Bayreuth in the summer to conduct at the festival for the third time. But Toscanini suddenly withdrew, unable to reconcile his own political convictions with Hitler's access to power. It was for Winifred a cruel blow. Criticism of her ability to run the festival, hinted at by the withdrawal in 1931 of the conductor Karl Muck and openly voiced by Wilhelm Furtwängler in the ensuing year, had already had its effect on advance bookings. The coming to power of the Nazi party had further deterred intending visitors from abroad. Now Toscanini's withdrawal proved an even stronger deterrent. A month before the festival opened, hardly more than half the seats had been sold. Hitler himself came to the rescue. In response to Winifred's direct appeal, he decided to attend the festival personally. He was present for the opening, and returned again for the first *Ring* cycle.

Wieland, now aged sixteen, could have had little appreciation of the difficulties his mother was facing or of the dangers she might be running in placing herself so trustfully in Hitler's hands. For Wieland himself Hitler's intervention was all gain. Unlike Tietjen, Hitler was impressed by his position as the eldest Wagner heir, and was quite ready to recognise it. Early in 1933 Wieland made his first representative appearance, accompanying his mother to a festive dinner in Leipzig in honour of Richard Wagner. Later in the same year he went alone to Dresden to represent his mother at the dedication of a Wagner statue. Lieselotte reported to her parents that he conducted himself very well and appeared for the occasion dressed in *Hitler Jugend* uniform.

But, flattering as such appearances might have been to his vanity and useful in bolstering his self-esteem against Tietjen's supposed indifference, they did not divert him from his true interest, which at this time lay in his painting. He had begun to move from straightforward landscape into the field of stage design, and in February 1934 Lieselotte was writing of a "splendid Valhalla" he had painted. True to his introspective nature, he worked alone, following his own ideas without the help of any regular teacher. With Emil Preetorius, Tietjen's stage designer, he had no significant contact. But the great Viennese stage designer, Alfred Roller, who came to Bayreuth in 1934 to prepare new sets for *Parsifal* (they had remained virtually unchanged since 1882), was a more fruitful influence. Later in his life Wieland acknowledged that it was Roller who taught him to prepare his stage designs as models rather than as drawings or paintings. But, if the lesson was learned, it was not immediately applied, and Wieland continued at that period of his life to design sets as paintings.

In any case, Roller's presence in Bayreuth was only brief. The artist Franz Stassen, who had been a close friend of Siegfried Wagner, was a more frequent visitor, and he took a fatherly interest in Wieland's efforts. Lieselotte wrote in 1934, "Wieland, as long as Stassen is here, will have none of me— that is to say, he'll do no more school work than is absolutely necessary . . . . Wieland slaves with him all afternoon. He has painted splendid *Lohengrin* designs, and also sets for *Kobold* and *Sonnenflammen* [operas by Siegfried Wagner]—really extremely talented and done with so much ease: ideas simply pour out of him. Stassen is only tolerated as a spectator. At every stroke he makes, the pupil watches anxiously, terrified of having his work spoiled."

Stassen was an artist of the *Jugendstil* school, the German version of *Art Nouveau*, and so by objective standards already somewhat outdated. But this was something that Wieland would have been unlikely to notice. Brought up in the nineteenth century atmosphere of his father's Wahnfried (which did not even contain a radio set until Winifred introduced one in 1932), he had passed straight into the restrictive artistic climate of Hitler's Germany, which labelled all modern artistic movements collectively as degenerate. Such official cultural education as Wieland received tended to be safely in line with ordinary German middle-class tradition: visits to towns like Jena, Weimar and Eisenach with all their historical associations; visits to the opera to see *Der Freischütz* and *Aida* and to the theatre for Schiller and Lessing—all of it essential to know, but scarcely a full preparation for a budding artist.

In 1934 a further representative trip to Leipzig in company with his mother to attend a stone-laying ceremony was made particularly memorable since on the return journey Wieland made his first journey by plane. The German Vice-Chancellor, Franz von Papen, whose plane it was, made a special round above the city of Berlin for the benefit of his young guest.

In the following year Hitler himself gave the seventeen-year-old boy a handsome present: a Mercedes car. Wieland went to Munich with Wolfgang to collect it. Hitler, who entertained them in his Munich flat, had to leave in the evening for Berlin. Lieselotte wrote to her parents, "Wieland and Wolf spent the night—would you believe it?—alone in the *Führer's* flat: Wieland in the *Führer's* own bed! It doesn't bear thinking of!"

According to Helmut Danzer, Wieland, though proud of his car, showed no particular emotion about the source from which it came, and certainly his school friends did not think there was anything sensational about it. Everybody knew that Hitler was a personal friend of his mother, and so what was so very remarkable about his gift? In his position he could afford it!

This seems indeed to have been Wieland's own attitude towards his powerful benefactors. He accepted their favours without feeling any obligation to make a return. Anything that took him away from his artistic preoccupations in fact rather bored him, and he stopped going to *Hitler Jugend* meetings or wearing uniform. Wagner children could do with impunity what less exalted families would find politically dangerous. Wieland certainly did not avoid the company of the prominent Nazis among whom his family moved. In addition to being a painter, he had developed an interest in photography, and his snapshots of these people, from Hitler downwards, had a definite commercial value. Wieland started to trade his photographs, and he was soon earning quite handsome fees from newspapers and periodicals. Most of this money, it appears, was spent on rather extravagant presents for Gertrud and for his mother, whom he still secretly worshipped. He once told Gertrud he would never marry any woman who was not like his mother.

Wieland's photographic skill had earned him the right during rehearsals in the *Festspielhaus* to take stage shots of the singers. But this was a long way from any real participation in the festival, and it may well have been despair of making any headway that caused him in his stage designs to turn his attentions to the operas of his father.

A projected production of *Der Bärenhäuter* in Lübeck gave Wieland his first chance of proving himself in public. He was invited to submit his designs to the opera house, where they found favour, and they were used as the basis for sets prepared in the opera house by the resident staff. Wieland had nothing at all to do with their preparation. And though Lieselotte proudly wrote in February 1936, "Wieland's decorations for *Der Bärenhäuter* in Lübeck have caused a real sensation", Wieland himself was not even present at the first performance. He was busy at school preparing for his final examinations.

With the help of Lieselotte and a private coach, Adolf Hopf, Wieland managed to master his weakest subject, mathematics, sufficiently to get through his *Abitur* successfully. In the other subjects he had less difficulty, as his final school report, dated March 1936, shows. "Among his written examination papers the German essay was very successful: he developed personal and individual ideas and revealed mature understanding. The translation from Greek was also very good, and the other

foreign language papers were well done, while in the mathematical papers his work was fair to good. . . . In the academic
subjects he managed by a combination of his very varied
interests and conscientious application to achieve very credit-
able results through almost the entire range, and among other
things he showed very considerable understanding for art and
literature. . . . During his stay at this school he won the high
regard of his teachers through his exemplary behaviour: he was
reliable, companionable and adaptable."

Wieland had now had enough of compulsory learning, and
he decided against going on to a university. Instead, he took the
calculated step, a few weeks before leaving school, of volunteering for the army. This was not due to any feelings of patriotism.
On the contrary, it was a deliberate attempt to reduce his
national commitments. All young Germans were obliged to do
a period of *Arbeitsdienst*—organised labour for the benefit of the
nation—and there were rumours going around that in the
following year conscription in the armed services would be
introduced. By volunteering for a year's army service and working in the *Arbeitsdienst* until called up for it, Wieland stood a
good chance of reducing the time wasted on his national
service obligations to a minimum.

School ended, Wieland set off for Lübeck, accompanied by
Stassen, to see his first stage designs in practical use. Before they
departed there was a party at Wahnfried to celebrate Wieland's
Abitur success. Lieselotte wrote to her parents, "Simply because
he is so modest, it is right that he should now and again be
accorded a little honour on suitable occasions. We shall now
really recognise, when his gentle warm presence is no longer
here in the house, how dearly we love him."

5

FIRST STAGE DESIGNS

1936–1938

DER BÄRENHÄUTER, LIKE all Siegfried Wagner's operas, is based on a fairy-tale. He followed the example of his teacher Humperdinck in using the full Wagnerian apparatus, with the result that his naïve and simple stories were in constant danger of being swamped by an over-portentous musical treatment. In *Der Bärenhäuter* Siegfried managed, however, to achieve an acceptable balance between music and action, and for that reason it has remained his most popular work.

Wieland's designs for the Lübeck production of *Der Bären-häuter*, as for the other works of his father painted at this time, were based purely on the texts. Though he liked the music and would play it to himself on the piano, his knowledge of music was at this stage of his life far too superficial to make him conscious of a significant connection between the musical substance of an opera and its visual realisation. He was content to take his father's works on their face value and match them with unproblematic fairy-tale designs in which charm was its own justification. Their success was evidence of his skill as a painter rather than of his dramatic sense, which was still completely undeveloped.

Wieland began his *Arbeitsdienst* in the labour camp of Grossenhain, not far from Dresden. Though clearly any labour camp would have proved a severe trial to a boy used to the relative luxury of Wahnfried, Grossenhain seems to have been more primitive in its conditions and harsher in its demands than most. According to Helmut Danzer, who served there with him, Wieland himself accepted his blistered feet, festered eyes and enforced grubbiness without complaint. But his mother, when she visited him, was so appalled that she set to work to get things changed. Once again Hitler came to the rescue, and Wieland was moved to another labour camp at Kulmbach, only a few miles from Bayreuth.

There he was within easy reach of the *Festspielhaus*, where in the festival of 1936 he was to make his first modest and un-publicised artistic contribution. Winifred's decision to replace Joukowsky's original designs for *Parsifal* in 1934—a decision which at the time caused a furore fully equal to that her sons experienced in 1951—had to some extent misfired, since the new sets designed by Alfred Roller had fallen short of expecta-tions, mainly for technical reasons. Roller returned to Bay-reuth in 1935 (a year in which there was no festival) to make improvements, but he was already a very sick man, and the work was uncompleted when he died later the same year. For the 1936 festival Tietjen decided to retain most of Roller's sets and costumes, but he insisted on new scenery for the Good Friday meadow. This was based on a painting by Wieland.

In the brilliant festival of 1936, the year of the Olympic Games in Berlin, Wieland's work passed virtually unnoticed, except by Lieselotte, who wrote to her parents that it received "general admiration". Not *Parsifal*, but Tietjen's lavish new production of *Lohengrin* was the main centre of attraction. It was conducted by Wilhelm Furtwängler, who had temporarily patched up his differences with Winifred, and, to mark the festive occasion, Tietjen restored the cut which Wagner himself had made in Lohengrin's narration in the third act. It is certainly evidence of Hitler's knowledge of the work that, on hearing the unaccustomed passage for the first time, he started up in alarm, thinking that something had gone wrong. The Wagner purists naturally seized the occasion to renew their protests, but Winifred no longer needed to worry about that: with Hitler seated at her side, her triumph over her enemies was demonstrably complete.

Winifred had extended her husband's little working annexe in the grounds of Wahnfried into a complete and sizable house, to be used as a residence for important conductors and singers until such time as she should relinquish Wahnfried to her successor and retire to it herself. In 1936 Hitler decided to use the annexe as his own residence during the festival, and the large Wahnfried garden was made over to him with it. Between the two adjoining houses there was a constant flow, Hitler going to Wahnfried for some meals, Winifred and the children going to the *Siegfried-Wagner-Haus* for others. Once during each festival Hitler would hold there a reception for the artists taking part in the festival. The *Künstlerempfang* in 1936, Lieselotte reported, went on till three in the morning.

The Nazi takeover was complete—at least as regards the outward show. Inside the *Festspielhaus*—as I have described more fully in my book *Wagner at Bayreuth*—there were people at work who refused to capitulate to the flagrant demands of the more fanatical Nazi officials. And though many fine singers had by now ceased to appear at Bayreuth, either because they were Jewish or Jewish-connected or because they were critical of the Hitler régime, they had been replaced by other singers sufficiently talented to make their absence less noticeable. Many of these were undoubtedly delighted to be invited to Hitler's *Künstlerempfang*, but, whether delighted or not, all of them knew better than to refuse. Frida Leider, who had a Jewish husband, was one of those who allowed her loyalty to Wagner and Bayreuth to outweigh her distaste for the outward show, but—as she reveals in her reminiscences—the strain eventually proved too great for her, and after the festival of 1938 she did not return.

*

Wieland's labour service in Kulmbach came to an end in September, when he was called up for the military service for which he had volunteered. Once again the authorities were accommodating: he was posted to an anti-tank company (*Tank-Abwehr-Kompagnie*) stationed in Bayreuth itself. Army service proved far more congenial to him than his labour service. He was surrounded by personal friends who had volunteered with him, and he could spend his spare time at home getting on with his painting. This was certainly more important to him than his military duties, which he could not take seriously at all. Danzer, who had remained at Grossenhain when Wieland moved to Kulmbach, but was now reunited with him at the barracks, told me that they amused themselves on parade making surreptitious fun of self-important NCOs.

The NCOs retaliated by separating them—but only on parade.

For the festival of 1937 Tietjen decided to have the sets for *Parsifal* redesigned completely. Emil Preetorius showed no inclination to take on the task. Wieland, having been found good enough to patch Roller's settings where necessary in 1936, saw no reason why he should not now be given a chance to do the whole work. Though Winifred herself told me, many years after, that both she and Tietjen approved the idea, Wieland himself did not gain the impression that their consent was willingly given. To Gertrud, who was now studying ballet in Munich, he complained that he had to fight fiercely for it. It is possible that his interpretation of the events was complicated by his growing dislike of Tietjen, whose attitude towards his mother (so he told Gertrud) was as domineering as it was towards himself.

However, once having gained his object, he went to work in a fully professional spirit. He was still not yet following Roller's advice of preparing all his sets as models: he painted the main scenes as pictures, which were then given to the stage carpenters and painters to translate into sets. His original paintings, some of which can still be seen in the *Richard-Wagner-Gedenkstätte* in Bayreuth, show a very fine regard for form and colour relationships. The stage photograph of his temple, reproduced opposite page 96, reveals how much gets lost in the adaptation of paintings to solid sets. The general approach, as this picture shows, is completely traditional, though there is a reduction in the amount of realistic detail which was a feature of the original designs by Joukowsky.

Wieland's realistic approach was in no way a concession to the taste of Tietjen and his mother. At that time he was himself a conscious traditionalist, and he tended to agree with those critics who complained that Tietjen and Preetorius were replacing Wagner's ideas with ideas of their own. In fact, he held to this view all his life, and he would speak disparagingly of what he called "Preetorius's Japanese tea-garden style".

Wieland showed a more revolutionary spirit in his attempt to solve the difficulty of the transformations between the two scenes of Acts One and Three, when Parsifal and Gurnemanz move from an outdoor scene into the temple. This had hitherto been done by a process of moving the scenery sideways while the singers marked time on the stage in front of it. Basically it is a cinematic idea, and Wieland decided to make actual use of cinematic techniques. Practical help came from Paul Eberhardt, a young lighting expert whom Tietjen had brought to Bayreuth. In the course of teaching Wieland to drive a car, Eberhardt had become a close personal friend, and he now designed for Wieland a special three-dimensional projecting apparatus which enabled three slides, prepared from Wieland's sketches, to be projected at differing speeds simultaneously through a single lens. The speed could be controlled to correspond exactly with the conductor's tempo. Eberhardt, who became one of Wieland's closest artistic collaborators from this time to the end of Wieland's life, told me that his apparatus worked well until it was broken by a clumsy manipulator.

Determined to make the most of his chance with *Parsifal*, Wieland did more than Tietjen had asked of him. Lieselotte Schmidt reported to her parents in June 1937 that she and a friend were busy sewing costumes for the Flower Maidens according to Wieland's designs. "He has been preparing them in secret, just in case the question of costumes gets serious." Consequently, when Tietjen asked Wieland to prepare some costume designs, he was able to produce not only designs, but actual garments on the spot, and they were paraded before Tietjen, Gertrud acting as model. According to Lieselotte, Tietjen approved the costumes and sent Wieland to the *Festspielhaus* to consult with the wardrobe master, Curt Palm. Lieselotte remarked gleefully, "For the first time we shall have classically beautiful Flower Maidens!" She spoke too soon. Palm, with whom I spoke in Bayreuth (and who, like Eberhardt, developed a lasting artistic relationship with Wieland), remembers that Wieland's costumes were not used in 1937: Roller's costumes were retained.

Memories are generally rather vague, but the probable reason for the rejection of Wieland's costumes was lack of time to prepare them in sufficient numbers, coupled with Wieland's own absence from the scene at the crucial time. Army manœuvres stole two and a half vital weeks of his rehearsal time, and he returned to Bayreuth only a few days before the first performance of *Parsifal* (with Furtwängler conducting) on 23 July.

Wieland (wrote Lieselotte) could be well satisfied with what
Hitler, who was present at the opening, said to him about his
scenery. He could also be satisfied with the newspaper reviews,
one of which remarked, "The monumental Temple of the Grail
and equally the outdoor scenes, full of contrast yet recognisable
as variations of a single fabulous landscape, are admirable.
They strike one as a visual realisation of the musical moods."

However, criticism came from another quarter. Daniela,
convinced that Winifred with the help of Tietjen and Preetorius was artistically betraying Bayreuth, demonstrated her
general disapproval by staying away from the festival. Supplied
with picture postcards of Wieland's new sets by friends in
Bayreuth, she sat down in Salzburg to write him a letter, four
pages of close typescript, describing in merciless detail every
divergence from the master's instructions of which she judged
him guilty. The letter ended as follows:

"With the works of the master, your grandfather, other
theatres may experiment as much as they please and as much as
their sense of responsibility will permit them. *But in Bayreuth
our sole duty is to carry out the master's will*, as laid down with all
clarity in the scores of his works, in countless essays and letters,
in a tradition that has been held sacred for nearly half a
century. Precisely because his wishes are no longer being
rigorously fulfilled in all purity and faith I have felt it necessary
to sever my connection with the present-day Bayreuth. I cannot
sit through a performance of *Parsifal* in which, beside countless
other misdeeds, *forty-eight* Flower Maidens appear instead of
the *twenty-four* called for by the master to provide with their
gentle movements the proper musical balance for the six solo
voices; in which the colour of the costumes worn by the
Knights of the Grail are arbitrarily changed. The master
selected these fine light shades with conscious artistry to match
both the instrumentation of his orchestra and the gently
glistening gold mosaic of his Temple. . . . Equally I cannot sit
though a *Lohengrin* in which, beside countless other transgres-
sions against the master's will, the long narration is sung which
he expressly said he did *not* wish to be used in the drama (consult the letters which he wrote to Liszt in 1850). For my attitude,
forced on me by circumstances, I have been mocked and
derided, outlawed and *slandered*—and have still to endure it...."

"It would have been so simple, so natural and so pleasant if, in making your designs, you had sought instruction and advice from me, knowing that I have been immersed in these works for as long as I can remember, and that from the year 1909 onwards I was your father's most loyal helper and colleague."

Making allowances for Daniela's understandable bitterness and even acknowledging the rightness of many of her views, one must nevertheless feel that it was an ungenerous letter to send to a young man just setting out on his career. At least she might have found a few words of encouragement to temper her criticism. Wieland was deeply wounded by Daniela's letter, as his reply, dated 24 August 1937, clearly shows:

"My dear Aunt Lulu—Regarding your letter I have this to say to you: in view of your great knowledge and experience of the work, I shall always be grateful for anything you can tell me which does *not* appear in the scores, piano arrangements and written material in the archives. You will always find me ready to respect everything that you learned directly from the master or his very talented assistant [*geniale Mitarbeiterin*: a reference to Cosima]. But you will understand that the eldest grandchild, embarking with open eyes and heart on the heavy tasks confronting him, must necessarily strive sharply to distinguish, in the knowledge he has to acquire, between what is authentically proven and the things people say.

"If you had been in the *Festspielhaus* yourself and had judged my *Parsifal* settings with your own eyes, your letter would have meant much more to me. But you have based your verdict on the reports of third persons who are opposed to my mother and to the present approach to the festival work, and on picture postcards and newspaper reports. If you could bring yourself in future not to judge the festival from Salzburg, but to view it with your own eyes, I should be very willing to accept any form of criticism or advice. With warm regards, Yours— Wieland."

The savagery of Wieland's reply might have owed something to his own feelings of insecurity, arising in part from his uneasy relationship with Tietjen and his mother, but more profoundly from his modesty—the innate modesty of an artist who is constantly aware of his inability to express all that he has inside him. Something of his true state of mind at this time might be discerned from a letter written to Daniela by an old Bayreuth visitor, Professor Golther, who spoke to Wieland just before the *Parsifal* opening. "Wieland said it was very rash of him to do the scenery for *Parsifal* at the age of twenty, and I was pleased with that remark. He went on to say jokingly that one should look at it first, then complain afterwards. I told him how happy I was to see the festival work back in the hands of a young Wälsung, from whom we might hope great things."

This last sentence was possibly intended as a gentle reproof to Daniela for having failed so dismally to give her young nephew a little sign of encouragement. She had sent copies of her letter to Wieland to a number of old friends, but only Golther had shown a faint distaste. Others, such as Daniela's sister Blandine and the conductor Karl Muck, wrote congratulating her on her outspokenness.

Wieland's reply to Daniela makes it clear that he definitely regarded the festival as his life's work, and that he was actively preparing himself for it in his own way. A voracious reader, he had already begun his study of Richard Wagner's writings and other books on the life and works available in the Wahnfried archives. Apart from that he had always had a ready ear for the reminiscences of his aunts Daniela and Eva, and spent many hours questioning them about earlier productions in Bayreuth. As yet, however, he had not concerned himself analytically with the music, a task for which he was not yet trained.

*

In November 1937 Hitler decided that Wieland should be released from the army at once, after only a year's service. He had managed only a month before his discharge to gain promotion to the rank of lance-corporal. But any ideas that Hitler might have had that the Wagner heir would now begin to take an active part in the running of the festival were not realised. Five years were to pass before Wieland was again invited to provide scenery for a new production there.

On his release from the army Wieland went straight into hospital in Bayreuth for a long delayed rupture operation. His brother Wolfgang was already there, suffering from rheumatic

Wieland, aged forty-eight, rehearsing Brünnhilde with Birgit
Nilsson in Bayreuth

Wieland, aged
forty-nine,
rehearsing Berg's
Lulu with Anja
Silja and Carlos
Alexander in
Stuttgart

fever. Though he made a quick recovery from the operation, Wieland, while still in hospital, was stricken with an embolism which severely affected his right lung, and for a while his condition gave rise to real anxiety. He was still in bed when Siegfried's opera *Schwarzschwanenreich*, with Wieland's scenery, was produced in Antwerp.

The year 1938, in which Wieland celebrated his twenty-first birthday, found him in a state of almost complete stagnation. There were two productions of Siegfried's operas for which Wieland designed the scenery: *Sonnenflammen* in Düsseldorf and *Der Bärenhäuter* in Cologne, and this last Wieland was able to attend, staying in Bad Godesberg as Hitler's personal guest. At length, his health fully recovered, he began to find his inactivity irksome, and he pressed his mother for a decision on his future.

Tietjen came forward with a complete plan: Wieland should join him at the *Staatsoper* in Berlin and learn production and the administration of an opera house, starting at the bottom. The whole course of training would take eight years. Wieland rejected the proposal out of hand and announced his own plan: to go to Munich and study art with a teacher of his own choice.

6

STUDY IN MUNICH

1938–1942

GERTRUD, WHO WAS studying ballet at the *Günther Schule* in Munich, run by Carl Orff according to a system based on the style of Mary Wigman, had a flat in the Kaulbachstrasse, and Wieland set up his studio in the same building. He had no desire to study at the *Kunstakademie*, but preferred to take lessons privately.

A picture by Ferdinand Staeger which he had seen at an exhibition in Bayreuth had attracted him through the artist's manipulation of light. According to Gertrud, it showed something of the technique of the French Impressionists, though the subject of the picture, peasants at work in the fields, was more in line with the sort of pictorial idealisation favoured by the Nazis at that time. Wieland visited Staeger in Munich and, in spite of the difference in their ages, they formed an immediate bond of sympathy. Staeger consented to take on the task of teaching the young man. The object was to improve Wieland's painting technique, and the question of subject did not enter into the bargain. In any case, Wieland's artistic intentions were not yet clearly defined, and he showed in his own paintings no desire to experiment, either in subject or form. His technical interests (Gertrud told me) lay in the gradations of light and shade, and his tendency was to produce pictures that were blueprints for stage productions rather than self-contained artistic expressions. The picture reproduced opposite page 40, painted in 1939 in the Munich studio, seems to support this opinion.

In the first two years after leaving Wahnfried Wieland spent most of the daylight hours working in his studio. Staeger would come in occasionally to inspect his work, and Gertrud frequently acted as his model. In the evenings Wieland would visit the opera, the theatre and the cinema, filling in the many gaps which his upbringing in the over-specialised atmosphere of Bayreuth had left in his general cultural education. When he first came to Munich, Wieland was inclined to scoff at Gertrud's interest in Bach and Mozart. He soon came to revise his views.

There was no definite break with Bayreuth, where, in spite of the outbreak of war, the festival was still being held every summer. It was in Wahnfried in the spring of 1940 that a meeting with Kurt Overhoff reminded Wieland of the inadequacy of his musical education. Overhoff, now a producer at the Mozarteum in Salzburg, described in a talk broadcast by the Austrian Radio in Salzburg in 1969 how one day in Wahnfried he saw a score of *Rheingold* lying on the piano. "I began to play it to Wieland and Wolfgang and to explain it. . . . That same evening Wieland implored me to come to Bayreuth permanently and to initiate him into the works of his grandfather. He complained bitterly about . . . Heinz Tietjen and about his own mother, and asserted that they were both deliberately keeping him in ignorance, in order to be able to reject his claims to future participation in the festival work."

Overhoff had first come to Winifred's attention in 1937 during a Wagner festival in Heidelberg, where he was musical director. A native of Vienna, he had scored an early success as a composer with his opera *Mira*, produced in Essen in 1925, when he was twenty-three. He studied conducting at the Vienna *Staatsoper*, where he came into contact both with Richard Strauss and Alfred Roller. He appeared on all counts to be well equipped to act as Wieland's tutor, and Winifred took him on the Bayreuth staff. He gave up his conducting post in Heidelberg and moved to Munich.

In the meantime Wieland's enthusiasm appeared to have abated, and Overhoff had some difficulty in reawakening his interest. Wieland's first concern was still his painting. "In matters of expression," he told Overhoff, "it is colour and form that count, not words and music." He continued to spend his days at his easel, allowing Overhoff only an hour or two of his time each evening.

Eventually, however, he became fascinated by Overhoff's

method of teaching, which was not confined to a dry analysis
of musical themes, but took into account tonal colour, rhythms
and key relationships, all used by Wagner for dramatic purposes in the realisation of his philosophical and psychological
ideas. The range of Overhoff's analyses can be seen in his book
Die Musikdramen Richard Wagners, which is based on the lessons he
gave Wieland during those Munich years. In addition, he taught
Wieland the techniques of score-reading and conducting. At
a concert in Heidelberg, where Overhoff still occasionally
appeared as a guest conductor, he gave Wieland an opportunity to conduct the overture to *Der Fliegende Holländer*.
Wieland, however, had no particular talent for or interest in
conducting, and he made no further public appearances as a
conductor.

*

While Wieland had been pursuing his studies in Munich,
protected by Hitler from taking any active part in the war, his
brother Wolfgang had been called up for military service. At
the very start of the Polish campaign he received a wound in
the left arm which severely impaired the use of his hand, and
he was discharged from the army. The injury put paid to his
ambitions of an engineering career. Tietjen offered to take him
on the staff of the Berlin *Staatsoper* to learn the business of
producing and administration over a period of four to five
years. It was in fact the same plan that had been offered to
Wieland and rejected, although spread over a shorter time.
Wolfgang accepted it. Relations between him and Tietjen
were cordial, and in the Bayreuth Festival of 1941 Wolfgang
was officially named as a musical assistant.

In a lengthy letter of complaint addressed to Winifred from
Berlin after this festival was over, Tietjen claimed to have
noticed a change of attitude in Wolfgang, who, he said, went
out of his way to avoid him during the festival. Tietjen put this
down to the influence of Wieland, who in his presence had
greeted a newcomer to the Bayreuth staff with the words,
"Welcome to this madhouse." Wieland had also told Tietjen's
daughter that Tietjen's conducting in *Die Walküre* had been

"a terrible mess", and he had openly complained to a member of the festival staff that Tietjen was purposely keeping him and his brother at a distance in order to prolong his own authority at Bayreuth. According to this report, Tietjen went on, Wieland intended to approach Hitler with a suggestion that he should now take over the running of the festival himself.

One can understand Tietjen's feeling, expressed to Winifred in this letter, that the time for a showdown had come. In particular he seemed hurt by the suggestion that he was deliberately attempting to prevent the grandsons from taking part in the festival. It had been reported to him, he said, that Wieland was keen to become a painter and would be delighted to be released from any obligations to the festival beyond designing scenery. Whether or not Tietjen really believed this, the fact remains that Wieland, by his voluntary withdrawal to Munich, had provided his enemy with a convenient argument. Indeed, he had timed the whole operation very badly, for neither he nor his brother Wolfgang were at that time qualified to run the festival unaided. Overhoff, to whom Wieland appealed for evidence to support his criticisms of Tietjen's supposed inadequacies as a conductor, advised him in the interests of the festival not to provoke Tietjen to the point of resignation. Wieland saw the wisdom of his advice and capitulated. An uneasy peace was restored.

Tietjen's document, Wieland wrote to Overhoff, had greeted him on his wedding day. He married Gertrud at the registry office in Nussdorf on 12 September 1941, both of them being at the age of twenty-four. In accordance with Wieland's wishes, the marriage was celebrated entirely without fuss, and three weeks later Gertrud departed for Italy to take up a language course for which she had booked long before the wedding.

Wieland returned to Munich alone. For a while he was deprived not only of Gertrud, but also of his music teacher, for Overhoff was suddenly called up for military service. Overhoff himself saw this as an act of revenge on Tietjen's part for the role he was suspected of having played in Wieland's abortive palace revolution, but it could of course have simply been a case of one government department not knowing what another was doing. However, his subsequent release to continue with Wieland's musical training was due to the intercession, not of

Winifred or Tietjen, but of Clemens Krauss, who was then musical director of the Munich Opera.

Wieland had come into close contact with Krauss at rehearsals for *Der Freischütz*, which he was invited to attend as a guest of the producer, Rudolf Hartmann. This was for him a valuable experience, and one that certainly helped to turn his own interests in the direction of production. At Bayreuth he had of course seen both his father and Tietjen at work, but probably in both cases his reactions had been too subjective to allow him to profit by his experience. Though in Munich he was playing only an observer's role, Wieland now found himself watching a major producer and a major conductor working on an opera which was not part of his own heritage. There were no family traditionalists to tell them what they must do: the work alone was important in determining the means of its expression.

Erik Maschat, who was Krauss's assistant at that time, remembered that during rehearsals Wieland showed tremendous interest, though he was too modest to say anything at all. Maschat's picture of Wieland, whom he said was well liked by everybody, contrasts strangely with the portrait so far presented of an aggressive, rather self-willed young man with a pronounced sense of grievance. But it is a version that will be met again, almost invariably outside Bayreuth. Wieland had the ability to relax completely only when he was at a safe distance from Wahnfried and the family.

*

Yet Bayreuth remained at the centre of his life. In the family history 1942 was an eventful year. Eva Chamberlain, the last survivor of the second generation, died; and on 12 June the first representative of the fourth generation was born. Gertrud returned to Bayreuth for the birth of her daughter, who was given the name of Iris Diana—the first documented indication that in the minds of her parents the family predilection for Nordic legend was yielding to a taste for ancient Greece.

At this time Wieland was working on scenic designs for a new production of *Der Fliegende Holländer* at Nuremberg and supervising their construction in the workshops at Bayreuth.

The first performance took place in November 1942 and earned Wieland considerable praise for settings which were traditional in approach, though, as in his *Parsifal* of 1937, they showed some economy of detail. The producer was the director of the Nuremberg Opera, Willi Hanke. According to Winifred Wagner, he chose a very naturalistic approach, even to the extent of showing Senta at one point seated on a table swinging her legs. Wieland was not happy with the production, and he resolved to design no more settings for productions other than his own. With the single exception of his *Meistersinger* sets for Bayreuth in 1943, he kept to this decision for the rest of his life.

It was one he could now afford to make. Overhoff's work with him, resumed in Munich after his return from the army, had progressed to the extent that Wieland was now ready to try out in practice what he had absorbed in theory. With the help of Dr Goebbels, an opening was found at Altenburg, not far from Leipzig. Early in 1943 Wieland was appointed chief opera producer at the *Landestheater* there, and at the same time Overhoff was made musical director.

7

PRODUCING IN ALTENBURG AND NUREMBERG

1943–1944

GERMANY'S WEALTH OF opera companies, of which there are still more than fifty active today, is the result of the country's historical development. Even up to Richard Wagner's middle years Germany consisted of a vast number of entirely separate kingdoms, principalities, duchies and markgravates. Their rulers built theatres and had their own resident actors and singers and musicians, and this naturally led to rivalry between them. The artistic standard of their theatre was a matter of pride and prestige. Though in 1918 the monarchs and princes and lesser nobility lost the last remains of their power, their palaces and their theatres remained, and the local tradition of theatre-going which they had built up continued. Hence that wide distribution of resident theatre and opera companies which is, even today, one of the most enviable features of the German artistic scene—not only from the theatregoer's point of view, but also from the practising artist's, since it is possible for actors, singers, conductors and producers to gain continuous practical experience in lesser, but still reputable, ensembles on their way to the great centres of Berlin, Munich, Hamburg, Stuttgart and Frankfurt.

Altenburg, though a town of only fifty thousand inhabitants, was one of these. There, with a resident company of singers and an orchestra of modest size but acknowledged excellence, Wieland was able to throw himself straight into the task of designing, casting and producing works from beginning to end on his own while his brother Wolfgang, as a single cog in the vast machinery of the Berlin *Staatsoper*, had to be content for the time being with stage management and coaching.

Reception hall in Wahnfried (*above*) in Cosima's days and (*below*) the same after post-war conversion (Wieland's daughter Iris on sofa)

Wahnfried (*above*) and the *Festspielhaus*, Bayreuth (*below*)

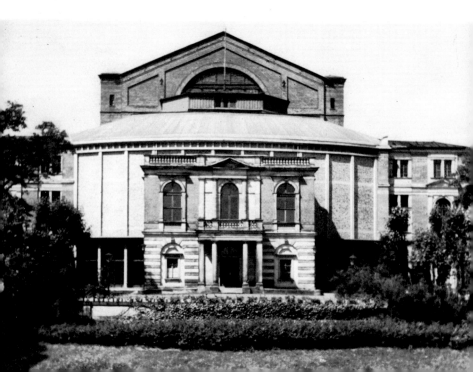

Wieland began his producing career with the most gigantic work in the whole operatic repertoire: *Der Ring des Nibelungen*—and not only in Altenburg, but simultaneously in Nuremberg. The director of the *Landestheater*, Ernst Lüsenhop, generously allowed Wieland to accept Willi Hanke's invitation to produce the whole cycle at Nuremberg as long as it did not interfere with his duties at Altenburg. In the same year (1943) Wieland was commissioned to design settings for Tietjen's new production of *Die Meistersinger* at the Bayreuth Festival.

The physical difficulties of coping with this huge amount of work, which would have been severe enough in peacetime, were still further intensified by the wartime conditions of air raids, housing shortages and rationing, both of food and petrol. Though Wieland eventually had a room of his own in Overhoff's flat in Altenburg, his main basis was Bayreuth, where Gertrud, now expecting her second child, was living. As far as she was able, Gertrud accompanied her husband on his journeys between Bayreuth, Altenburg and Nuremberg, helping him privately with choreographic work on stage.

*

Wieland himself often said that his production of the *Ring* in Altenburg contained the seeds of his later development. Of the Nuremberg production he had nothing to say, probably for the reason that it was on the whole traditional: a large production employing sets constructed in the Bayreuth workshops and making use of the excellent technical facilities with which the Nuremberg stage was equipped. The stage in Altenburg was very much smaller, the resident company less experienced in Wagner singing and consequently more malleable, and he was working with a musical director with whom he had studied the works in detail. Obviously, if there was any experimenting to be done, Altenburg was the right place to do it, particularly since it was further from Bayreuth than Nuremberg and less in the glare of general publicity.

The first of the *Ring* productions to reach the stage—in June 1943—was *Die Walküre* in Nuremberg. A programme note which Wieland wrote for it throws some light on his approach:

C

"*Kinder, schafft Neues!* (Children, create new things): this alleged statement by Richard Wagner is always pressed into service to justify any arbitrary decision on the part of the producer or other deviation from the composer's score. But in fact what Wagner said was, '*Kinder, macht Neues*'—'Children, do new things—and only new things. If you stick to old things, the devil of unproductivity will get you, and you will be the most miserable of artists.' Wagner spoke these words when he observed Joachim Raff busy revising an old work, and consequently they can be taken to refer simply and solely to *musical* creation in his own time. The urge to 'create new things' in presenting a Wagnerian music drama can only stem from a desire to present the dramatic idea of the work in a way *different* from that laid down by the composer. Any such attempt must lead sooner or later to discrepancies between the music and the action, since these form—and formed from the very moment of their conception—one single, indivisible whole. Wagner's composition sketches show quite clearly that during the process of creation he heard the sound and at the same time saw the stage action vividly in his mind. In consequence the happenings on the stage must be made to correspond exactly with the music. The nature of the dramatic action demanded by each musical motive is not of course specified, and it cannot be defined according to one particular style. Thus the producer is at complete liberty to seek new forms of expression in line with the personality of the singer concerned. It is of little significance if the chosen forms sometimes run counter to so-called tradition (which is anyway seldom verifiable in detail), since *above* every tradition there stands the will of the creator as clearly laid down in the score. One has only to think, for example, of the *Feuerzauber*: it has become 'traditional' in performance to increase the height of the flames right up to the fall of the curtain. That means that, in order to achieve a purely external effect, both music and stage directions are ignored. These clearly require the flames to sink out of sight behind the rock and night to fall."

Wieland seems here to be giving expression to a literal purism outdoing even Daniela in its pious regard for the composer's wishes. But a closer examination reveals the basic principle from which Wieland claimed later in life never to have deviated: namely, a return to the original source, which is the work as written down, and not to any single interpretation of it, even if that interpretation came from the master himself. The sentence, "The nature of the dramatic action demanded by each musical motive is not of course specified, and it cannot be defined according to one particular style," is a direct criticism of the methods of Cosima, the chief architect of the "tradition" Wieland so much despised. It is also, more positively, a vindication of his own departures from tradition. His argument that the producer is free to invent action as long as it arises from the musical motive is the first step towards his later contention that the producer is free to invent action as long as it arises from the *psychological situation* which the musical motive illustrates. But in 1943 he had not yet come, as he subsequently did, to separate the functions of words and music and to seek the dramatic reactions of the actors in the meaning of the words alone, leaving the music to supply its own comment without visual aid. He was still tied, though less tightly than Cosima, to the conviction that the singers on stage had to illustrate the music with matching gestures.

Wieland's triumphant dig in his programme note at the traditionalists for ignoring the composer's instructions regarding the Magic Fire music was a legitimate point to make, though it has in fact nothing to do with his main argument, which concerns the actions of the singers on stage. The treatment of the *Feuerzauber* is in fact a scenic problem, and it raises the question whether Wagner's wishes can be met at all in the framework of a realistic setting. Since the Nuremberg production of *Die Walküre* was a realistic one, Wieland probably felt it wiser in that context not to pursue the question. But he was shortly afterwards to deal with it in practice in his production at Altenburg.

An extract from Professor Richard Reinhardt's review in the *Bayerischer Kurier* of 30 June 1943 gives some idea of the impact made in Nuremberg by Wieland's *Die Walküre*:

"The young scenic artist strikes out more boldly into new territory in the wild and rocky mountain scenery of the second act, which has the quality of genius. The huge rock on the left, with its steep, jagged high walls, has a genuinely unearthly character. Wotan's heroically tragic decision to abandon his new world plan, revealed for the first time in the great narration, seems even stronger against the background of these Cyclopean rocks, since it shows Man (the superman Wotan) as even greater than mighty Nature. In the third act Wieland Wagner has made use of Nuremberg's great cyclorama to create a vast picture, presenting a view from the mountain top past the clearly visible fir tree to the distant peaks from which Wotan's wrath comes storming. Brünnhilde's fate, usually sealed on a narrow mountain summit, is here brought out into the wide world, which does after all play a prominent role in the drama."

Here, certainly, one sees the first tentative move towards that clearing of the stage which was to lead to Wieland's subsequent master stroke, in his first Bayreuth production of *Die Walküre*, of laying Brünnhilde down to sleep virtually on the summit of the world. But dramatically he was clearly still far from his later interpretation of the figure of Wotan. This picture of the heroic god, more powerful than Nature itself, was the work of a young German who had not yet experienced disillusionment. The Wotan of *Die Walküre* in Altenburg was out of the same mould: in the words of one critic, "a unified character who in anger, despair or love always remains what he is: a god".

*

Siegfried followed in Nuremberg in August, and then in the following month Wieland began his *Ring* production at Altenburg with *Die Walküre*. This was followed by *Götterdämmerung* in December and *Siegfried* in January. In April 1944 Wieland added *Götterdämmerung* to his Nuremberg *Ring*, then returned to Altenburg to complete the cycle with *Rheingold* in May. In the midst of all this he found time and energy to produce *Der Freischütz* in Altenburg. In the circumstances it is not surprising that the *Freischütz* production, for which Wieland himself did not design the scenery, was cast in a traditional mould. While reasonably successful, it made no lasting impression on the minds of the three people with whom I discussed it: Ernst Lüsenhop, Kurt Overhoff (who conducted it) and Gertrud

Wagner, whose main memory was of rehearsing the peasant dances while in the last stages of her pregnancy.

The impact of the *Ring* production in Altenburg was far more permanent, and memories tend to confirm Wieland's claim that it contained the seeds of his later ideas, though opinions differ regarding the extent to which these ideas were due to design or accident. Wieland himself once told me that in Altenburg the existing scenery for the *Ring* was in a poor state and, since he was unable to obtain new scenery, he contented himself with leaving out as much as he could—"and nobody seemed to mind". He told the same story with further embellishments to the Parisian critic Antoine Goléa, whose book *Entretiens avec Wieland Wagner* appeared a year after Wieland's death. "I had to make do with the existing theatre properties," he told Goléa. "I was not allowed to spend any money at all. . . . Since I could not provide anything of my own, I contented myself with taking out more and more of what was there. I worked pragmatically and with a certain amount of caution. At every rehearsal I simplified the background. On the last day nothing was left at all—and it went all right. Nobody tried to stop me."

This is totally at variance with the facts as recalled by Ernst Lüsenhop, the artistic director of the Altenburg *Landestheater* at the time. There was never any intention, he told me, that Wieland should use the existing scenery, which was both old and old-fashioned. The *Landestheater*, though modest in size, possessed modern equipment and had its own resident staff of technicians, carpenters, scene painters and costume makers. It also had a healthy budget. Altenburg was fully alive to the distinction of having a grandson of Richard Wagner working in its midst, and Lüsenhop found no difficulty in procuring from the town and provincial government an additional financial subsidy for a new production that was regarded from the start as a prestige affair. The extra money, amounting to 110,000 marks (about £10,000) was intended to cover the costs of engaging guest singers for the main roles, reinforcing the orchestra and providing new scenery and costumes. Wieland was given a free hand to spend the money as he wished. In fact, Lüsenhop told me, he did not spend it all: at the end something like 40,000 marks remained unused. It is possible,

Lüsenhop added, that Wieland was sometimes unable, owing to wartime shortages, to obtain the exact materials he wanted, but this was certainly not due to lack of financial means.

Lüsenhop's account, confirmed by Overhoff, leads one to conclude either that Wieland subsequently forgot the true circumstances of his time in Altenburg, or that he deliberately invented his version of it. Though this second speculation seems the more likely, one wonders why he should have preferred fantasy to facts, which flatter him far more by suggesting that his new ideas owed their origin to choice rather than necessity. Possibly the urge arose from his wish to preserve intact, in his own mind as well as in the minds of outsiders like Goléa and myself, the impression that he owed allegiance to nobody but himself. His distrust of the past, which had been the cause of so much frustration in his early life, was a powerful censor.

Gertrud Wagner today recalls that the stage at Altenburg was too small to permit any elaborate architecture, and certainly in comparison with the vast dimensions of the *Festspielhaus* in Bayreuth or even the relative largeness of the Nuremberg stage, it must have seemed to Wieland very cramped. With the available projectors he could conjure up a Valhalla, for example, but otherwise he had to rely for scenic effects on painted backcloths, which he himself helped to paint, and on the use of platforms covered with stage grass.

Overhoff's training had done its work in making Wieland conscious of the wealth of colour and imagery which Wagner had built into his orchestral scores. In his efforts to match them visually, Wieland had come to realise that, from the dramatic point of view, painting has one great disadvantage: it is a static form of art. A visual background which fits exactly the mood of one dramatic moment is likely to be quite wrong in the next. Lighting can help to provide fluidity, and has always been used in that way since means of controlling it were invented. Wieland now took this process a stage further. Realising that, as long as definite objects are visible, lighting must be related to them, he began by the process of trial and error to remove these objects one by one from the stage as they became disturbing in the continuous dramatic development.

This was the first cautious step in the direction of the "empty space" idea which Wieland was later to develop so strikingly at Bayreuth. It was based on the feeling that lighting, freed from the restrictive task of illuminating realistic objects, could act significantly on the subconscious emotions and thus convey essential meanings more important to Wagner's purpose than the external framework. Wieland was in fact now beginning to use lighting in the same way that Wagner used his orchestra: as a commentary on the stage action and not as a direct description of it.

His process of taking out more and more of the static properties with which he began was certainly not due to the fact that they were poor objects in themselves, as he asserted both to Goléa and to me, but simply an attempt to see how much literal realism could be eliminated without destroying the intelligibility of the action. Basically his approach to the drama was still realistic, but it was realism reduced down to its barest essentials in order to leave his lighting free to create its emotional effects. Lüsenhop recalls that Wieland spent long hours rehearsing with the lighting technicians, and before the first performance of *Götterdämmerung* Lüsenhop kept the theatre closed for a full week so that Wieland could rehearse his lighting effects to the full.

In the *Altenburger Zeitung* of 13 September 1943 Arthur Schmolitzky wrote of *Die Walküre*: "The elemental force of the action unfolds against a background in which all that is needed on stage is transformed into art. We are presented with 'pictures', with all the qualities we expect in them. Rocks, which usually lie around in a purposeless way, here become living entities in a heroic landscape. Sensitive lighting helps to provide a moving experience."

A more literal-minded critic, Friedrich Preuss, writing in the *Altenburger Zeitung* of 20 December 1943 about *Götterdämmerung*, reveals the distance to which Wieland had gone in his policy of leaving things out. "Certainly we ask ourselves why the composer's detailed stage instructions are so often ignored. Why do the Norns stand, almost motionless, when according to Wagner the first is seated under a fir tree (which was not there), the second reclining on a (missing) stone bench and the third seated on a rock? The rope broke in the music—but not on the stage. Curtains, used in the palace of the Gibichungs, are always a makeshift device, and a tree, however large it may be, does not constitute a forest scene. And we do not want to see the rock formations of the Valkyries' mountain appearing again outside Gunther's palace on the Rhine." But then the critic himself dismissed these as "only slight blemishes" and added, "These apart, the general impression was one of faithfulness to the composer's intentions."

In Altenburg Wieland had his first opportunity of using costumes of his own designing. According to Overhoff, he dispensed right away with helmets and breast-plates and clothed his Valkyries in tights "with hair blowing violently in the wind" (Salzburg broadcast). It is curious, in reading the reviews, to find no mention of this startling innovation. All that Schmolitzky had to say on the subject was: "Stylish costumes show an awareness of the symbolic significance of colour, and fit into the prevailing mood."

There was much in his use of scenery, costumes and lighting to suggest that Wieland had already learnt from the writings of two men whose influence he later acknowledged: Gordon Craig and the Swiss designer Adolphe Appia. Though Houston Stewart Chamberlain's attempts to interest Cosima in Appia's ideas on the interpretative use of lighting had been witheringly rejected, Appia's books found their way into the library at Wahnfried, and Gertrud recalls with what avidity Wieland used to study them in his youthful days. Siegfried Wagner had been interested in Gordon Craig, and Craig's books were also on the shelves at Wahnfried. But, according to Gertrud, Wieland's interest in both Appia and Craig was only partial: he entirely rejected their use of cubistic or abstract sets.

However, these were only two of the many scenic artists whose work Wieland had studied attentively in his younger years. He read all the books on stagecraft on which he could lay his hands, and he learned in this way about the experimental work of Alfred Roller and Oskar Strnad in Vienna and of Ludwig Sievert, who had used lighting as the basis of a production of the *Ring* in Freiburg before Wieland was even born. Sievert was also the designer of the scenery for the production of *Der Freischütz* which Wieland witnessed in Munich in 1940, and they had many conversations together. According to Gertrud, Wieland rejected Sievert's later work as too ornate, but this would not have prevented him extracting from it, as he did from Appia and Craig, certain technical aspects which he could adapt to his own use.

The well-known guest singers considered necessary to grace a prestige production which was attracting attention far outside the normal boundaries of Altenburg were selected by Wieland himself. They were Margarete Bäumer (Leipzig) as Brünnhilde in *Die Walküre*; Helena Braun (Munich) as Brünnhilde and Ferdinand Frantz (Vienna) as Hagen in *Götterdämmerung*; Paul Kuën (Dresden) as Mime in *Siegfried* (he was also singing this role in Wieland's Nuremberg production); and Friedrich Dalberg (Leipzig) as Fasolt in *Rheingold*. Wieland wanted Julius Pölzer (Munich) to sing the title role in *Siegfried*, but Pölzer's last-minute indisposition led to the engagement of Gotthelf Pistor, who had sung the role at Bayreuth in Siegfried Wagner's days.

In fact Wieland would willingly have dispensed with the star singers, who arrived only a day or two before the performance and consequently could not be rehearsed with the thoroughness he considered necessary. The resident singers with whom he worked included Wolfgang Emil Ritz (Wotan and Gunther), Kilian Danner (Loge, Siegmund, Siegfried in *Götterdämmerung*), Margarete Katz (Sieglinde and Brünnhilde in *Siegfried*) and Helene Oertel (Fricka, Erda, Waltraute). These and others in the company Wieland subjected to prolonged individual and collective rehearsals far more exhausting than anything to which they had previously been used, but he managed in the process to retain their goodwill and arouse their respect. Lüsenhop, who had started his career as an actor, was delighted to see his young producer working with a care for detail more usual in the preparation of drama than opera, and he gave Wieland his full support and encouragement.

The result of Wieland's efforts was registered by Schmolitzky in his review of *Siegfried* in the *Altenburger Zeitung* of 1 February 1944: "The opera-goers of this town . . . have seen how his activity has transformed singers with whom they are familiar and caused them to grow beyond recognition. We have felt the presence of a man who does not compromise, who does not follow routine or take the easy way out, and who uses all his suggestive power to transmit to his artists the life at the centre of a work of art."

Schmolitzky might have cited a practical instance of Wieland's intense dedication to his work if he had known of it. Lüsenhop revealed to me that shortly before a performance of *Die Walküre* one of the Valkyries was taken ill. It was impossible to drill her substitute in the intricate movements of the scene in the time available. Wieland thereupon dressed himself in the Valkyrie's costume and played the part on the stage during the performance, while the singer sang her role from the wings.

If Wieland had impressed Altenburg audiences through the high quality of his work, he had also won over his colleagues inside the theatre through his personal modesty and charm. There was never any suggestion in his manner that he regarded himself as above the rest by virtue of his birth or position as the prospective heir of Bayreuth. He was punctilious, Lüsenhop recalls, in his observance of the rules of etiquette and careful to seek the permission of his theatre director for any matters that went outside the competence of his position as senior producer. He always worked in close collaboration with Overhoff, his musical director, who was present at all rehearsals with the singers.

Certainly nothing was done from above to single Wieland out as a person of special importance while he was in Altenburg. Hitler did not attend any of the performances of his productions there, and nor indeed did Winifred Wagner. But their excellence had been noticed outside Altenburg, and this led, following a hint from Lüsenhop, to an invitation to Wieland from Karl Böhm in Vienna to undertake a production of the *Ring* in the *Staatsoper*. Wieland went to Vienna to discuss the project, and on his return to Altenburg confessed to Lüsenhop his disappointment with the scanty facilities of the *Staatsoper* stage. Nevertheless, he accepted Böhm's invitation.

By now the war had reached a perilous stage for Germany. On all sides the allied armies were closing in, and air raids were causing increasing devastation. Yet still the opera houses remained open, and in June 1944, the seventy-fifth anniversary of Siegfried Wagner's birth, both his sons were invited to celebrate the occasion with productions of his operas. In the Berlin *Staatsoper* Wolfgang brought out *Bruder Lustig*, while for the *Landestheater* in Altenburg Wieland chose *An allem ist Hütchen schuld*.

This was the work in which Siegfried had immersed himself during the former world war, and it was first produced at Stuttgart in the winter of 1917, the year of Wieland's birth. Wieland's reasons for choosing it were, however, based less on such extraneous considerations than on a genuine delight in the work itself, which Winifred Wagner has called Siegfried's "sunniest" opera. It introduces a string of well-known fairy-tales by the brothers Grimm, linked together by an elf named Hütchen, who takes pleasure in creating mischief and upsetting things, but in the end brings about a general reconciliation with the words *Alle Leiden, allen Schmerz zwingt ein kindlich reines Herz* (All suffering and pain yield to a pure and child-like heart). Certainly a good escapist theme for a country on the verge of catastrophe, and Gertrud, who was responsible for the choreography, told me that Wieland spent some of his happiest days in designing fairy-tale scenery for it and producing elves and animal figures on the stage. Following the first performance in Altenburg the whole production, with Overhoff as conductor, was transported to Bayreuth, where around the date of Siegfried's birthday it was given six performances in the baroque splendours of the *Markgräfliches Opernhaus*.

It was to be Wieland's last production for seven years. Shortly afterwards all theatres and opera houses throughout Germany and Austria were closed, and with that went both Wieland's chance of completing his *Ring* in Nuremberg and of producing the *Ring* in Vienna. Actors, singers, musicians, conductors and producers were now called on to take a more active part in the war. Overhoff was recalled to the army and sent to the Russian front. Wieland, still protected by Hitler's decree, went to work in a research establishment in Bayreuth. Before starting work there he wrote a letter to Overhoff, dated 15 September 1944:

"Dear friend Overhoff—With *Götterdämmerung* in Nuremberg I have completed in style a slice of my life which was devoted almost entirely to the *Ring*. Since then I have used my time in 'adapting' myself inwardly, catching up gradually on my correspondence debts of the past five years and—for the first time without work to do—devoting myself to what is called family life. After reporting to the labour exchange I have a few days to go before my 'new life' begins.

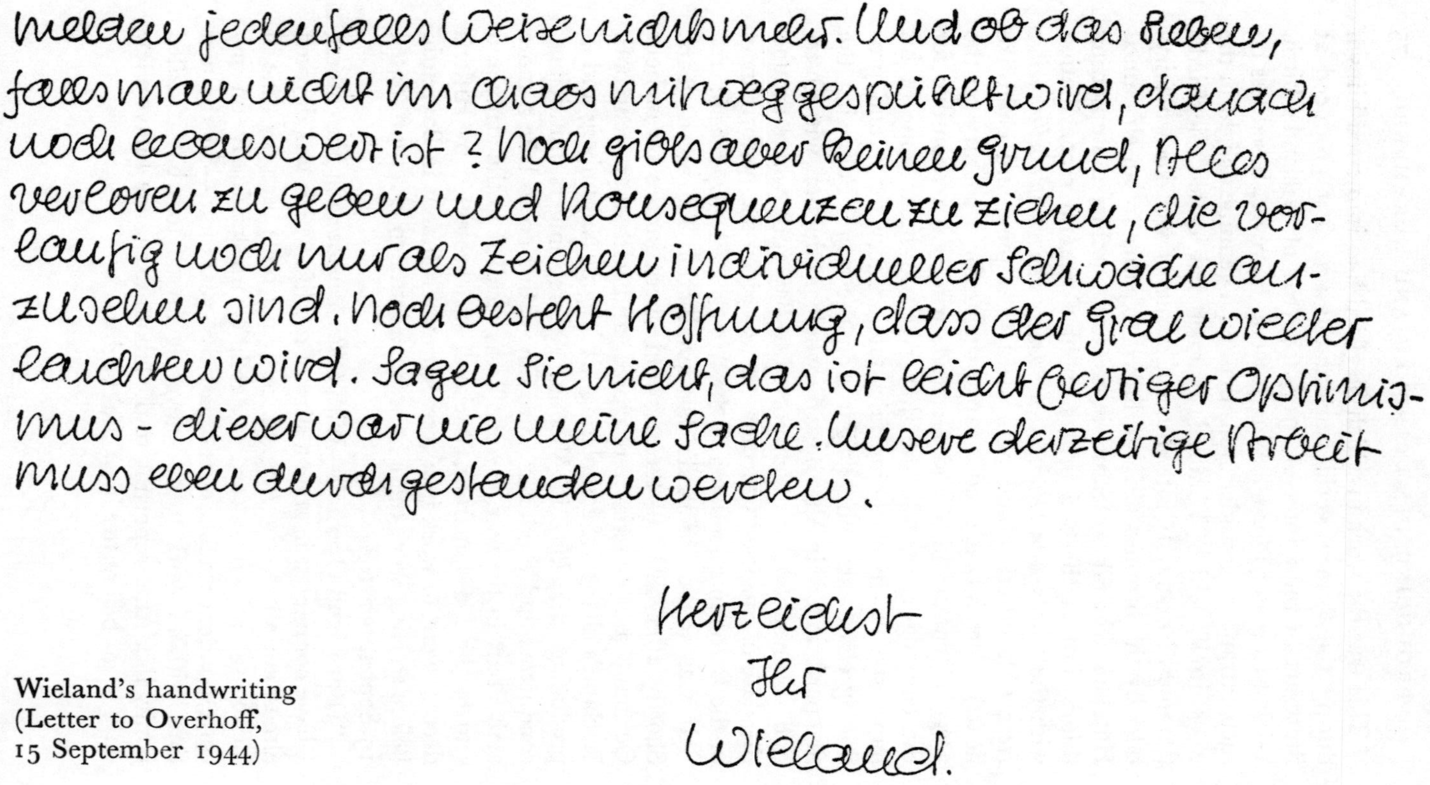
melden jedenfalls Weise nicht mehr. Und ob das Leben, falls man nicht im Chaos mitweggespült wird, danach noch lebenswert ist? Noch gibts aber keinen Grund, Alles verloren zu geben und Konsequenzen zu ziehen, die vorlaufig noch nur als Zeichen individueller Schwäche anzusehen sind. Noch besteht Hoffnung, dass der Gral wieder leuchten wird. Sagen Sie nicht, das ist leicht fertiger Optimismus – dieser war nie meine Sache. Unsere derzeitige Arbeit muss eben durchgestanden werden.

Herzlichst
Ihr
Wieland.

Wieland's handwriting
(Letter to Overhoff,
15 September 1944)

"Through the relentless pressure of war our work together has now been torn apart, but, however far in distance or long in time our separation may be—perhaps indeed for ever—there remain both friendship and gratitude. These arose in both pleasant and difficult hours from our joint work and joint enthusiasm for all that is true and beautiful in art.

"I owe you a great deal. Without ever thinking of yourself, you have helped me to find a path that I could not have trodden without you. You have given me as much of your ability and knowledge as was humanly possible in so short a time. How much this was I know better than any other, and I also know only too well that I did not at the start make things easy for you.

"Whether it will again be granted to us to renew our work together—and this time not under primitive conditions and inhibited by external fetters—who can now say? The future lies all too darkly over us all—*der Welt melden jedenfalls Weise nichts mehr*. And who knows whether life afterwards, if we are not swept away in the general chaos, will be still worth living? Still, there is no reason yet to give up all for lost and to draw conclusions which can only be interpreted as signs of individual weakness. Hope still remains that the Grail will glow again. Do not call this frivolous optimism—that was never my way. All we can do now is see our present work through to the end. Yours affectionately—Wieland."

8

END OF AN ILLUSION

1944–1945

On 6 December 1943 Wieland's own family had been
increased by the birth in Bayreuth of his son, Wolf Siegfried.
In the same year both his brother Wolfgang and his younger
sister Verena had married.

Verena's husband, Bodo Lafferentz, was born in the same
year as her mother Winifred. He had been entrusted by Hitler
with the running of the movement *Kraft durch Freude* (Strength
through Joy), which organised recreational facilities for German
workers and their families. At the outbreak of war he extended
his activities to troop welfare, and in this capacity he was
responsible, among other things, for selecting audiences for the
wartime festivals in Bayreuth from serving soldiers and arma-
ments workers. It was to his influential brother-in-law that
Wieland owed his assignment after the closing of the theatres
to a research establishment in Bayreuth dealing with optical
instruments.

The increasing violence of bombing raids on Germany had
turned the thoughts of the war leaders in the direction of
improving the anti-aircraft defence system, but a shortage of
research scientists was proving a serious handicap. A number
of highly qualified men were, however, languishing uselessly in
concentration camps, and it was felt that, given sufficient
inducements, these people might be persuaded to forget their
grudges for the moment and help their country in its hour of
need. A special camp was set up in Bayreuth, and the scientist
prisoners were put to work devising a new plane tracking
system.

Wieland worked in this highly secret establishment for the
rest of the war, though—since he was no scientist—he could

not contribute usefully to the research. In fact, according to Lafferentz, he spent most of his time there constructing stage models and working out lighting systems for them, a task in which the optical experts proved of great help to him.

During these months Wieland, who was now living permanently in Wahnfried, often returned home from work in a state of deep preoccupation. He was under a pledge of secrecy not to talk of the camp or the work being done there, and he maintained this pledge even in his home. But he did say vaguely that he had heard things at work he would never have believed possible. It can be assumed that, in view of its purpose, the Bayreuth camp bore little resemblance to the concentration camps from which its inmates had been drawn. But no doubt, in the intervals of helping him with his stage lighting problems, the prisoners talked to Wieland of their experiences elsewhere.

In December 1944 Wieland met Hitler for the last time. Not even Winifred had seen him personally since his last visit to Bayreuth in the summer of 1941, when he had attended a performance of *Götterdämmerung*. Wieland's visit to Berlin, on which he was accompanied by Gertrud, Verena and Lafferentz, was not purely a friendly one. Hitler had in his possession a number of original Wagner manuscripts, and the family, believing these were likely to be safer in Bayreuth than in the beleaguered *Reichskanzlei* in Berlin, hoped to persuade him to hand them over. The visitors found Hitler looking tired and worn, but he still showed all his usual concern for the Wagner family and was particularly anxious to know whether they had adequate air raid shelters in Bayreuth. As for the manuscripts, he preferred to keep them himself.

The manuscripts have not since come to light. Almost certainly they were destroyed in the final attack on Berlin. In later years Winifred Wagner was accused of having presented them to Hitler and thus being indirectly responsible for their loss. Wieland came to his mother's defence in a letter published in the newspaper *Die Welt* on 19 February 1958. The manuscripts (he wrote) had all been presented by Richard Wagner to King Ludwig II between the years 1865 and 1872. They consisted of the original orchestral scores of *Die Feen*, *Das Liebesverbot* and *Rienzi*; the orchestral sketch for *Der Fliegende*

Holländer; original fair copies of the orchestral scores of *Rhein-gold*, *Die Walküre* and the third act of *Siegfried*; and copies of the orchestral sketches of *Götterdämmerung*. These manuscripts had been sold in 1939 by the executors of the former Bavarian royal estate to the *Reichswirtschaftskammer*, which presented them to Hitler. They were thus legally Hitler's personal property.

By February 1945 allied bombers had begun to turn their attention to Bayreuth, and Winifred decided that it was no place for expectant mothers, of whom she had three in her family: Gertrud was now awaiting her third child, Verena her second and Ellen, Wolfgang's wife, her first. Winifred sent Gertrud, with Iris and Wolf Siegfried, and Verena, with her daughter Amélie, to her house in Nussdorf on the Lake of Constance. Ellen, however, chose to remain in Bayreuth with her husband, and she was with Winifred in the cellar of the adjoining *Siegfried-Wagner-Haus* when on 5 April 1945 an American bomb fell on Wahnfried, demolishing about a third of the house. There were no casualties.

Shortly afterwards Wieland and Lafferentz left to join their families in Nussdorf, while Winifred moved to her little week-end cottage at Oberwarmensteinach in the nearby Fichtel-gebirge. Wolfgang stayed on in Bayreuth to keep an eye on the damaged house. Wieland and his brother-in-law travelled in a car loaded with precious Wagner manuscripts from the archives, and on arrival in Nussdorf stored them away in secret places in the house and garden.

9

THE CREATIVE BLACK YEARS

1945–1948

THE HOUSE ON the lake at Nussdorf was Wieland's home for
the next three years, and here, surrounded by his growing
family (his second daughter Nike was born on 9 June 1945), he
spent what he afterwards described as the "creative black
years" of his life. The blackness refers not only to material
circumstances, but also to the spiritual crisis induced by the
now inescapable realisation that Hitler, the man who had
virtually taken the place of his father in his thoughts and to
whose protection during the war years he possibly owed his life,
had been one of the most brutal criminals in history. He faced
the evidence of the concentration camps and the gas chambers
squarely and accepted it as true. His acceptance of Hitler's
guilt was summed up in a phrase he later used: "After Ausch-
witz there can be no more discussion about Hitler."

Winifred stuck to her belief that Hitler had been betrayed by
his associates, and she submitted without complaint to the
menial tasks of clearing rubble which she, as a known Nazi, was
forced to perform. Wieland escaped such indignities, probably
because in Nussdorf he came under a different authority—
Nussdorf was in the French zone of occupation, whereas
Bayreuth was in the American—and also because he had not
occupied a prominent position of authority during the Nazi
years. Allied policy at that period was directed mainly against
party members of the earliest vintage, against holders of senior
offices and against members of such notorious organisations as
the SS. This left most people of Wieland's generation un-
touched, as far as punishment was concerned, but of course it
did not free them from their own personal problems of conscience.

Years later Wieland told the journalist Willy Haas: "My old mother has had to pay very dearly for her mistaken beliefs. She is probably the only woman in the whole of Germany who, without ever having harmed another human being, has done full penance for her mistakes" (*Welt am Sonntag*, 30 July 1961). It is not necessary here to go into the question of whether, by her association with Hitler, Winifred brought harm to anyone, directly or indirectly. But Wieland's words reveal something of the conflict that existed in his mind, his love for his mother struggling with his exasperation for her misplaced loyalties. The already troubled relationship was only intensified and was to become even worse as the years went on.

The "creative" aspect of these post-war years was the opportunity his enforced idleness afforded Wieland to prepare for the future. That his thoughts were still very much on producing is shown by a letter to Kurt Overhoff from Nussdorf, dated 1 December 1945. Overhoff, returning to Altenburg in May from the Russian front and expecting to resume the post of music director which he still officially held, had also found himself out of a job. The town authorities informed him curtly that, in view of his close relationship with the Wagner family and his activity as "a guardian of the most decadent form of German music" (by which—in case it is no longer self-evident—the authorities in the Soviet zone of occupation meant Richard Wagner), his services were no longer required. Overhoff eventually found asylum in Garmisch-Partenkirchen in Bavaria, where Richard Strauss engaged him as musical tutor to his grandson. From there Overhoff wrote to Wieland, who replied:

"Gertrud and I were delighted to hear direct from you at last after so long a time. . . . How pleased I am for you that you have found your Ithaca, if only for a while. . . . I do not need to assure you that we should have loved to offer you a home here, but there is no chance in the foreseeable future of our requisitioned rooms being freed, quite apart from the fact that one never knows what the next day will bring in this connection. Nussdorf is occupied by a large Moroccan force, and the flood of refugees from the east is still to come. We must expect to be given 'preferential treatment' in this respect.

"At the moment I am working on *Tristan*, as far as I can, and could often make good use of your help. In the summer I memorised *Parsifal*. Apart from that I spent the summer working hard in the garden, looking after children, drying plates and learning French. Only today Elfriede [Gertrud's sister] brought me some paints from Bayreuth, and I mean now to get down to my painting again. . . .

"I have been thinking a lot recently about that old pet wish of mine, which I suggested once to the maestro and which would have been possible as things were at that time. Dr Strauss promised then to go through the whole of R.W.'s works with me—all one would need would be someone to play the piano. The few sentences he spoke to me about *Die Walküre* in Vienna once were so instructive that I have at last made up my mind to ask him. I wonder if you could find an opportunity to sound him out on the possibility of putting this plan into effect? But on no account do I want to be a burden on him or his family, and you should make a point of emphasising that: you know what I'm like. . . .

"If you should happen to be able to put your hands on a copy of Kierkegaard's *Either—Or* I should be grateful if you could send it to me on loan. . . ."

Wieland did not know that Strauss was no longer living at his home in Garmisch, but had moved to Switzerland. The plan to go through Wagner's works with him never materialised. Wieland continued his study of the works alone, with the help of what books he could find. Verena remembers that in the evenings, when the children were in bed, Wieland and Gertrud would settle down on the floor of the living-room they shared with Verena and her husband to discuss the psychology of the characters in Wagner's dramas and the problems of expressing it in terms of movement and gesture. Gertrud, with her choreographic training, was able to demonstrate possible methods, while Wieland looked on, offering intensely critical comments. Ocassionally he would ask Verena how the passage under discussion had been done at Bayreuth in former days, relying on her memory, which was better than his.

At this stage of their marriage Wieland and Gertrud were very close. Neither of them could be described as compromising persons, but fierce argument rather than admiring approval was what Wieland needed to set his imagination alight. Later, in the days when his ideas were accepted, admired and copied, he tended deliberately to provoke opposition—a habit which earned him a reputation of seeking sensation for its own sake.

During the day, when the children were about, Wieland, besides doing a share of work in the house and garden, devoted himself to his painting. This was on the whole a more profitable activity since, according to Lafferentz, Wieland was not good at the sort of cunning and opportunism which in those days of shortages and primitive living made material existence easier. If he were to slip into the woods to gather forbidden fuel, he would invariably be spotted and foiled. His paintings, on the other hand, proved useful as objects of barter. He took to copying well-known portraits of Richard Wagner, Cosima and Liszt, each of which could be exchanged for a sack of potatoes or something else of that kind. A number of these portraits he sent off to his sister Friedelind in America, with instructions to sell them and buy food parcels. Unfortunately the pictures were packed before they were dry and arrived in America inextricably stuck together.

Beside copying, Wieland painted some original works: a portrait of the local miller's daughters, for example, in exchange for a sack of flour. He also painted a self-portrait, which he gave to Gertrud when she moved to Bayreuth temporarily in November 1946 for the birth of her fourth and last child. This portrait, reproduced opposite page 40, shows a spare, long face very unlike photographs of Wieland taken before and since. However, according to Gertrud, it is a good likeness of her husband at that time, when he lost the last remains of his youthful stoutness.

They named their new daughter Daphne, partly to conform to their pattern of choosing Greek names for their daughters and partly to honour Richard Strauss, whose opera *Daphne* was a favourite of theirs. Strauss was much touched by this tribute.

Though by now Wieland had accepted that he would never make his mark as a painter pure and simple, painting provided him with an occupation he could pursue during the long winter months in the single living-room, undisturbed by the children crawling around his feet. He was a patient and devoted father, and would keep Iris and Wummi (by which name, invented by his sisters, Wolf Siegfried was and still is known) entertained with games and stories while Gertrud was busy with the babies.

In March 1946 Wieland wrote to Overhoff again:

"Have you had any news at all from Altenburg? I still keep thinking of our work there: a pity we can't simply start up again there—but without the *Arschgesichter* (literally, arse faces) in Weimar. Do you know any anti-Fascist in Altenburg to whom I could write some time about some scores I left in the palace? They are the *Ring* scores with remarks written in by my father. . . .

"I am lying in wait for spring to release me from the awful congestion of this one heatable living-room. So far as menial household duties and the screaming of children allow, I have been busy getting to grips with *Tristan* and *Parsifal*; you won't mind if I send you a list of questions and problems which I haven't been able to solve? I very much miss Kurth's book on the harmony in *Tristan*, but things like that can't be got in the desert regions of the Lake of Constance. At least some one has now given me a few piano scores. I've been trying, also in vain, to get hold of Schopenhauer, in order to catch up on what I have missed.

"Have your future plans begun to take on a more definite shape? My future is truly dark and foggy—and optimism, according to Spengler, is nothing but cowardice. It looks too as if Bayreuth will continue in the future to be a woman's affair. For I am in no illusions about my sister's plans—though Mama seems to be. However, I shan't give up the fight any more than I did against the Berlin system—but one is simply condemned to inactivity—and forced to remain negative.

"During a music-less year I have at last come fully to appreciate Mozart—the reward of a lifetime for which I gladly bear all the unpleasantness of the past year. As a result I feel infinitely removed from all things Italian—even my beloved *Carmen* suddenly seems over-perfumed. . . ."

This letter also contains news of Tietjen himself (who is of course meant in Wieland's reference to "the Berlin system"). Tietjen had recently married a ballet-dancer—an attempt, in Wieland's prejudiced mind, to create an alibi for himself. "The rats are leaving the sinking ship. But at least it clears the air. . . . How many difficult hours this gentleman has cost us both!" The plans of his sister for Bayreuth were not Friedelind's own, but attempts on the part of the American authorities to transfer authority for the festival to her, since she was now an American citizen. It was one of several plans—another involved Isolde's son, Franz Beidler—all of which came to grief on the terms of Siegfried's will, which legally bound the festival to the person of Winifred. Since the occupying powers had no intention of allowing her to reopen the festival, Wieland's feelings of depression were fully justified. His reference to the *Arschgesichter* in Weimar was a general rather than a specific attack on Nazi bureaucracy. The provincial government (so Lüsenhop told me) had kept a tight hand on the finances of the Altenburg *Landestheater*, but it was Overhoff, with his demands for expensive soloists for his symphony concerts, rather than Wieland who had suffered from it.

In the spring of 1947 Wieland obtained permission to leave the French zone of occupation and move temporarily to the American zone for the purposes of study. He went to Richard Strauss's house in Garmisch, where he spent several weeks in April and May working with Overhoff on *Tristan und Isolde*. In the following year Overhoff published a little book entitled *Richard Wagners Tristan-Partitur: eine musikalische-philosophische Deutung* (Richard Wagner's *Tristan* Score: a Musical and Philosophic Interpretation), which contains the essence of his teaching on the subject. A short extract from the passage concerning King Marke gives some idea of the method:

"There are two sound symbols which relate chiefly to King Marke: first, the motive of the king's love:

seventh

"This motive is first heard when Brangäne speaks to Isolde of the king's love. As tonal atmosphere we hear it only once in the actual presence of Marke: in the third act—*Warum, Isolde, warum mir das?*

"One sees immediately that this motive is only another variation of the love theme itself. The longing seventh, reaching deep into the heart and eye of the beloved, is familiar to us from the motive of Tristan's eternal love in the orchestral prelude:

'Love' seventh

"The interval of the seventh denotes in metaphysical terms directed desire, as does also the ninth (note, for example, the passionate ninth in Erda's entreaty to Wotan in the third act of *Siegfried*.). Here the seventh denotes sensual desire. The application of this motive to King Marke proves that 'traditional' representation of Marke as a world-weary old man is wrong. This representation stems from the fact that the motive of the king's love is usually ignored entirely, and the traditional portrayal is based on the second symbol alone: the resignation motive:

"It is at once apparent that this resignation motive stems musically from the same root as the love's embrace motive:

It expresses the king's painful renunciation of this embrace—a proof that he longs for the bliss of intimate union with Isolde. His renunciation thus illustrates only one side of his character, whereas the sound symbol of the love motive shows him as filled with desire and in no mood for resignation. This musical fact is almost invariably ignored in the stage representation, and in this way a plaintive, spineless ancient usually emerges, complaining tremulously of the injustice done to him by inconsiderate youth. I have no idea where this traditional nonsense comes from, but I know for a certainty that there is nothing in the master's score to justify it. On the contrary, the role of King Marke demands the sharpest contrasts in its dynamic and psychological accents. The king in his reproach to Tristan must be trembling with repressed anger."

This is just a very small, and indeed an unusually straightforward example of Overhoff's method, and my reason for choosing it is simply to show that in his musical analyses Overhoff does not indulge in musical and philosophical speculations for their own sakes, but has his eyes firmly fixed on their physical expression. In working along these lines with Wieland, he does not claim the teacher's privilege of infallibility. In fact, in the foreword to his book he pays tribute to his pupil, "to whose penetrating powers of observation and empathy I owe many valuable ideas".

The atmosphere of sympathetic collaboration that existed between teacher and pupil is illustrated by a note concerning the book written by Wieland just after leaving Garmisch:

"I find both your added pages fine now as they are, though I think they should be completed with a *third*—and very significant!—motive transformation: in the second part of the death

motive: —you know what I mean. If you could

manage to get this into your interpretation, the old problem of this controversial motive would at last be *unanswerably* solved.

"Could you not also find a musical derivation of the *second* motive in the introduction to the Tristan-Isolde scene? It must surely be there.

"If you have a bit of time to spare, perhaps you could give some thought to the following questions. They concern the mimed action after the love potion in Tr., Act I:

"1. How could one interpret the tremolo passage in the cellos? (Certainly not as the throwing away of the cup!) From the conflict motive—but wouldn't that be rather drastic?

"2. And the ascending violas?

"3. What is the significance here of the second part of the death motive in the bass clarinet?

"4. The harp chord (in the third bar of the slow 6/8) must then have some special significance. A realisation on Tristan's part? Could this be where he at last understands that Isolde wants to die with him? (Everywhere else he is always thinking only of *himself!*) But it worries me that this happens so late. But what else is going on psychologically?"

This is admittedly rather cryptically expressed and is introduced here not for its own sake, but as an indication that Wieland had more knowledge of and concern for Wagner's music than he is usually credited with.

Wieland's close study of the works themselves was supplemented by extensive reading on more general lines. As he told his biographer Walter Panofsky, his reading consisted of "books which were not available in Wahnfried—or rather which were not permitted in Wahnfried". The authors included Freud, Jung and Klages. In addition to these he developed an intense interest in the poets of ancient Greece. "All of a sudden I became conscious of deep mythical relationships. In the Rhine Maidens I discovered foster-sisters of the ocean nymphs, and I recognised in the conflict between Wotan and Brünnhilde a repetition of the story of Creon and Antigone. Zeus and Semele must have been the mythical prototypes for *Lohengrin*, just as much as Perseus and Andromeda. Siegfried was Herakles. And what with all the other astonishing discoveries I made, I became a real Greek in those creative black years—a Homer fan, if you like."

Perhaps the most astonishing thing about these "discoveries" is that Wieland should have found them astonishing at all. The parallels between ancient Greek and Nordic legend are too obvious to be regarded in the light of a revelation, and Wieland's surprise can only be seen as evidence of the narrowness of his general education. This could be attributed more to the Nationalist Socialist period in which he grew up, with its absolute insistence on Nordic supremacy, than to the shortcomings of Wahnfried. The ancient Greeks were certainly not unknown there: Wagner himself often acknowledged his debt to them and paid them the compliment of building his *Festspielhaus* in imitation of their amphitheatres. Cosima too, with her French classical upbringing, could certainly not be accused of having ignored them. But of course the Wahnfried in which Wieland grew up was no longer theirs. It had become the shrine of a god named Wagner, who was for all his adorers sufficient in himself, and nobody bothered to inquire into his real origins. It is a demonstration of the remarkable strength of

Wagnerismus that it took its intensification by Hitler to the point of caricature and its catastrophic downfall to induce even a rebel like Wieland to recognise the simple reality behind the illusion.

*

While Wieland was in Nussdorf, his brother Wolfgang remained in Bayreuth looking after the family property. With his wife, and daughter Eva, he had been living since the end of the war in the chauffeur's annexe, a little building in the Wahnfried grounds. Here, on 13 April 1947, his son Gottfried was born. Wahnfried itself was empty. Together with some friends Wolfgang had laboured physically to clear the bomb damage from the back of the house, but there could be no question of rebuilding yet: Winifred's capital had been frozen pending the outcome of denazification proceedings against her.

The *Siegfried-Wagner-Haus* had been taken over by the Americans as an officers' club. The Americans had also requisitioned the *Festspielhaus* itself, and unaccustomed things were happening on its hallowed stage, ranging from variety shows for the troops to a performance of *Madame Butterfly*. But by the latter part of 1947 life in the town was beginning to return to normal. Among other things a symphony orchestra was formed, and, at Wolfgang's suggestion, Overhoff was appointed to conduct it. He left Garmisch to settle down in Bayreuth, where he began to organise concerts in which, for reasons of tact, the music of Wagner played no part. However, he succeeded in obtaining the use of the *Festspielhaus* for his symphony concerts, thus saving it further indignities.

In 1947, Winifred, who was still living in Oberwarmensteinach, appeared before a denazification court. In spite of the evidence of a number of witnesses who described how she had personally intervened to save them from Nazi persecution, she was found guilty of collaboration with Hitler. On appeal, exonerating circumstances were acknowledged which brought her into a less incriminated category, but she was still denied the right to reopen the festival, and her confiscated assets in Bayreuth were not yet returned to her.

In autumn 1948 Wieland and his family moved back to

Bayreuth. There was still no prospect of any producing work for him there, but he had the advantage of being within physical reach of Overhoff, to whom he was now addressing questions concerning *Parsifal* on the lines of those about *Tristan und Isolde* which have already been quoted.

In this period of virtual stalemate there arose the possibility of restarting the festival in another country, at least as a temporary measure. Interest was certainly shown, for instance, in Monte Carlo. The danger of losing the festival may at last have spurred the Bavarian authorities to find a practical solution to the whole problem. Winifred put forward a suggestion that she should appoint her sons jointly to run the festival; she would lease the *Festspielhaus* and Wahnfried to them and withdraw from any active participation.

Somewhat to her surprise, as she now says, her suggestion was accepted. In 1949 plans could at last be made to reopen the festival in Bayreuth.

10

PREPARATIONS IN BAYREUTH

1949—1951

WAHNFRIED'S ORIGINAL baronial splendours might have suited both the taste and the way of life of Richard Wagner, but Wieland lacked all feeling for the social graces. What he wanted was a home in which he could work in peace and quiet and live a close family life with his wife and four small children. He took advantage of the damage caused by American bombers to reconstruct the house as far as possible in accordance with his own taste. The part that had been destroyed included a large portion of the main salon in which Wagner had received his guests. This was not restored. The exposed inner walls became outer walls with a series of large windows looking out over the garden. What remained of the salon Wieland enlarged by taking space from the great entrance hall, thus creating an oblong room of generous but not inhospitable size, which he furnished and decorated in a bright modern style. The entrance hall, which had originally extended right up to the roof, with galleries at first floor level, vanished entirely, giving way to a plain vestibule of modest dimensions: simply a place, as in most ordinary houses, to wipe one's shoes and hang up one's coat.

Where Cosima's former *Lila-Salon* had been he constructed an open terrace with paved paths and flower borders. Around it he erected a high wall, cutting it off from the rest of the Wahnfried garden. Winifred, who was now living in the *Siegfried-Wagner-Haus*, resented this wall. Her own house had an open terrace facing the Wahnfried garden, and the wall seemed to her to be a deliberate attempt on Wieland's part to erect a barrier against her. His act was probably nothing more than the wish to ensure a small area of family privacy, understandable in view of the fact that he had, in those early years, to share the Wahnfried garden not only with his mother, but also with his brother and his family.

However united in the common cause of preserving the festival, the Wagner family has always tended to be quarrelsome. The inclination to form rival groups was just as strong among the grandchildren as it had been in the second generation. But the brothers themselves, now jointly responsible for the reopening of the festival, had little time for family feuding. While Wieland was preparing the opening productions—*Parsifal* (which had been dropped from the festival at the outbreak of the war on Hitler's command) and the *Ring*—Wolfgang was busy organising the administration and arranging the finances. This was of vital importance, since with rising costs the festival could no longer hope to be self-supporting. There were government and town authorities to be seen and subsidies to be negotiated, industrial concerns to be coaxed into giving grants. Wolfgang, with his easy manner and his talent for mixing with people, was far more suited to these tasks than the austere and withdrawn Wieland, who neither drank nor smoked and considered small talk a waste of time. Wolfgang crowned his considerable success in setting the machinery going with the formation of an organisation called the *Gesellschaft der Freunde von Bayreuth* (Society of the Friends of Bayreuth), a group of Wagner devotees from nineteen countries who guaranteed to make good any deficit left over at the end of each yearly festival.

Since all this work left Wolfgang no time for producing, Rudolf Hartmann was invited to stage *Die Meistersinger* at the opening festival.

*

The task of restoring Bayreuth's artistic image after Hitler had so disastrously compromised Wagner in the eyes of the world was a formidable as well as a perilous one. There was now a certain advantage to Wieland in the fact that he had been denied the opportunity during Winifred's régime to make his mark in the *Festspielhaus*. He was virtually an unknown quantity, and thus any new approach in his presentation of Wagner's works was less tinged with the suspicion of political expediency than it might have been if his former production work had been better known.

New approaches based purely on political considerations have, however, little chance of finding permanent acceptance. If Wieland had not himself believed in the validity of the ideas he had worked out for himself in the "creative black years" of Nussdorf, it is unlikely that they would have succeeded for long.

He explained his ideas in an essay entitled *Überlieferung und Gestaltung*, which appeared in the handbook (*Festspielbuch 1951*) published to coincide with the first post-war festival. The essay, under the title *Tradition and Innovation*, appeared in English in the brochure *Life, Work, Festspielhaus* the following year. Since this was Wieland's first open declaration of his aims, it is worth quoting extensively. He started with a very definite statement: "Basically, the works of Richard Wagner tolerate no change. Like all elemental works of art, they remain inviolable and sufficient unto themselves. . . . The actual staging—and it alone—is subject to change. To avoid change is to transform the virtue of fidelity into the vice of rigidity."

After this vigorous opening, Wieland went on to discuss the problems of translating inviolable works into effective modern terms. "A single technical invention—electric light in the form of the spotlight—has effected . . . a revolution on the stage. . . . Scenic design is determined by the spotlight to much the same extent that it was formerly determined by painting. Illuminated space has replaced the lighted canvas. An attempt to preserve elements of an epoch already outdated by technical developments would be foolish. The task before us is to create the essential mood with new means.

"The stylistic methods employed in achieving this mood . . . can take various forms. . . . *Die Meistersinger*, for example, calls for a certain naturalism (imposed by a historically fixed time, a geographical place and human beings of flesh and blood). *Parsifal*, on the other hand, requires mystical expression of a very complex state of the soul, rooted in the unreal and grasped only by intuition. To present both works in a similar way, as seemed natural in earlier days, appears to us neither possible nor even remotely desirable. The gap between them arises from the innermost core of their differences, and it cannot and must not be bridged.

"Wagner's stage directions reflect the taste of his age. . . . He himself was tragically disappointed with the realisation of his own instructions. His lines to King Ludwig II, written from Wahnfried in May 1881, are revealing: 'Everyone thinks he can do better and make more beautiful things than I can, when all I want is a definite something, a clear poetic effect, but no theatrical pomp. Scenery, for instance, is invariably designed as though it were to be looked at for its own sake, as in a panorama, whereas I see it as a silent facilitating background and setting for a certain dramatic situation.'

"Strict devotees of tradition cling to every comma in Wagner's stage directions as though therein lay the clue to perfection. But how far did the productions of 1876 (the *Ring*) and 1882 (*Parsifal*), though under Wagner's personal direction, deviate from his own sacrosanct instructions! The Valkyries' rock corresponded to them as little as the grotesque costumes of the Flower Maidens; the Rhine Maidens were so ornately dressed that even the most modern machinery would have made swimming impossible. How could Wagner have felt when he saw the airy rainbow of his imagination reduced to a rickety bridge? And what had become of those creations of his inner vision? The demon Klingsor depicted as a small-town conjuror; the arch-temptress Kundry wearing a tight-laced flowery evening gown; Fafner, the wild serpent, degraded to an almost ridiculous pantomime dragon!

"Should one keep on blaming these defects exclusively on the insufficient technical facilities of the period? Certainly the argument would not hold true in regard to the costumes. The shortcomings suggest that Wagner's stage directions represent inner visions rather than practical demands, and that these, through the dictates of current taste and the practical limitations of realisation, changed of their own accord from imagined perfection to the best that was possible in the circumstances— the price any lofty vision must pay when it insists on assuming visible form. . . .

"But the essential problem of producing Wagnerian music drama is not solved by this admission alone. It lies far deeper than that: in the music itself. It is music which transmits Wagner's visions in so expressive a language that it is well nigh impossible to duplicate those visions for the eye. The watcher will invariably fall behind the listener, however happily the scenic problems may have been solved. Today, after seventy-five years of rapidly improving technical methods—the development of lighting undoubtedly represents the peak of scenic design—we must still admit that the stage can, at its best, provide only a sparse reflection for the eye of what the orchestra pit is triumphantly conveying to our ears. No amount of theorising, no pseudo-philosophical treatises on the problems of staging, no arguments between fanatical followers of tradition and innovations will ever alter this fact. Scenes like the cosmic catastrophe of *Götterdämmerung*, the spring night of *Die Walküre* or the *Rheingold* thunderstorm—to cite just a few examples—can never convey a visual impact to match their musical expression.

"The path to the future lies neither in an attempt to employ all the most modern devices in achieving a cinematic realisation of Wagner's inner visions, nor can it be found in an infantile reversion to former 'tried and true' methods. The conventional image of bygone days may summon up wistful memories of a notable era to many faithful and deserving veterans, but to the generation which has risen since the quantum theory and atomic science this image has lost its value."

Looking back on this essay in the light of after-events, one cannot avoid a feeling of surprise at its inherent modesty. It makes the damaging admission that "the stage can, at its best, provide only a sparse reflection for the eye of what the orchestra pit is triumphantly conveying to our ears", thereby implying that Wieland's own attempts at staging were as doomed to failure as any that had gone before. It does not define to what use Wieland planned to put the revolutionary spotlight, and—most noticeably—it has nothing at all to say about the psychological interpretation of character, which had been his main preoccupation during all his years of study and was to become the main basis of his production method.

It is in fact, apart from the occasional tendentious adjective, a very cautious document, and it suggests either that Wieland's ideas were not yet fully clear in his own mind, or that he was deliberately trying to soften the blow to the traditionalists in and outside the Wagner family, on whom he still at that time depended for help in the practical realisation of his plans. There

Parsifal, 1937: The Temple of the Grail (*above*)
Parsifal, 1951: The Temple of the Grail (*below*)

Rheingold, Scene Two: first Bayreuth production (*above*)
Rheingold, Scene Two: second Bayreuth production (*below*)

were conductors, singers, orchestral players, coaches to be found. In searching for these, Wieland needed the help of the older generation, either because, like Tietjen, who was now again in charge of the opera house in West Berlin, they had the authority to grant or deny him the singers he coveted, or because they could give him advice concerning new singers of whom he knew little. In these matters Wieland was man of affairs enough to realise the value of discretion in a position of weakness.

There were not many people who believed in him implicitly at that time—possibly no more than his wife, Overhoff and his former friend from the time of his mother's régime, Paul Eberhardt, who had helped Wieland with his early lighting experiments and who now returned from Africa to help him again in Bayreuth.

Between Wieland and Overhoff relations were, however, becoming strained. Overhoff had ventured to criticise Wieland's design for Klingsor's castle in the second act of *Parsifal*. Its horse-shoe shape seemed to him, he told Wieland, more appropriate to the variety stage than to the Bayreuth *Festspielhaus*. "I saw at once that Wieland took my remark as a personal insult," Overhoff said in his Salzburg broadcast. "His attitude towards me had radically changed, and in place of our long-standing frank and open comradeship he was suddenly demanding the relationship of reigning monarch and loyal servant."

They had in fact reached the painful point at which the pupil outgrows the teacher. Wieland was feeling the need now to go forward on his own, while on his side Overhoff was beset by misgivings. As he himself later said, it appeared to him that Wieland was no longer concerned to continue the reform they had begun together in Altenburg: he was intent rather on making a sensation. The sudden gap which arose between them extended beyond their personal relationship. Overhoff, who was still the conductor of the town's choir, though the symphony orchestra had now been disbanded, had entertained hopes of being invited to conduct at the festival. Failing that, he expected some public acknowledgement of his work as Wieland's music teacher and adviser. Neither hope was realised. In the festival handbook of 1951 Overhoff's name appeared as only one of eleven musical coaches.

D

*

Wieland's avowed aim of rescuing the music dramas from their traditional nineteenth century associations extended to the orchestra as well as to the stage, and consequently the choice of Hans Knappertsbusch as his first conductor strikes one with surprise. Knappertsbusch's weighty and deliberate approach to the works would seem to be exactly the sort of approach that Wieland most wished to avoid. If on the one hand the choice can be regarded as evidence of the caution beneath Wieland's iconoclasm, it reveals equally the extent to which personal sympathy played a part in his decisions. Knappertsbusch's obstinate integrity, which had brought him into disfavour with the Nazis, and his air of solid self-assurance, from which pomposity was banished by a pronouncedly dry sense of humour, aroused Wieland's intense admiration. "Do you know why I love Kna?" he once said. "He *does* nothing— he just *is*."

Wieland had not known Knappertsbusch personally before his appointment to Bayreuth. Wilhelm Furtwängler, on the other hand, was well known to him from his boyhood days, and it is probable that his admiration for Furtwängler's artistic gifts was enhanced rather than diminished by his memories of the difficulties that had beset Furtwängler's relations with Tietjen and his mother in pre-war days. Wieland invited Furtwängler to share the conducting duties of the first festival with Knappertsbusch, and was very disappointed when Furtwängler, after veering to and fro for several months, eventually declined. The most he would consent to do was to reopen the festival with a performance of Beethoven's Ninth Symphony.

The search for a second conductor ended with the appointment of Herbert von Karajan, whom Gertrud had admired since she heard him at concerts in Munich during the war. Then in his early forties and as yet relatively unknown, Karajan might have seemed the predestined answer to Wieland's wish for a conductor of outstanding talent who would be prepared to match his experiments on stage with a similarly modern approach to Wagner's scores. Wieland soon discovered, however, that the modern attitude towards Bayreuth was not necessarily imbued with that selfless attitude to the Wagnerian cause which could make a man of the older generation such as Knappertsbusch feel honoured by an invitation to appear there. Younger conductors, who now had the choice of several summer festivals, were liable to raise the question of fees. For all his rebelliousness, Wieland was in this respect an old-fashioned Wagnerian. He was shocked, and from the start he regarded his second conductor with a certain amount of reserve.

To Karajan, Wieland owed the discovery of Wilhelm Pitz. Pitz was chorus master of the opera in Aachen, where Karajan had conducted in the Thirties before his promotion to Berlin, and to which he returned for a while after the war. Wieland, who once described himself as a "choral fetichist", wanted in his chorus singers with sufficient intelligence and open-mindedness to grasp the vital stage role he was preparing for them. Pitz visited the opera houses of Germany in his search for suitable singers and presented them to Wieland after a few rehearsals. According to Wilhelm Kemp (*Tannhäuser* programme 1967), Wieland remarked, "Pitz is the greatest choral talent I have ever met. If everything is as good as this, I shall have no fears for the success of the festival."

Through Karajan, Wieland also came into contact with Walter Legge, the founder of the Philharmonia Orchestra, who was at that time Artists and Recording Manager of the EMI gramophone group. Legge, who was to become one of his few close friends in the following years, was a valuable help to him in the search for singers. Wieland made full use of his former contacts in the opera world to discover promising newcomers, who were then invited to the *Festspielhaus* to give an audition—a necessary precaution, since, owing to its peculiar acoustic conditions, many excellent voices prove ineffective there. He also kept an eye on the newspapers, and many singers were invited to Bayreuth for an audition on the strength of a favourable review.

Of the singers who had sung in Bayreuth during his mother's time only one was invited to return in 1951: Kirsten Flagstad, who had sung Sieglinde and Gutrune in the festivals of 1933 and 1934. As a boy Wieland had fallen in love with her voice, and he tried hard to persuade her to accept the role of Brünnhilde in his own production. Kirsten Flagstad declined the invitation on the grounds that she felt past it, but she warmly recommended for the role a young singer named Astrid Varnay, who was then singing in New York. It is an indication of the strength of Wieland's respect for Kirsten Flagstad that he instantly engaged Astrid Varnay to play Brünnhilde without ever having seen her or heard her sing.

Martha Mödl owed her initial discovery to Wieland's habit of reading newspaper reviews. He later wrote in Walter Erich Schäfer's book *Martha Mödl*: "I was looking in 1951 for a new and truly undefined Kundry for the first festival, and had read in the newspapers about her Carmen and particularly her Magda Sorell in Menotti's *Consul*. It was in the Hamburg *Staatsoper*, playing Venus, that I saw her for the first time—saw rather than heard for, as she later confessed to me, she had had a bad cold and during the overture had drunk a hot lemon, which robbed her of the last vestiges of her voice. I then invited her to give an audition in Bayreuth. . . . Her acting ability, the deep sense of tragedy she gave to Kundry's narration, her timbre and her personality made my decision to engage her for the opening festival truly an easy one."

Gradually in the years between 1949 and 1951 Wieland built up his initial team, drawing his singers not only from the major opera houses of Germany and abroad, but also from such relatively minor ones as Koblenz, Linz, Lübeck, Oldenburg, Saarbrücken, Viersen, Weimar and Wuppertal. Some of his singers were already established: Sigurd Björling (Wotan), Bernd Aldenhoff (Siegfried), Günther Treptow (Siegmund), Hermann Uhde (Klingsor and Gunther), Ludwig Weber (Gurnemanz and Hagen), Elisabeth Höngen (Fricka) and Elisabeth Schwarzkopf who, engaged by Hartmann as Eva in his production of *Die Meistersinger*, showed a true appreciation of the old Bayreuth spirit by taking on the role of one of the Rhine Maidens in addition. With two of his singers Wieland had worked before in his Altenburg days: Friedrich Dalberg (Fafner) and Paul Kuën (Mime). The remainder were relatively unknown, though many of them subsequently achieved international fame, among them Leonie Rysanek (Sieglinde), who was at that time singing in Saarbrücken, Hertha Töpper (Flosshilde and Siegrune), Wolfgang Windgassen (Parsifal and Froh) and Gerhard Stolze (Knappe in *Parsifal*).

Inevitably in so large a team built up from scratch there were some disappointments. Wieland demanded a high standard of ability from his singers, but equally important to him were personal relationships. His loyalty to the chosen few with whom he could work in harmony was as striking as his ruthlessness in discarding those with whom he could make no sympathetic contact, however great their talents. What he required from his singers is illustrated by a short note which he published in the *Rheingold* festival programme of 1955. He prefaced it with a quotation from Richard Wagner: "The basis of acting talent is truthfulness. The art of noble deception as practised by the born actor cannot be attained through mendacity, and this is the point at which the true artist parts company with the bad actor." Wieland went on:

"Seven 'actor-singers'—all true artists—can look back this summer on five continuous years in the Bayreuth *Festspielhaus*: Martha Mödl, Astrid Varnay, Paul Kuën, Gerhard Stolze, Hermann Uhde, Ludwig Weber and Wolfgang Windgassen. They made the reopening of the festival possible in 1951, and they form the seed from which, through tireless work and enthusiastic dedication to the task in hand, the artistic and human community of the new Bayreuth has grown."

*

Stage rehearsals for *Parsifal* and the *Ring* began in the *Festspielhaus* in May 1951, two months before the opening of the festival. A glimpse of the sheer hard work in which Wieland was now involved is given in a tribute which he wrote to Paul Eberhardt many years later. Published in the *Rheingold* festival programme of 1966, it is the only piece of autobiographical writing, as far as I have been able to discover, in which Wieland ever indulged:

"From May 1951 onwards, year by year, day by day, often night by night—I remember with pleasure the times in which we would take leave of each other at the stage door at dawn, tired out and completely colour blind—we would sit for weeks on end in the still chilly auditorium, feebly warmed by electric fires, and busy ourselves with the nuances of a shade of green or blue, a filter mixture, or the exact musical plan for a lighting transition: always trying and trying again.

"I did not make things easy for you. I confronted you with something new: the empty room, whereas before, up to the last festivals during the war, you had been illuminating decorations which in form, volume and colour filled the stage of themselves. My stage rooms could only become the musical rooms I had envisaged for the Wagnerian music drama through the medium of your light—and lighting *changes*. How new that concept was is recalled by the much quoted anecdote about Hans Knappertsbusch: asked reproachfully by guardians of the old Bayreuth tradition why he had consented to conduct this disgraceful production of *Parsifal*, he replied that he had imagined during the dress rehearsal that the stage decorations were still to come. . . .

"To our joint work you brought great musical feeling and a knowledge of the piano arrangements of the entire operatic repertory of which any conductor might be proud. In addition you possessed the rare gift of intuition, a sort of sixth sense for my ideas and my aims . . . which were at first often vague and imprecise technically. . . . You, my dear Paul Eberhardt, were for me the best imaginable, that is to say, the ideal colleague."

The warm personal affection that speaks from these lines was fully reciprocated by Eberhardt, whom I visited in his home in Bayreuth, its walls decorated with his own African landscapes and one or two paintings by Wieland himself. With a vigour belying his seventy-odd years he spoke of his work with Wieland as the crowning experience of his life, for which he had gladly sacrificed his beloved Africa. Wieland's sense of colour, he told me, was remarkably acute. In his efforts to apply it through lighting to the music he would play passages on the piano while Eberhardt, at the lighting desk, would try out various combinations. And so they would continue, for hours at a time, until Wieland was satisfied.

His work with Eberhardt, vitally important as it was, represented only a small fraction of the task in hand. He spent hours on end with his singers, in individual discussions as well as in stage rehearsals, trying to instil in them an awareness of the psychological implications of their roles which would result in a physical interpretation free of the usual stereotyped gestures.

In 1951, however, he had not yet mastered the art, which he later developed so successfully, of physically demonstrating to his singers what he required of them. Astrid Varnay, his first Brünnhilde at Bayreuth, remarked: "Although he knew exactly in his own mind what he wanted, he could not . . . demonstrate it to us in action. All moments of excitement he portrayed with clenched fists, outstretched arms, legs wide apart, and shaking head, thrown back or hanging down. I personally could do nothing with it. Certainly not the shaking head, which got in the way of my singing. When I told him this he simply laughed and said I must translate it into my own terms. Gradually, by watching his face carefully, I learned to grasp what he meant with his unsatisfactory gestures. He approved my 'translation' and accepted the movements that I thought out for myself" (Bayreuth Festival *Rheingold* programme 1967).

In any case, Wieland's gestures were not meant to be slavishly copied. They were suggestions, which the singer was permitted to accept or reject as he thought fit—though what was put in their place had naturally, in the interests of the overall style, to earn Wieland's approval. The main object was to agree on the psychological interpretation of a role, and to achieve this Wieland would often paraphrase Wagner's high-sounding language in terms of similar situations as they might occur today. He would, for example, describe Nothung as "Wotan's secret weapon" and equate Valhalla with Wall Street—anything, however mundane, that might make the situation real to the singer and provoke, in expression and gesture, a natural reaction.

By the time I myself came to observe Wieland at work, some ten years later, this method of procedure had certainly become more important to him than the demonstration of a preconceived gesture. But by that time his style was well established. In the early stages of its evolution it was inevitable that he should think to some extent in terms of fixed visual patterns.

11

FIRST BAYREUTH PRODUCTIONS

1951–1952

"THIS WAS NOT only the best *Parsifal* that I have ever seen or heard, but one of the three or four most moving spiritual experiences of my life." Thus Ernest Newman wrote in the *Sunday Times* of Wieland's production with which the festival of 1951 opened. Of the same production a German critic wrote: "What the master's grandson has conjured up for us is a symphony in gloom, a formless play of patterns and shadows which dispenses with individual dramatic relationships, confines itself exclusively to symbols and thereby becomes wearisome." These are two extreme views of a production which tended, as all Wieland's work did from this time on, to evoke either tremendous praise or harsh criticism. A middle course scarcely existed. One was either passionately for the "new Bayreuth style", as it soon came to be called, or passionately against it: a convincing proof that something radical had been discovered, an uncompromising new approach that defied any cautious attempts to hedge.

The facts of the German critic's description were not entirely unjust. The lighting was dim, the movements patterned, and such few physical objects as were used were symbolic rather than realistic in appearance. But the patterns were not formless, and there was no lack of individual dramatic relationships. These had simply been transposed to other than the customary levels, and the critic failed to recognise them.

As Wieland had pointed out in his essay on tradition and innovation, *Parsifal* "requires mystical expression of a very complex state of the soul, rooted in the unreal and grasped only by intuition". In this conception of it neither time nor place have any relevance. Yet on a stage these can never be entirely eliminated. Wieland attempted to reduce their impact by avoiding all geographic and period detail in both scenery and costumes. There were no solid sets apart from some plain columns in the temple. The dim outlines of the forest, Klingsor's castle and the meadow were all suggested by lighting, and otherwise the stage was bare except, in the temple, for a raised chair and a round table. On this the Knights of the Grail gradually converged, appearing out of the surrounding shadows with slow, almost indiscernable steps. The Flower Maidens were mauve wraiths undulating against a dim background that made no attempt to suggest an actual garden.

In the festival handbook of 1951 Wieland published, under the title *Parsifal's Cross: a Psychological Pattern*, a design which he described as "an attempt to express in graphic terms the fundamental ideas of the work, the relationship of the characters to each other and their place in the drama; and in doing so to find an objective basis for the production of this work during the festival of 1951".

This rather forbidding and at first sight cryptic design (reproduced on the next page) is worth careful study. *Parsifal*, looked at purely as a narrative, undeniably lacks clarity, and the lazy opera-goer is usually content to regard it as a sort of general parable on the subject of Christian redemption. Those who are willing to penetrate a little further into its symbolic mysteries can easily lose their way, baffled particularly by the character of Kundry, who is without doubt Wagner's most enigmatic creation.

By putting an action—the kiss—at the centre of his psychological plan and building in all directions from there, Wieland found a starting-point in his search for coherence. "Parsifal's spiritual and mental development," he explains, "unfolds within the magnetic field bounded by the four poles of 'Mother', 'Saviour', 'Klingsor' and 'Titurel'—symbolically represented by swan, dove, spear and cup. It forms a complete 'mirrored arch', the centre of which is Kundry's kiss—simultaneously the mystical core, climax, nadir and crisis of his salvation."

Above and below the horizontal line of his cross Wieland set out the individual experiences of the persons involved in the drama. In Parsifal's case they form a sort of mirror symmetry. In this way he establishes enlightening parallels

PARSIFAL'S CROSS

A psychological pattern by Wieland Wagner

THE SAVIOUR

The divine paternal spirit of all-embracing love

The suffering divinity weeps for man's shame

The "Divine"

Spear and Grail united
Symbol: the dove

PARSIFAL

Experiences the knights' despair and enters into the maternal community of the Grail

Experiences the atonement of man towards Nature on the Grail meadow

Conscious of the sacred precincts: despairs over his guilt of Titurel's death. Atonement and anointed as king with Kundry's help

Desperate struggle in vain search for Titurel's Temple of the Grail and ordeal through experiencing the sufferings of mankind

Leaves Kundry—wanders astray

Capture of the spear: destruction of the castle

Hostile meeting with Klingsor

Retreats before Kundry

Conscious of his mission

Sees woman as "corrupt destroyer"

Experiences the sufferings of Amfortas

Recognition of his guilt towards the Saviour

Torment of sensuality

"Sinful nature"

The woman

Decisive experience ("the Fall—sin"): meeting with the Saviour

Failure:
in relation to the Divine.
In her natural destiny:
her laughter

Her longing: renewed meeting with the Saviour

Her guilt: profanation of the "Cup"

Her curse: "at the height of salvation to languish for the fountain of the damned"

Symbol of her dual nature: the "Wound"

KLINGSOR

Belief in nothing

Chaos of egoism

Desperate struggle against sensuality (the "bad"):
Castration

Magic Castle

Flower Maidens (naturally unchaste, can be redeemed)

In possession of the spear (after the loss of the spear: no longer existent)

His error: chastity = subduing sensuality

Hatred of woman (feminine element)

Misuse of the spear as magic weapon to achieve power

"Terrible distress"

KUNDRY

Distorted by cruel laughter

In Klingsor's ban:
enchantress against her will (hallucination: salvation = physical surrender to imagined saviour)

In the service of Titurel:
Messenger of the Grail against her will (hallucination: salvation through distorted service to the Grail as penitence and atonement)

Torment, madness, despair:
Cry for pity

Message: "Whoever withstands thee, sets thee free"

Her salvation: to serve freely

Liberating experience: Parsifal captures the spear

Expiation: tears at the sight of the smiling meadow

THE KISS

Despair, torment

Recognition of his guilt towards his mother

Experiences the sufferings of his mother

Sees woman as "mother"

Kundry bestows a name on him

End of his anonymity

Retreats before the Flower Maidens

Hostile meeting with Klingsor's knights

The lure of the magic castle

Flight from the Grail: wanders astray again

Torment in Titurel's Temple of the Grail and failure to understand the experience of mankind's sufferings

Unconfessed guilt of mother's death. Therefore, unconscious of the sacred precincts, fails to grasp the meaning of his trial admittance to the holy community of the Grail

Kills the swan and recognises his guilt through the sufferings of Nature inflicted by man in the forest of the Grail

Meets the shining knights and flees from his mother = astray = forgotten

PARSIFAL

Parsifal and Herzeleide united
Symbol: the swan

"Goodness"
Suffering Nature weeps at Parsifal's flight
The Eternal Woman—primal origin

THE MOTHER

The "fallen spirit"

The Man

Decisive experience ("the Fall—sin"): meeting with Kundry

Failure:
in relation to woman.
In his spiritual destiny:
loss of the spear

His longing: meeting with the Saviour

His guilt: profanation of the spear

His curse: "at the height of salvation to languish for the fountain of the damned"

Symbol of his dual nature: the "Wound"

AMFORTAS

Distorted in cruel self-torment

In Titurel's ban:
Protector of the Grail against his will (hallucination: salvation through spiritual surrender to the—imagined—Saviour)

Torment, madness, despair:
Cry for pity

Message: "Await him, whom I have chosen"

His salvation: liberation at the sight of the Grail

Liberating experience: return of the spear through Parsifal

Expiation: rapture as the wound heals

TITUREL

The pure faith

Ethos of the law

Bitter struggle against unbelief ("Evil"):
Revelation

Castle of the Grail

Knights of the Grail (unnaturally chaste, corruptible)

In possession of the Grail (without sight of the Grail: no longer existent)

His error: chastity = repression of sensuality

Hatred of woman
(feminine element)

Misuse of the Grail for mental satisfaction and prolongation of life

"Fear and misery"

between the fate of Kundry and the fate of Amfortas, as well as between the "white" magic of Titurel and the "black" magic of his opponent Klingsor. The psychological pattern is based very closely on Richard Wagner's use of *Leitmotive*, which in *Parsifal* are compound in structure. As Kurt Overhoff points out in his book *Richard Wagners Parsifal*, Wagner frequently used musical mirror formations for dramatic purposes. Overhoff's book, like his previous one on *Tristan und Isolde*, was the outcome of his work on the score with Wieland, to whom it is dedicated.

Wieland's psychological pattern must be regarded as a producer's blueprint rather than as a guide to the audience, who would find it unrewarding to follow during performance. It was Wieland's basic guide in planning the physical movements of his actors just as much as their psychological understanding. The movement of a character from one part of the stage to another was not for him a matter of mere convenience, but a deliberate dramatic factor, and here for the first time he was employing the principle of geometry to achieve it. He recognised that the distance between one character and another had its significance in the expression of dramatic tensions. However, he took care to conceal from the audience his basic geometric patterns. In a large scale movement, such as the entry of the Knights of the Grail or the Flower Maidens, he would start in rehearsal with a completely symmetrical pattern and then, like a painter in the final stages of a picture, he would with a few touches subtly soften the outline in order to conceal it from the conscious eye, while leaving its basic function intact.

But probably to no one in the audience during that first postwar festival was any of this clearly apparent. The analyses and interpretations of Wieland's techniques came long afterwards.

*

In contrast to *Parsifal*, Wieland's *Ring* production of 1951 contained a number of compromises with the old traditional style. Even in 1953, when I myself saw it for the first time, it still contained a huge dragon with hinged jaw, though the tree under which Brünnhilde was laid to sleep, visible in 1951, had by then disappeared. Wieland was so dissatisfied with certain aspects of his production that he subsequently put a ban on photographs taken in that first year: the existing photographs of his so-called 1951 production were taken at performances in later festivals.

Still, as I wrote in *Musical Opinion* in 1953: "Criticism . . . pales in the memory of many superb moments. There is the impressive rosy projection of a distant Valhalla at the beginning of the cycle and its breathtaking dissolution into flame at the end; the grey-green Rhine Maidens, no longer swimming in the air, but flitting away in an instant into the gloom of deep water; the moving tragedy of Wotan taking leave of the sleeping Brünnhilde, alone on the great bare stage against a background of raging flame; the wonderful impression of the hall of the Gibichungs, two bronze-gleaming projections of light against the general blackness, fading out at the end so that only Hagen's white face can be seen (a moment of amazingly sinister power); and the last picture of all, after the general hotchpotch of the

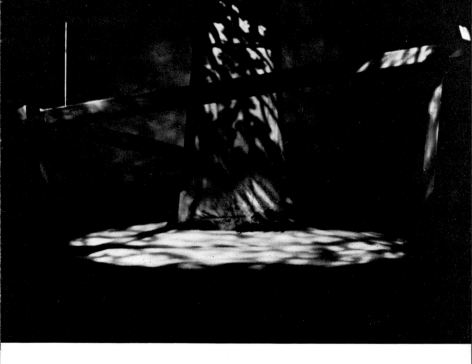

Die Walküre, Act One: first Bayreuth production (*above*)
Die Walküre, Act One: second Bayreuth production (*below*)

Tristan und Isolde, Act Three: first Bayreuth production (*above*)
Tristan und Isolde, Act Three: second Bayreuth production (*below*)

rising Rhine (an impossible thing to stage by any standards), where, encircling the space where Valhalla had stood, a huge reflection like a moon-ring mirrors in a grey-green sky the now deserted disc which had been the basic element of all but the first scene of the four dramas."

This disc was of course the unifying factor of the whole production, and its symbolic meaning, both in relation to the world and to the ring, was clear. In a conversation I had with him in later years Wieland said rather ruefully, "The *Weltenscheibe* which I introduced in 1951 has since been copied almost *ad absurdum* on all the stages of the world. One is almost ashamed to see it nowadays. It has become the common thing." The symbolic disc was, in other words, a very successful discovery, which proved at the time imaginatively rewarding and only later was to become an embarrassment, when its inherent possibilities, as a means in itself, had been fully exploited.

More noticeable in the *Ring* than in *Parsifal* was Wieland's disregard of many of the composer's stage directions which seemed in no way out of keeping with a production that did not break entirely with the realistic approach. To take one example, earlier versions of Hunding's hut may have appeared ludicrously elaborate, but Wieland's solution of a central tree trunk surrounded by a triangle of open beams at roof level on an otherwise empty stage was no effective substitute. Here Wieland could be accused of leaving out essential as well as inessential things. The meeting of Siegmund and Sieglinde must take place against a more recognisably human background than the meeting of Siegfried and Brünnhilde, not only to gain contrast, but also to emphasise the difference of their significance in the drama. Wieland's setting for this latter encounter, on the curved rim of an empty stage that suggested the top of the world, was one of the great moments of the production, and its success lay in the perfect integration between the event and its place in the cosmic drama as a whole. In contrast with the Siegmund-Sieglinde scene, it reflected the infinite potentiality of true simplicity rather than the false simplicity of baffled imagination.

In his essay on tradition and innovation Wieland had defined Wagner's stage directions as inner visions rather than practical demands, and his refusal to interpret them literally, on the grounds that the works deal in psychological states rather than historical events, was logical within the context of his generally non-realistic approach. Wagner did, however, on occasions introduce physical details into the text itself. Wotan's lost eye, his broad-rimmed hat, the sleeping Brünnhilde's armour: these are referred to in the text, and Wieland's decision, in the interests of the non-realistic production as a whole, to present a hatless, two-eyed Wotan and a Brünnhilde without armour would logically have obliged him to alter the text.

His excuse for leaving the words unaltered was that Wagner's words were an inextricable part of the corporate sound. They could not be altered or eliminated without damage to the over-all texture. True though this may be, it was not the only reason for Wieland's abstention. Rebel or not, he had in 1951 a firm respect for the basic traditions of Bayreuth. As a member of the Wagner family one did not tamper with the words and music of the master.

Much of the inconsistency in Wieland's treatment of the *Ring* could be attributed to the lack of time available to trans-late his ideas fully into stage practice. But part of it arose from the fact that he had not yet worked out in his own mind an overall thematic conception of it. If his main purpose had been more political than artistic—namely, to strip the *Ring* of its romantic Nordic associations and to reveal the universality of its subject—then he very largely succeeded. In particular he recognised the fallibility of Wotan: this was no longer a god, but a man whose downfall is the result of his own weaknesses rather than the cunning of his enemies.

*

Wieland's third production at Bayreuth was *Tristan und Isolde*. It opened the festival of 1952, in which all the productions of the previous year were repeated. However mixed the recep-tion had been of these, Wieland had resolved to follow the excellent advice which Albert Schweitzer, a friend and admirer of Siegfried Wagner, had given him in a letter of good wishes from Lambarene in Africa: "Answer criticism with achieve-ment".

Of his three productions *Tristan und Isolde* represented the most consequential application of the "new Bayreuth style".

Scenery was almost entirely banished. The basic structure was a slanting oval with raised sides, which did service in the three acts as a ship, a garden and a castle courtyard. Isolde's tent in the first act was a cloth screen, with a bed before it. In the second act there was a bench for the lovers, and in the third act a bed for Tristan. The persons on stage were reduced to seven—Isolde, Brangäne, Tristan, Kurwenal, King Marke, Melot and the shepherd—and the sailors and courtiers were kept completely out of sight. The spotlight was used extensively. In the second act the lovers sang their duet with only head and shoulders visible in the general blackness, and Isolde sang her *Liebestod* with Tristan lying invisible at her feet. It was a very intimate and romantic production that reflected Wagner's first conception of *Tristan und Isolde*, defined in a letter to Liszt, as a memorial to love—"the most beautiful of all dreams".

Much of the extraordinary emotional force which Wieland's production generated may have been due to the superb musical quality achieved under the direction of Herbert von Karajan with a cast including Ramon Vinay as Tristan and Martha Mödl as Isolde—both at that time at the height of their vocal powers and both sensitive actors with whom Wieland liked to work. But the philosophical basis of the drama, its simple dramatic structure and above all its perfect integration between sound and vision, make *Tristan und Isolde* of all Wagner's works the most amenable to non-realistic treatment. In two letters written by Wagner, Wieland found what seemed a complete justification, if that were needed, of his new approach. They were addressed to Eduard Devrient, the manager of the opera house in Karlsruhe, and concerned the projected first performance of *Tristan und Isolde*, which would have taken place in 1859 at Karlsruhe if Wagner and Devrient had not eventually quarrelled. Wieland had these two letters printed in the *Tristan und Isolde* programme of 1952, in which they were described as "hitherto unknown".

In these letters Wagner described his work as "the most musical I have ever written or ever will write. Its dramatic truth and relevance is in every respect at one with its flowing musical sound." Pleading with Devrient for a larger orchestra than the Karlsruhe opera normally employed, he wrote: "More than anywhere else the orchestra in *Tristan* is a power in the realm of ideas, comparable perhaps in importance with the Greek chorus, though with the added significance that it does not just reflect on the happenings, but experiences them to the full and expands them beyond the bounds of imagination. Only through it can the whole spiritual process be realised in all its strength and subtlety."

About his scenic requirements Wagner wrote: "As far as the ship is concerned, I think I am more interested in its symbolic purpose than in its technical reality." The action in the first act takes place inside Isolde's tent, and Wagner felt that any attempt to widen the perspective by depicting the ship on which it stands "would rob the scene of all intimacy. As soon as the tent is closed at the back, we should pay absolutely no more attention to the ship and its crew, but remain in the intimate atmosphere of a private room." When Brangäne pulls back the flap at the beginning, we can see that we are on a ship at sea—"and that is sufficient for the moment. . . . After this disclosure, I have no desire that the ship's characteristics should be seen in great detail. It is only at the end of the act that it should make a real impact."

Though, to judge from the pictures of Wagner's own first production of *Tristan und Isolde* in Munich in 1865, Wagner himself had apparently forgotten his remarks to Devrient on the symbolic character of the work, Wieland could justifiably claim to have (at least in part) the composer's own authority for his treatment of it in 1952.

12

REPERCUSSIONS

1953

AFTER THE FESTIVAL of 1951 Wieland and Gertrud had travelled to Italy for a holiday. Yet for all his interest in classical art, Wieland did not feel at home in one of its principal breeding grounds. The dry atmosphere had an oppressive effect on him. In the following year he switched his attention to the North Sea island of Sylt, a long and at that time only sparsely populated strip of sand-dunes off the coast of Schleswig-Holstein, where it was possible to find solitude and freedom from civilisation, and in the sight only of seagulls to strip off one's clothes and plunge into the sea. This was far more in line with Wieland's solitary nature than the sophisticated, comfort-addicted world to which his sudden emergence to fame had opened the doors.

Year after year he returned to the sand-dunes of Sylt, where he could forget his work for a short while and find time for his children. They saw little of him in Wahnfried, since for hours on end he would be locked away with his gramophone, getting ideas for his new productions, after study of the text and the printed music, from the sound in its full colouring. During such sessions or when he was immersed in books, of which he read enormous quantities, the children would be kept out of his sight and hearing. Fond as he was of them, he had that quality of single-mindedness which insisted that he should give his complete attention to whatever was occupying him at a given moment, and this called for a tight control of domestic arrangements. Wieland was not prepared to tolerate distractions, from whatever direction they came. Having no need of social contacts himself, he did not encourage them among the members of his family, and his children, if they wanted to see their own friends, were usually persuaded while Wieland was at home to meet them outside Wahnfried.

This did not prevent a very affectionate relationship, in fact it rather intensified it. The children paid tribute to his appetite for work by nicknaming him *Bieber* (beaver), and by that name they continued to address him for the rest of his life. Their fierce loyalty towards him once caused them in their younger years to stay away from their grandmother for a time after they had heard her criticising one of their father's productions. Winifred, though she scrupulously adhered to her undertaking not to intervene in the running of the festival or to make any public statements, saw no reason to conceal her private views from her personal friends, and within her own four walls she did not, in her forthright way, err on the side of discretion. Wieland was apt to respond with equally tart comments, and the relationship between him and his mother, though never broken off, became increasingly strained.

Wieland had not yet learnt to ignore criticism though, so long as it was confined to details of his productions and did not question the sincerity of his approach, he would bear it with a good grace. Any suggestion, however, that reflected on his integrity as an artist or implied that he was deliberately trying to create sensations in order to draw attention to himself would rouse him to a fury, and he would retaliate with a cold unforgivingness which could sometimes amount to cruelty. The particular target of his retribution, now that success had put him in a position of power, was the group of old Bayreuth loyalists around his mother. "I wish I knew," he once told his biographer Walter Panofsky, "what Richard Wagner did to deserve all these supra-national secret societies and pseudo-Germanic women's organisations and all the other busybodies swarming round the *Festspielhaus*." The fact that many of these busybodies had been kind and encouraging to him in the past did nothing to soften his hostility towards them. Possibly indeed his consciousness of past obligation might even have intensified the savagery with which he threw it off.

One of the principal victims of this unforgiving streak in Wieland's nature was Kurt Overhoff. Finding himself now virtually unemployed in Bayreuth, he took to writing about Wieland's productions in the capacity of a music critic. His judgments were not always favourable and Wieland, hurt more than he would have been by criticism from less close a source, made it clear to him that the time had come to part. Overhoff left Bayreuth. From then on Wieland cut him completely out of his life, even to the extent of suppressing his name entirely when speaking about his earlier life.

Schweitzer, in his letter to Wieland and Wolfgang which I have already quoted, had another piece of advice to offer: "Let people discuss you in speech and in writing. Keep your own counsels. Do not attempt to join in the discussion and to influence them or to justify yourselves." This advice the grandsons did not accept. They introduced the modern institution of the press conference into their festival schedule, and many of the questions that were flung at them were far from friendly. Master of the sarcastic retort that he was in private, it took some years for Wieland to accustom himself to making use of it in public, and in the first few conferences he left the talking mainly to his more extrovert brother.

I was myself present at the press conference in 1953. It was the first time I saw Wieland, and I cannot remember a word he said on that occasion. Possibly he said nothing at all. The main figure on the platform, seated between the two brothers, was Paul Hindemith, who had in that year conducted Beethoven's Ninth Symphony at the opening of the festival. Hindemith's engagement, as Wieland told Panofsky, was a deliberately provocative act. Following the controversies of the two opening years, a group of old-school Wagnerians had formed a Society for the Faithful Presentation of the Dramas of Richard Wagner (*Vereinigung für die werktreue Wiedergabe der Dramen Richard Wagners*). Hindemith, a leading figure of the modern musical world who had shown in his acts that he was anti-Nazi and in his music that he was anti-Wagnerian, was the grandsons' reply to the loyalists. How well he conducted the symphony was, in Wieland's view, of secondary importance. "The main point is that he should conduct it here. We must put an end once and for all to this rotten old cult" (Panofsky, *Süddeutsche Zeitung*, 19 October 1966).

Such acts of retaliation were certainly more profitable than Wieland's vain efforts to stifle a Bayreuth critic, Alfred Pellegrini, whom he suspected of playing a leading role in the

Society for the Faithful Presentation of the Dramas of Richard
Wagner. Beside complaining to the editor of the paper for
which Pellegrini wrote, Wieland refused him press tickets for the
performances. The quarrel assumed ludicrous proportions and
even came before the courts. In the final result Wieland was
the loser, since he had to pay the court costs and in addition he
lost a lot of public sympathy. No more jealous upholders of the
freedom of the press exist than the German newspapers of the
post-Hitler period.

*

It was predictable after his sudden rise to fame that Wieland
should find himself sought after by other opera houses. The
first to approach him, even before he had made his mark in
Bayreuth, was the director of the Stuttgart opera, Walter
Erich Schäfer. In his book *Wieland Wagner: Persönlichkeit und
Leistung* Schäfer writes: "Some people . . . who knew about
his early plans had drawn our attention to him. We wrote to
him and he came, sat shyly opposite me, breathing shallowly,
and asked me to be good enough to wait until his first Bayreuth
productions had appeared and had either succeeded or failed.
In principle he would like to say yes. And I think it was precisely the fact that I did not press him that brought us so near
to each other."

There is a mixture of modesty and caution in Wieland's
reaction to Schäfer's proposal that must ring true to anybody
who came even cursorily into contact with him. The aggressive
front he often showed to the outside world concealed an inner
humility which even success did not dispel. At the time Schäfer
met him he had of course every reason to be modest, since he
had no real achievements behind him, but all the same it
requires considerable strength of character in a young man to
reject so alluring an opportunity as that which Schäfer was
offering him.

Not Stuttgart, however, but Munich was the scene of
Wieland's first post-war production outside Bayreuth. Rudolf
Hartmann, who had produced *Die Meistersinger* in the *Festspiel-
haus* in 1951, had been appointed artistic director of the
Munich opera, and one of his first acts was to invite Wieland

Tannhäuser, Act Two:
first Bayreuth
production

Tannhäuser, Act Two:
second Bayreuth
production

Fidelio
at Stuttgart,
1954

to produce Gluck's *Orfeo ed Euridice* there. Hartmann, whose *Meistersinger* at Bayreuth had been completely traditional, had observed Wieland's more revolutionary approach with great interest. Though, as he later told me, he did not agree with all that Wieland did, he had a high regard for his artistic capabilities and was curious to see how he would apply his ideas to a work that was not written by Wagner.

Munich's main opera house, the *Nationaltheater*, destroyed during the war, had not yet been rebuilt, and *Orfeo ed Euridice* was presented in March 1953 at the *Prinzregententheater*, a more solid replica of the Bayreuth *Festspielhaus*. During its temporary use as a stage for the entire operatic repertoire the hood that concealed the orchestra from sight had been removed, so that Gluck's work was not subjected to the full test of being presented as a Wagnerian music drama. But Wieland approached it in the same spirit, and he had no inhibitions about doctoring it very considerably.

He wrote in the programme: "Orpheus's mourning, his defiance, his test and his defeat have been depicted by Gluck in a spirit wholly in keeping with Greek tragedy, with an almost ascetic avoidance of all operatic devices and an unusual economy of external action. The music is at one and the same time delicate and clear-cut, lyrical and intense. . . . Both for the musician and the producer *Orfeo* presents a unique stylistic problem. It is as far away from Handel as it is from Mozart, and my aim has been to find a form of presentation for Gluck's work which will ensure its survival in the German theatre now and in the future."

This was a large and, it must be admitted, unnecessary claim. Gluck's work has managed to hold the stage for two centuries without too much interference from producers. However, one can grant that it survives on the beauty of its music rather than on its handling of the classical legend, and there is scope for improvement in the dramatic framework. Wieland's first step was to banish Calzabigi's happy ending entirely. It had been tacked on to the legend, he claimed, simply to suit the theatrical conventions of Vienna in 1762, and nowadays it was quite intolerable. Wieland also felt that musically Gluck's ending was inferior to the rest, and consequently he had no qualms about leaving it out. In its place he simply repeated the mourning scene with which the work opens, thus—as he told Antoine Goléa—giving it "that dramatic and human unity of which Gluck too must have dreamt".

Since anything that smacked of convention was liable to arouse instinctive hostility in Wieland, he clearly gave some thought to the question whether the role of Orpheus should be sung by a male or female singer. This time he came down on the side of convention for what seemed to him a valid dramatic reason. A male Orpheus, he felt, would introduce an element of eroticism that was foreign to the work. It was a legitimate argument for his own particular production, which was severely classical in style, sombre in colouring and restrained in movement. The Munich audiences received it with marked approval.

In his programme note Wieland pointed out the basic resemblance between *Orfeo* and *Lohengrin*, in both of which the drama depends on a fatal veto: Orpheus must not look at Eurydice, Elsa must not demand to know Lohengrin's name. *Eros thanatos*, the kind of love that finds fulfilment only in death, was, as Wieland remarked, an obsessional theme with Richard Wagner. It runs through all his works from *Der Fliegende Holländer* to *Parsifal*, finding its fullest expression in *Tristan und Isolde*. With Wieland himself *Eros thanatos* also became an obsessional theme, and in almost all the non-Wagnerian works he chose to produce he found evidence of it.

*

At the Bayreuth Festival of 1953 Wolfgang Wagner made his debut as a producer with *Lohengrin*, while Wieland contented himself with making minor adjustments to his existing productions of *Parsifal*, the *Ring* and *Tristan und Isolde*. His most urgent task, however, was to solve the crisis that had arisen among his conductors.

Hans Knappertsbusch had never been happy with Wieland's production of *Parsifal*, and he had tried from the start to persuade Wieland to restore to it such (in his view) essential objects as the swan, the dove and Klingsor's spear, which Wieland had preferred to leave to the imagination. Wieland had managed in the first two festivals to satisfy him with half-promises. He had even introduced a visible model of a dove, though he suspended it so high above the stage that, though Knappertsbusch could see it from the conductor's desk, the audience behind him could not. This little piece of chicanery was of course supposed to be kept a secret, but whether or not Knappertsbusch discovered it, he came to the conclusion that Wieland had no intention of meeting his demands, and in consequence he rejected the invitation to conduct *Parsifal* or any other work at Bayreuth in 1953.

Herbert von Karajan had also decided after the 1952 festival to sever his connection with Bayreuth. This left Wieland with only one conductor: Joseph Keilberth, who had been engaged in 1952 to conduct the *Ring*. Since Keilberth was now occupied with Wolfgang's new production of *Lohengrin*, Wieland was faced with the need to find two new conductors.

One of them was immediately at hand. Wieland would in fact have invited Clemens Krauss to Bayreuth from the very start if he had been free to do so. Krauss, whom he had known since his student days, had to Wieland's ear a lightness of touch in his approach to Wagner's music which corresponded to his own taste. Knappertsbusch, whose position in Munich had been taken over by Krauss following Knappertsbusch's quarrel with the Nazis in 1936, was unwilling to share the Bayreuth Festival with him, and Wieland had to make a choice between them. Now that Knappertsbusch had withdrawn, Wieland was free to invite Krauss to take his place.

Krauss confirmed Wieland's estimate of his lightness of touch during the 1953 festival by negotiating *Parsifal* faster than any other conductor in the history of Bayreuth. He also conducted one cycle of the *Ring*, Keilberth retaining the other. For *Tristan und Isolde* Wieland engaged Eugen Jochum, a well-known conductor whose true interests lay in the concert hall rather than the opera house. The appointment does not seem to have been regarded by either as anything more than a temporary solution.

Following the festival Wieland went to Naples, to supervise his production of the *Ring* cycle at the San Carlo. Little need be said of this production, spread over two separate seasons. It was identical with Wieland's existing production at Bayreuth. Its main significance was that he used it to try out new singers in important roles. In Naples Martha Mödl sang

Brünnhilde for the first time and Hermann Uhde Wotan. It was a pattern that Wieland followed from then on: all his productions of Wagnerian works outside Bayreuth served in one way or another as models for future productions in the *Festspielhaus*.

13

EDITING MASTERPIECES

1954

DIFFICULTIES WITH CONDUCTORS again arose to threaten the Bayreuth Festival of 1954, which was to open with Wieland's first production of *Tannhäuser*. According to advance publicity, Clemens Krauss was to conduct both cycles of the *Ring*, Eugen Jochum *Parsifal* and Joseph Keilberth *Lohengrin*. For *Tannhäuser* Wieland had engaged Igor Markevitch, a young conductor of considerable promise who had made a great impression on Gertrud with his conducting of the music of Ravel. Wieland, himself an admirer of Ravel's music, had hopes of a *Tannhäuser* in which the orchestral sound would have a Gallic delicacy.

The death of Clemens Krauss in May, two months before the festival was due to open, was a severe blow to Wieland, not only in relation to the impending festival, but to all his future plans. Of the conductors with whom he had so far worked he had found Krauss the most sympathetic, both in his musical approach and his personal relations. But for his death there can be no doubt that Krauss would have become the major Bayreuth conductor in the post-war years.

His death had one consolatory result: it healed the breach with Hans Knappertsbusch, whose personal affection for Wieland overcame his artistic scruples at a difficult time. He returned to Bayreuth to conduct *Parsifal*, and from 1954 onwards he appeared at every festival up to his own death in 1965, conducting *Parsifal* regularly and other works—*Der Fliegende Holländer*, the *Ring* and *Die Meistersinger*—occasionally.

Keilberth took over the *Ring*. But further troubles lay ahead. Shortly before the festival opened Markevitch withdrew from *Tannhäuser* and left Bayreuth. Officially he was said to be ill.

It may certainly have been true that Markevitch, like many other conductors making their first appearance in the *Festspiel-haus*, had difficulty in accustoming himself to its peculiar acoustic conditions. The resulting nervous strain can then communicate itself to the singers, leading to nervous crises and ultimatums all round. On such occasions—and there were several of them over the years—Wieland had to decide whether to support his singers or his conductors. Since personal inclinations played so large a part in his decisions, he usually came down on the side of the singers, with whom he worked more closely than with his conductors. Markevitch left, and the task of conducting both *Tannhäuser* and *Lohengrin* was taken over by Keilberth and Jochum.

Audiences, faced with the finished product, can seldom have any idea of the difficulties behind the scenes that have preceded it or of the unhappy compromises which a producer has been forced by circumstances to make. Successful as they had been in re-establishing the Bayreuth Festival, Wieland and Wolfgang were not able, after their initial effort, to relax. Unlike their predecessors, they could not count on having the automatic pick of the best conductors and singers of the day. Competition with other festivals—Salzburg, Munich, Vienna and Edinburgh among them—led to a great deal of hard bargaining, and contracts had frequently to be negotiated years ahead. Competition had also obliged the grandsons to make the festival an annual event, and they were in consequence denied the luxury, enjoyed by their predecessors, of having one year off in every three to prepare a new production. To keep the festival in the news they had to provide a new production every year. In the fifteen years up to 1965 Wieland was responsible for eleven of these. Wolfgang's burden was no less large for, beside his four productions (*Lohengrin* in 1953, *Der Fliegende Holländer* in 1955, *Tristan und Isolde* in 1957 and the *Ring* in 1960) he had the entire administration and finances of the festival to look after, as well as the task of restoring the frail fabric of the *Festspielhaus* which—built as a temporary structure by Richard Wagner—had long outlasted its projected life.

Artistically the brothers worked independently. In the matter of expenditure, however, Wieland was ultimately dependent on Wolfgang's ingenuity in raising funds. Wieland was not remarkably considerate, and he tended to answer all Wolfgang's appeals for economy with the argument that, to retain its position in the world, Bayreuth must offer nothing but the best—in materials as well as artistic effort. In this department of the festival work Wieland gave his brother many difficult hours.

*

Tannhäuser was the first of Wagner's early works that Wieland had attempted, and he offended the loyalists right from the start by rejecting the Paris version, which had hitherto been used at Bayreuth, and making a version of his own. He found two reasons to justify his boldness: first, Wagner's words to Cosima in the last year of his life—"I still owe the world *Tannhäuser*"; and second, Wagner's own readiness in his earlier years to tamper with the works of other composers, including even Mozart's *Don Giovanni*. Wieland made use of both these arguments in a note which he wrote for the 1954 *Tannhäuser* programme, though he struck that note of modesty and caution which we have noticed before, when he stated that the Bayreuth version (as he termed it) was put forward "for discussion".

Wieland's solution was to retain the overture in its complete concert form and to use the Paris version of the Bacchanal, followed by the early Dresden version of the scene between Venus and Tannhäuser. In the second act he restored Walter von der Vogelweide's contribution to the singers' contest; and in the final scene of the opera he attempted, while making use of the changes of instrumentation in the Paris score, to find a method of presentation that would convey the poetical idea in effective dramatic terms. Wieland maintained that both Dresden versions and the Paris version of the final scene were unsatisfactory. "The reports we have of Richard Wagner's angry discussions with his friends . . . prove this explicitly." And in a further note in the programme on his ideas concerning *Tannhäuser* Wieland tried to explain, as he saw it, what Wagner was aiming at:

"Wagner's main creative urge from *Der Fliegende Holländer* to *Parsifal* is to explore 'the true nature of love'. This theme is common to each of his works, but the presentation changes in relation to the state of intellectual maturity reached by the composer at the time of writing it. All Wagner's works can be considered in Goethe's sense as 'fragments of a grand confession'. But, however the problem is presented, the answer remains always the same, whether spoken by a young revolutionary or by a man on the threshold of old age. It is of eternal validity and can be expressed roughly thus: true love is a deliberate, dedicated and selfless surrender to the identity of the beloved. In *Tannhäuser* the negative factor that has to be overcome is the characteristic egotism of the male in the face of the unquestioning devotion and self-sacrifice of the female. This, rather than the problem of eroticism in itself, is what the work is about.

"The tragedy of Tannhäuser is the common tragedy of mankind in the age of Christianity, seeking the way back to the original unity of God and Man in the conscious knowledge of the split between his mind and his instincts. The cross he bears is the mistaken belief that he can find happiness either in extreme intoxication or in extreme asceticism. Yet the experience of these two extremes brings him, in place of the redemption he longs for, the curse of both worlds:

> *Venus:* Seek salvation but find it never!
> *Pope:* So you are damned forever!

"Tannhäuser fails to achieve 'true love' in his decisive meeting with Elisabeth, but the realisation of his guilt towards her enables him to seek and find 'the path to salvation through love', which in Wagner's conception lies for the man in the woman, who still lives in the original state of unity between God and mankind. It seems significant that Tannhäuser finds redemption as he dies—that his death is in fact directly identified with redemption. Thus we find in this transition work an artistic anticipation of the *Tristan* idea, a presentiment of the redemption theme in *Parsifal* (Kundry).

"And it is significant that in the proclamation of salvation ('Hail to the miracle of grace: the world is accorded redemption') Wagner presents his hero Tannhäuser as the symbol and representative of all mankind: Tannhäuser's individual fate is indicative of the destiny of all human beings. Only personal recognition, gained through guilt, of 'the true nature of love' can release the individual from the prison of his own ego. This recognition by souls on the threshold of parting is the prerequisite for the gift of divine grace, which enables the 'sinner' to resume his place in the eternal order."

Wieland's words about *Tannhäuser*, based as they are on extensive reading of the essays and letters of Richard Wagner as well as the writings of Baudelaire, Jung and others, would have been of lesser concern if he had not managed so successfully to translate them into effective stage terms. To me personally his *Tannhäuser* came as a revelation. In a work so overloaded with luscious musical moments, with opportunities for spectacle and grand gestures, his severely disciplined approach imposed a wholly praiseworthy coherence and raised the work beyond its usual heights.

Wieland's handling of the chorus in *Tannhäuser*, particularly in the second act, showed the radical difference between the new Bayreuth style and the old. Where Wagner had called for groups of individuals entering and paying their respects to the Landgrave and his niece, Wieland provided a grave procession of uniformly clad men and women who moved quietly to their places on either side of the stage. On a superficial view this was precisely what Wagner had not wanted: he had once written scornfully about choristers who enter from each side, cross the stage and form up opposite each other. However, Wagner was attacking a comfortable tradition that saved the trouble of rehearsal, whereas Wieland's efforts, painstakingly rehearsed, were directed towards an expressive use of his chorus as a dramatic background to the mounting tension of a climactic scene. Here were no separate human beings, but a mass expression of human prejudice, a wall against which Tannhäuser's reckless praise of carnal love resounded with all the force of blasphemy.

The formalism of the scene, which had this paradoxical effect of heightening the human passion that lay beneath it, was reinforced by the severe geometry of the setting, with its background of straight pillars and curved arches and its chequered floor. Wieland did not make the mistake of moving his actors around on this floor with the mathematical precision of a chess game—that would have been too obvious—but he certainly made full use of hidden tensions arising from the conscious use of lines, angles and distances in the pattern of movement. These were employed with equal effect in the procession of pilgrims: small and subtly varied groups of men in monk's robes, who moved diagonally across the stage, leaning forward on their way to Rome, upright on their return: a simple but effective depiction of guilt and redemption.

The contrasted world of the Venusberg was presented in this first production of *Tannhäuser* with an equally formal restraint. Scenically it was dominated by a series of conical patterns, rather like the inside of a shell, against which dancers clad in unadorned tights to suggest nudity mimed acts of love. It was a detached sort of miming that gave the impression rather of jaded memory than present enjoyment, a mood underlined by the fact that Tannhäuser was separated from Venus by the full depth of the stage.

The choreography of this scene was done by Gertrud Wagner (who had also been officially acknowledged since 1952 as responsible for the choreography of the Flower Maidens in *Parsifal*). It was no ballet in the usual sense. Gertrud, trained in the Mary Wigman style of expressive dancing rather than in classical ballet, saw its function as a heightening of normal movement within the dramatic context, and its pattern was evolved as much from the psychological situation as from the music itself.

In the valley of the Wartburg Wieland relied entirely on lighting and colour to provide the mood of the natural environment. The green of the first act, enlivened towards the end by the brilliant red costumes of the hunters, expressed the renewal of hope in Tannhäuser's heart; the autumnal shades of the third act his resignation and despair. After his death, by the simple device of assembling his choristers unseen in a pyramid formation behind a gauze and then gradually illuminating their haloed heads, Wieland achieved an ethereal atmosphere in which one could see Tannhäuser as "the symbol and representative of all mankind".

This production, important for its revelatory treatment of *Tannhäuser* as a drama of ideas, also gave proof of Wieland's growing confidence as a producer. For the first time—in particular in the second scene of the first act—he gave us a brilliant burst of bright colour. The objection that he tended to present most of his scenes in darkness or semi-darkness was here stilled. It was an important advance: Wieland's predilection for dim lighting might have been due to a certain extent to the extraordinary sensitivity of his own eyes, which could detect differences in shades of colour to which the ordinary mortal is blind; but it also owed something to his absorbed, self-communing nature. Here he gave scope to a new quality of showmanship, using the word in its most positive sense.

*

After *Tannhäuser* Wieland went to Stuttgart to fulfil his early promise to Schäfer. *Fidelio* was the first of sixteen productions he eventually made in an opera house which he himself called his "winter Bayreuth". Stuttgart provided him not only with a sympathetic chief who was willing to give him a free hand, but also with an ensemble which contained many of his favourite singers. In his *Fidelio* cast he had Gré Brouwenstijn (who had sung Elisabeth in his *Tannhäuser*), Wolfgang Windgassen as Florestan and Gustav Neidlinger as Pizarro.

Having now dared to edit Wagner at Bayreuth, Wieland had no scruples about subjecting Beethoven to the same treatment, on the grounds that Beethoven, like Wagner with *Tannhäuser*, had been dissatisfied with his own work. Wieland's tamperings with *Fidelio* were so radical that even Schäfer showed signs of alarm, though he loyally supported his producer to the extent of collaborating in the most drastic of Wieland's changes: the introduction of a masked narrator to replace all the spoken dialogue. The narration was written by Schäfer himself.

Wieland also made radical changes in the musical structure. For the overture he chose *Leonore No. 2*, and he used musical numbers from both the 1805 and 1814 versions of the work, including a trio for Marzelline, Jacquino and Rocco which Beethoven himself had cut out. He altered the order in which Marzelline's solo aria and her duet with Jacquino are sung. He employed a single set for the whole opera: a central arena surrounded by prison bars, and the various scenes were indicated only by lighting changes. The persons in the drama were presented as impersonal types: Florestan, the freedom fighter; Leonore, the loving, self-sacrificing wife; Pizarro, the political tyrant; Rocco, the money-loving opportunist; Marzelline, the simple, infatuated girl. The prisoners, all dressed alike, were the faceless victims of political oppression. There was a minimum of movement on stage.

Wieland explained to Erich Rappl in an interview in the *Bayreuther Tagblatt* (March 1955) what he had been aiming at in his production. The producer's job, he said, was to establish the essential style of the work itself and then to translate it into practice. *Fidelio* is not a drama, but a sort of situation. Its characters are drawn in black and white and undergo no psychological development. The universality and timelessness of its theme transcend both the weaknesses of the action and the place in which it occurs: any Spanish colour would clearly be irrelevant. In fact, the absence of colour in any sense in his settings had been dictated by what Wieland called the "objectivity" of Beethoven's music. He contrasted it with the more subjective music of Wagner, which calls for the use of colour and light in the interpretation of its changing moods.

There is sufficient good sense in these remarks to absolve Wieland from the reproach of simply trying to be different in his treatment of *Fidelio*. He very clearly acknowledged the greatness of the work to the full, but he felt that Beethoven had been inhibited by his inadequate libretto. The mistake that Wieland made was to attempt to impose on *Fidelio* the classical conceptions of dramatic unity, taking his cue from the final scene which, as he rightly said, is closer in character to oratorio than to opera. But, as Wieland later acknowledged with a new production of *Fidelio* in Brussels in 1965, there are more ways than one of achieving dramatic unity.

Though the press gave his first *Fidelio* the usual mixed reception, it was a success with the public in Stuttgart. When, however, the Stuttgart opera took the production to Paris in the following spring, something like a riot broke out in the opera house, and at one performance the police was called in to restore order. The reception in London in September 1955, when the production was presented at the Royal Festival Hall, was more decorous, though not less divided. Ernest Newman was on Wieland's side, but Victor Gollancz, in his book *Journey*

*Die Meister-
singer, The
Festival
Meadow:
first Bayreuth
production*

*Die
Meistersinger*,
The Festival
Meadow:
second
Bayreuth
production

Towards Music, attacked the production bitterly as "ruinous", "the most perverse of all *Fidelio* productions", "highbrow preposterousness". Possibly Peter Heyworth's judgment might be accepted as fair: "Wieland Wagner . . . made us experience *Fidelio* in the light of recent history. A partial view of an 'eternal' masterpiece, you may say. But surely a relevant one?"

14

THE THEATRICAL IDEA

1955–1956

THE YEAR 1955 was spent mainly outside Bayreuth. There were visits to Paris and London with the Stuttgart production of *Fidelio* and, between them, a visit of the complete Bayreuth Festival ensemble, together with the Bamberg Symphony Orchestra, to Barcelona, where in June three of Wieland's existing productions—*Parsifal, Die Walküre* and *Tristan und Isolde*—were presented at the *Gran Teatro del Liceo*. Wieland found time between his official engagements to do some sightseeing and even to go to the cinema, where the British film *The Tales of Hoffmann* was being shown. Wieland was so fascinated by it that, together with Paul Eberhardt, he saw it three times. He spoke of his desire to produce the work himself on the stage, but he never did.

Back in Bayreuth for the festival, he touched up his existing productions, particularly *Tannhäuser*, for which he had now found a new conductor: André Cluytens of the Paris opera. Wieland was pleased with his discovery, and in all the festivals up to 1958 Cluytens appeared regularly.

In November 1955 he began his production of the *Ring* at Stuttgart with *Rheingold*, and in December staged Gluck's *Orfeo ed Euridice* there. Neither of these productions differed essentially from his previous versions in Bayreuth and Munich.

Stuttgart was also the scene of Wieland's next new production, his first with the work of a living composer. Wieland had first met Carl Orff in his student days in Munich, when Orff had been in charge of the school at which Gertrud was studying ballet. In spite of the difference in their ages, they had remained friends ever since. (It is noticeable that all Wieland's friends were much older than himself. Apart from his school companion

Danzer, he appears to have had no close friends among his own generation.)

On the occasion of Orff's sixtieth birthday in July 1955, Wieland wrote in the Bayreuth Festival *Tannhäuser* programme: "You have created new things: new in the sense of Richard Wagner, who warned all those who 'clung to old things' that they would fall into the clutches of the 'devil of unproductivity'. Thus you performed the miracle of presenting the contemporary stage in your *Carmina* with a work which, twenty years after its first performance, still exercises a persistent fascination over us. With your *Antigonae* (to speak only of the two extreme poles of your work) you performed the even greater miracle of creating, by means of a completely new sound of startling vigour, a convincing new interpretation of the phenomenon of Greek tragedy for modern consumption. You have brought to our ears new rhythmic experiences and to our eyes visions of a truly elemental theatrical effect—but still more: the happy consciousness that a creative person who believes in the theatre can still, in this age of cultural pessimism, set his intuition and his knowledge of essential truths to work to make nonsense of the warnings of all the professional prophets of woe. Continue steadfastly on your way, untroubled by all dogma, conventions and schools. It is the right way, for its goal is the same as that of all the great masters of the past: theatre in its original meaning of a magic centre for the preaching of spiritual realities."

Wieland's literary style, as opposed to his speech, often suffers from the German failing of portentousness, but the pompous words do reveal the nature of Wieland's interest in the works of Carl Orff and particularly in *Antigonae*, a setting of Hölderlin's German translation of the drama by Sophocles. It was this work, first produced at the Salzburg Festival of 1949, that Wieland produced at Stuttgart in March 1956. As he later told Goléa, *Antigonae* struck him as a truly revolutionary work. "It seemed to me above all like a return to the absolute origins of rhythm. . . . Also the new sounds and colours that Orff used appealed to me. I found the whole work provocatively new, and all the more remarkable in that this newness seemed to match the antique drama completely. It was a truly explosive work that convinced through the boldness of its stark simplicity."

This indicates a purely theatrical approach, in which the music was seen simply as one ingredient of a total experience, and not as an end in itself. A few years later, in Panofsky's biography, Wieland defined his attitude to the role of music in the theatre more definitely: "With all the great composers who wrote for the theatre the initial impulse was not the music, but the theatrical idea. The music is secondary in the sense that without the dramatic idea it would never have been written. The idea itself inspires the music, which is consequently not the dominant factor, but only one of the components to which the visual realisation has to conform. The relationship between music and scenic interpretation is not one of cause and effect. The scene, the idea is paramount: scenic action and musical development do not run parallel to each other in any direct sense, but correspond with one another on a spiritual plane . . . (Music) can and should serve only to illuminate the mind or state of mind of the stage character, to reveal the psychological background."

It is important to keep this statement in mind in considering all Wieland's achievements as a producer. One can see in it the basic cause of his break with his teacher Overhoff, as Wieland gradually began to deny Wagner's music the right to dictate to the last detail his scenic approach. As his ideas crystallised, Wieland grew ever bolder in his attempts to interpret the dramatic idea of a work by means other than the music.

The statement also helps us to understand Wieland's apparently arbitrary choice of works, outside the Wagner canon, which he felt inspired to produce—a choice which included Orff but ignored any other living composer, which restricted Richard Strauss to *Salome* and *Elektra* and which left Mozart (whose music he much loved) entirely out of account. It is true that *Don Giovanni* was among his unrealised plans, as also were Debussy's *Pélleas et Mélisande* and Schönberg's *Moses und Aron*. But, whether realised or unrealised, one recognises in all Wieland's choices (including some, such as *The Tales of Hoffmann* and *Tosca*, which may have been no more than idle fancies), a guiding principle that was not primarily musical. It was always what he called "the theatrical idea" that first aroused his interest.

However, it would be wrong to assume from this that Wieland was basically unmusical. Though in opera he accorded music only a secondary role, he was always keenly aware of the importance of its function in realising the dramatic idea. Without that musical sense he would, like many of his contemporaries in the operatic field, have been no more than a theatre producer turning his attention for a change to opera. Wieland was exclusively and by choice an operatic producer, and he rejected all invitations to stage plays, even when they came from such devoted friends as Schäfer.

Wieland's production of *Antigonae* was succeeded in the following year at Stuttgart by another of Orff's works: an Easter passion with the title *Comoedia de Christi Resurrectione*. This was a first performance and was the only completely new work that Wieland ever produced. His enthusiasm for Orff's works had now reached such heights that he seriously considered presenting some of them in the *Festspielhaus* in Bayreuth. Orff himself applied the brake. Wagner's theatre, he told Wieland, must be kept for Wagner's works alone.

Eventually Wieland's interest in Orff's operas waned. "What I felt to be genuine in *Antigonae* seemed to me in his *Oedipus* and then in his *Prometheus* to have become a mannerism," he told Goléa. But the personal friendship between them remained intact.

*

Back in Bayreuth after launching his *Antigonae* in Stuttgart, Wieland started work on what he himself knew to be a difficult undertaking: his first production of *Die Meistersinger von Nürnberg*. In his essay on tradition and innovation he had acknowledged in 1951 the essential difference between Wagner's only comedy and his other works: "*Die Meistersinger* calls for a certain naturalism, imposed by a historically fixed time, a geographical place and human beings of flesh and blood."

This had served very well to justify Rudolf Hartmann's orthodox production at the festival of 1951, but Wieland himself had no intention of following that with another production in the same style. What he aimed to do, he said in an interview published at the time in the Berlin *Musikblätter*, was "to free the work from the German sentimentality into which convention has delivered it and bring out the romantic irony which Wagner put into it".

This was certainly in line with the composer's own view of his work. After the dress rehearsal for the first Munich production of 1868 he had written to King Ludwig of "the deep melancholy, the tears, the distress call of poetry in chains" that lay beneath its surface humour. King Ludwig had been sensitive enough to recognise the serious undertones, but succeeding audiences had become increasingly obtuse. Seventy years after its first production *Die Meistersinger* had become—to use Wieland's own vigorous phrase in an interview in the *Hessische Nachrichten* of 27 July 1956—"a dangerous mixture of Lortzing and the *Reichsparteitag*".

True to his principle of presenting a work on the basis of its theatrical idea, Wieland attempted to put this idea into words in a programme note under the title *Ein Kind wird hier geboren* (Here a Child is born):

"An ardent hymn significantly provides the starting point of Richard Wagner's 'masterpiece' and illuminates with its evangelistic power considerable stretches of the dramatic development. It deals with the baptism of Jesus Christ by the biblical John on the banks of the Jordan. It is to a John from Nuremberg—the Jordan becomes the Pegnitz and John becomes Hans—that Wagner in *Die Meistersinger* entrusts the ceremonial baptism and naming of a 'child'. This *selige Morgentraumdeutweise* (blessed song interpreting the morning dream), symbolising the creative act of a genius, forms the central motive of the drama. The 'living father' of the song is Walther von Stolzing, ecstatic dreamer and irrepressible revolutionary—a clear self-portrait of the young Wagner.

"If the 'child' is to become a 'masterpiece' it needs the help of tradition, an inspiring model from the great past (here Walter von der Vogelweide). It requires the wise teacher and mature man, Hans Sachs, who persuades the genius, kindly but firmly, that dreams without reflection and ecstasy without form do not add up to art. It requires the *femme inspiratrice* (Eva), who alone is able through her feminine presence to arouse the latent creative force of the male Eros. It requires the snobbish opposition and complacency of respectable guild members no less than the redoubtable Beckmesser, whose positive function it is to provide the true artist unwittingly with provocation and incentive. And, last but not least, it requires a bold sponsor (Pogner) who idealistically uses his commercial talents to serve art.

"And when has a'new song' ever been created without a public outcry, panic among the intellectuals and nocturnal brawling between active and passive midwives—in other words without that quality of 'madness' to which a mature and knowledgeable philosopher-artist (Richard Wagner at the age of fifty) attributed a considerable share in the creation of a work of art?

"Night watchmen (contemporaries who see nothing of what is going on); untalented but for that reason all the more ambitious aspiring artists, such as the ever hungry David; and all too understanding, motherly sweethearts like Magdalene complete, in an almost parodistic way, the ensemble for Richard Wagner's 'little art theatre'.

"And finally the people: for the democrat Wagner the supreme judge in the world of art. It has an instinctive feeling for the true work of art and has the power to decide between triumph and defeat. On an imaginary 'festival meadow' the 'new song' receives its accolade—once again a choral hymn proclaims new awakening!—from an all-embracing human community in which the genius and the people are united in the name of art."

Valid as this undoubtedly is as an analysis of the underlying theme of *Die Meistersinger*, it is perhaps too intellectual to provide a practical basis for the presentation of a favourite comedy. In particular, Wieland's temerity in laying hands on the cherished festival meadow scene proved too much not only for his avowed opponents but also for many sympathisers who had accepted without a murmur—and often with genuine admiration—his impressionistic church of the first act, his houseless second act with its glowing lilac bushes and rich purple lighting, and the severe but beautifully proportioned room in Sachs's house. Now, in place of the final jubilation of the meadow, they found themselves confronted with a huge tribunal of seated choristers, uniformly dressed as if assembled to sing an oratorio, while the entry of the guilds was mimed. When the curtain finally fell, booes were heard—for the first time in the history of Bayreuth.

Wieland's presentation of this final scene, however logically it might have fitted in with his general conception of *Die Meistersinger* as a dissertation on the function of art, was an example of the dangers of allowing theory to overcome theatrical common sense. He was certainly carrying out the composer's intention in showing the people as the final judge of the genuineness of a work of art, but his attempt to emphasise the point by playing the meadow scene virtually in a courtroom brought about its own downfall, since it gave insufficient visual expression to the colourful, joyful music of which the scene is so full.

However, the failure of Wieland's attempt to cerebralise it should not—and did not—overshadow the many excellences of the production, and in particular the atmospheric magic of the second act. "This second act," Wieland said in an interview published in the Austrian newspaper *Neue Zeit* of 3 July 1956, "is Richard Wagner's *Midsummer Night's Dream*—an enchanted unreal world of elves and goblins. A background of comfortable, old-fashioned houses would destroy its atmosphere." The comparison with Shakespeare is just, and Wieland might profitably have followed it in his production more closely than he did. The description of Wagner's characters in his programme note suggests that he regarded them as types rather than as individuals, and consequently he lost much of the humanity and humour with which Wagner, modelling himself here on Shakespeare, had invested them.

Wieland's first production of *Die Meistersinger* was, as he himself was aware, by no means a complete expression of the work. However, he did succeed, as he intended, in stripping it of its nineteenth century conventions. This was something that many found harder to swallow in regard to *Die Meistersinger* than to any other of Wagner's works—in part because Wieland had failed to find a completely convincing alternative, but mainly because it is a work for which Germans have a very special affection. One member of the Society of the Friends of Bayreuth, a German civil servant, was so appalled by Wieland's handling of it that he resigned from the society. This was not

Die Meistersinger von Nürnberg, he said, but a show called *Kiss Me, Eva*.

A family footnote: Gertrud arranged the choreography for this production and, as a member of the crowd in the festival meadow scene, Wieland's eldest daughter Iris, now fourteen years old, made her stage debut.

15

COMPLETING THE CANON

1957–1959

BY NOW THE post-war Bayreuth Festival had been running for six years, and in that short time all Wagner's work from *Der Fliegende Holländer* to *Parsifal* had been presented in new productions, two of them (*Tristan und Isolde* and *Die Meistersinger*) twice. Wieland and his brother found themselves faced with a problem. To retain its dynamism, the festival had to mount a new production every year, yet there were only seven works to choose from (reckoning the *Ring* as one). This meant that existing productions would have to be replaced whether or not there were sufficient new ideas to justify a change. The grandsons would before long have to choose between the risk of repeating themselves or earning the reproach of inventing change for its own sake.

This problem caused Wieland seriously to consider extending the festival repertoire by at least one of Wagner's three early works: *Rienzi*. There was a legal difficulty: Siegfried had laid down in his will that only Wagner's works from *Der Fliegende Holländer* onwards should be presented in the *Festspielhaus*. A way might, however, be found around that obstacle if *Rienzi* could be proved worthy of promotion to festival status. Wieland, with Schäfer's approval, decided to put it to the test in Stuttgart.

The drastic cuts and alterations that Wieland made in the work might have suggested that he despised it. In fact, there was very much in it that he admired. Rienzi's prayer, he told Goléa, was one of Wagner's most deeply-felt compositions, while the part of Adriano contained rich and significant foreshadowings of both *Tannhäuser* and *Lohengrin*. He considered

Adriano to be psychologically one of Wagner's most effective creations, and for that reason he gave the role to a male singer, believing that Wagner had written it for a female voice mainly in order to make use of the fine acting abilities of Wilhelmine Schröder-Devrient.

The main purpose of Wieland's surgical operation was to bring out the parts of Wagner's overlong grand opera in which the seeds of his later development were clear to see. This was not easy, since *Rienzi* is essentially a historical opera, and regard had to be paid to its narrative coherence. His final version, the result of many reluctant sacrifices as well as restorations of passages which Wagner had himself cut after the first production in Dresden, was something in the nature of a music drama on the timeless, yet very topical theme of freedom threatened by terrorist power. To emphasise its symbolic character, Wieland made an alteration to the ending. Rienzi does not die, as in Wagner's text, beneath the ruins of the burning Capitol: he is struck down on the street by assassins and his body desecrated by the rioting crowd.

As history has shown in the case of operas by other composers as well as Wagner, attempts—however successful they may seem—to rehabilitate imperfect works prove of only temporary appeal, and Wieland's efforts to rescue *Rienzi* did not succeed in restoring it to favour. There was no further thought of presenting it at Bayreuth. The significance of the production in the framework of Wieland's artistic development is that it showed for the first time some relaxation of what threatened to become a doctrinaire approach to all the works he touched. Though, as earlier with *Orfeo ed Euridice* and *Fidelio*, he tried to force *Rienzi* into the mould of Wagnerian music drama, he recognised that in its outward form it retained some characteristics of other traditions, and these found expression in his scenery, in which there were many traces of straightforward realism.

*

A more rewarding task awaited him in Hamburg immediately afterwards: his first attempt at *Lohengrin*, in which he planned to try out his ideas for a production in Bayreuth the following year.

The invitation to Hamburg came from his old adversary, Heinz Tietjen, who had now succeeded Günther Rennert as artistic director of the *Staatsoper*. For Tietjen the advantage of a production by Germany's most successful young opera producer was enough to outweigh any personal reservations, while Wieland too could only profit from an appearance at one of Germany's leading opera houses. Amicable relations were quickly restored: Wieland was now mature enough to acknowledge that in the disputes of the old days the faults had not all been on Tietjen's side. He even revised his opinion of Tietjen's ability as a conductor—at least as far as *Lohengrin* was concerned. Tietjen conducted the performances in Hamburg, and in 1959 was invited by Wieland to conduct some performances of his subsequent *Lohengrin* production at Bayreuth.

Wieland's *Lohengrin* was the purest expression of the classical spirit that he ever achieved. Its inspiration was the story of Zeus and Semele. It was not only Wieland's own love of antiquity that had led him in this direction. In reading Wagner's autobiography he discovered that, at the very time the composer was working on *Lohengrin*, he was making his first serious encounter with the dramas of Aeschylus and with Goethe's *Iphigenie*. Aware as Wieland was of the strong autobiographical element in his grandfather's work, he came to the conclusion (as he told Panofsky) that Wagner himself had seen his Lohengrin with the eyes of a Greek.

Wieland's production of *Lohengrin* was cast in a very static form. Scenery was reduced to a minimum of functional requisites, over which were suspended friezes suggestive of the historical setting. Colour was provided entirely by lighting and by the costumes: silver for the men, blue for the women and black for the villainous pair, Telramund and Ortrud. Movement was restrained, even the fight between Lohengrin and Telramund in the first act being little more than a few formal gestures. The direction of the movement was for the most part frontal, whereas in *Tannhäuser* it had been diagonal. The use of angles and distances, so effectively applied in that work to create dramatic tension, was confined to the figures of Telramund and Ortrud, though even then it was sparingly applied. The chorus was used as in a Greek tragedy, to comment on the action rather than to participate in it—most strikingly at the first entry of Lohengrin.

Wagner's stage directions call on all but Elsa, Ortrud and Telramund to go to the river bank to watch Lohengrin's arrival. In Wieland's production everybody on stage was facing the audience as Lohengrin, accompanied by the cinematic projection of a formalised swan, stepped ashore behind them. It was a complete rejection, not only of the composer's instructions, but of any form of realism. Wieland later explained to me his reasons for treating the scene in this way:

"One cannot really localise miracles. As far as I am concerned, a miracle takes place everywhere at once, behind and before the spectator. In addition, there is a purely practical reason. The Swan Chorus is one of the finest choral pieces that Wagner ever wrote, and I find it horrible when this whole piece is sung towards Lohengrin standing at the back of the stage, just for the sake of conventional stage realism. The members of the chorus have their backs to the conductor, and so the whole thing is always ragged musically. On top of that I do not like the chorus to turn their backs on the audience when miraculous things are happening. It does not help the miracle at all, but rather weakens its effect. . . .

"Wagner's theatrical style cannot be thought of in terms of stage realism. All his works are—I should almost say—subject to the laws of the mystery play, and mystery plays have different laws from realistic opera. If I think in realistic terms, I must tell myself that Lohengrin actually sailed . . . from the direction of Spain along the coast of France, through the Straits of Dover; that he then turned off into the river Schelde, and the unfortunate swan had to tow him upstream all the way to Antwerp. I just do not believe it, and nowadays you could not make an audience believe it. Then there is the changing of Herzog Gottfried into a swan, in which form the Knights of the Grail use him as a sort of outboard motor—I just won't accept that. That is why I reject any form of realism for this work, and that is also why the chorus may sing about miracles facing forwards."

It is a typical Wieland statement in its mixture of scorn and aggression, of down-to-earth common sense and cynicism, none of it—and least of all the slangy language in which it is expressed—concealing for a moment his underlying seriousness and sense of dedication to the work in hand. He had a deep respect for *Lohengrin* and did not attempt, as in *Tannhäuser*, to edit either score or text, apart from the elimination of a choral passage in the final act which appeared to him too nationalistic in flavour. But he felt there were some dramatic weaknesses in it.

"It is difficult," he told me, "to make living characters out of Ortrud and Telramund, since they are simply traditional types. Yet as a producer I must try to find a way of bringing out as strongly as possible the elements hostile to the virtuous pair, Elsa and Lohengrin. I see Telramund as one of those typical knights who figure in all Wagner's works as a contrast to the hero. He is the politician, the egotist who bases his whole existence on concepts of personal honour, might and fame, as against the hero, whose basic motive is love. Wagner conceived Ortrud too as a contrast to his love-motivated heroine. He himself called her the 'political' woman—the woman who cannot love, the frigid woman, the woman impelled by intellect, by hate and by instinct."

To express all this in the limited scope that Wagner allows for it demanded not only resourceful production and considerable acting skill from the two singers concerned, but also a radical departure from Wagner's stage directions—the division of the second act into two separate scenes: a narrow set of a plain castle wall and a full stage dominated by a flight of steps. This led in Wieland's production to the loss of one of the most magical scenes of the work, the dawn transformation, the music being played while the curtain was down. Wieland's explanation, in his conversation with me (printed in full in *The Listener* of 7 February 1963), shows the same characteristic mixture of practicality and concern for deeper values which marked his treatment of Lohengrin's arrival:

"In the night scene Ortrud and Telramund are scarcely to be seen on a large and empty stage. They are just obscure figures in a huge void, and so the whole scene carries far too little weight. That is one reason. The other reason is that, according to Wagner's stage directions, several things happen during the dawn transformation: the gate is opened, maidens go down to the well (it used to be done that way in Bayreuth once), water is scooped up, a whole lot of men come in. And what do they do? In the good old German way they clap each other on the shoulder, they shake hands. And none of it has anything at all to do with Lohengrin. The music is not suited to it either. . . . So one can say there is an intellectual reason for my decision: to focus the Ortrud-Telramund scene and to bring the singers as close as possible to the audience—particularly in the tremendously important scene between Elsa and Ortrud, in which Elsa with the innocence of a girl in love invites the very serpent itself into her room. Here again Wagner gives us an example of unquestioning love, which is capable of taking even evil into its protection. And this scene, too, loses its effect in the huge courtyard."

Elsa was in fact the central figure of Wieland's production of *Lohengrin*, which he saw as an aspect of Wagner's constant preoccupation with the problem of the true nature of love. "In *Lohengrin* he comes to it—to the conflict between man and woman—only in the third act. The bridal chamber is therefore the key scene in *Lohengrin*, and all that goes before is simply building up to it. We see Elsa's development and the events that lead up to this bridal chamber scene, in which Elsa is forced for the sake of love to destroy Lohengrin with her question about his identity. According to Wagner there can be no anonymity in matters of love. Lohengrin himself cannot establish a true personal contact. In this scene lies his final defeat. In Elsa, on the other hand, Wagner gives us a symbol of true love: for the sake of love she must destroy it."

I find this an illuminating definition of what *Lohengrin*, beneath its fairy tale exterior, is basically about—and worth the loss of certain spectacular settings to discover. Spectacle was in fact not lost: rather it gained, through its very simplicity, a new emotional quality. The foremost image that remains in my mind of this production is the frail figure of Elsa slowly descending the steps to the cathedral, completely alone between a row of static choristers who were not even looking at her. One sensed at this moment the terrible loneliness of the individual, even at moments of happiness, a sense heightened by the knowledge that Elsa's bliss was very shortly to be shattered by the evil Ortrud waiting at the foot of the steps. By isolating

Elsa at this point and focussing attention on her figure rather than on the wedding procession as an impressive crowd spectacle, Wieland succeeded in heightening the drama of the scene while at the same time sustaining the austere spiritual quality of the whole production.

*

In the festival programme for *Die Meistersinger* in 1959 Wieland published a letter addressed to Otto Klemperer:

"Dear Dr Klemperer—It is with great regret that I received the news that your present state of health forbids you to conduct the Bayreuth *Meistersinger* this summer. You had chosen this work yourself, and I know that *Die Meistersinger* under your direction would have been a musical event, of almost inestimable significance both for Bayreuth and for the interpretation of Wagner's works as a whole. This *Meistersinger* would have been the first of Wagner's works that you had conducted on German soil since your *Tannhäuser* at the Berlin *Staatsoper* in January 1933. Bayreuth is well aware of the special significance of this resolve and will be very happy when, some time in the future, you conduct a work of your own choice in the *Festspielhaus*."

The regret Wieland here expressed was much more than formal. Even if the "new" Bayreuth was now firmly entrenched, its identification with an internationally renowned conductor who had in the Twenties done so much in Berlin to break from the rigid confines of old Bayreuth tradition would have been a major victory. But Wieland's interest in Klemperer was not merely tactical. He had heard him conduct a concert and had asked Walter Legge to bring them together. The meeting resulted not only in the invitation to Klemperer to conduct at the *Festspielhaus*—though there would have been physical difficulties in getting the incapacitated Klemperer into the conductor's seat in the sunken orchestra—but also to conduct the production of *Tristan und Isolde* which Wieland was doing for the Holland Festival of 1959. From this too Klemperer was forced to withdraw following an accident in which he received severe burns. Though the two remained friends—if that is the word to use of two men who were both masters of the biting phrase, against outsiders as well as each other—they never worked together on a production.

Klemperer was not the only conductor whose loss Wieland had to make good in the festival of 1959. Cluytens, disappointed at not being chosen to conduct Wieland's new production of *Der Fliegende Holländer*, decided to stay away entirely. To fill the gaps Erich Leinsdorf and Lovro von Matacic were summoned to Bayreuth.

Wieland had invited Wolfgang Sawallisch to conduct *Der Fliegende Holländer*. Sawallisch, who had first come to Bayreuth in 1957 to conduct Wolfgang's production of *Tristan und Isolde*, had made a swift rise to fame via the opera houses of Aachen, Wiesbaden and Cologne. He was the first conductor with whom Wieland continuously worked who was actually younger than himself, and they shared the same modern unsentimental approach to the works of Richard Wagner. Sawallisch raised no objections when Wieland decided to return to the original Dresden version of *Der Fliegende Holländer*, which does not include the romantic apotheosis at the end. The remarkable success of this production at the festival of 1959 raised hopes that, in Sawallisch, Wieland had at long last found the conductor with whom he could work in complete accord.

For Wieland's views on *Der Fliegende Holländer* it is necessary to look, not to the programmes of the Bayreuth Festival, in which he remained completely silent, but to an essay he wrote for his almost identical production of the work in Copenhagen in 1961:

"With this ballad about love, exile, sacrifice and redemption Wagner discovered not only his life's theme—the conquest of egoism through love—but also his own poetic and musical form. . . . The Dutchman—referred to frequently in an early draft as 'the stranger'—has fallen out with God. Like Prometheus before him, he has rashly and arrogantly cursed the Almighty. As punishment he has been condemned to live eternally in the torture of loneliness. His suffering is further intensified by the constant hope of redemption. The change in the sinner occurs only when a young woman gives herself selflessly and unconditionally to him. His infinite egoism is overcome in his encounter with and his love for Senta. For the sake of his love for this young girl he is prepared to accept his fate as a voluntary act of repentance, and thus the condemned man regains divine love and is forgiven.

"The portrait of the suffering man has exercised a magic power over Senta's life. This young girl is impelled by pity to accept her vocation. She fulfils it with her voluntary death for the Dutchman's sake. Erik, her betrothed, and Daland, her father, cannot deflect her from her purpose. The young girl's connection with the Dutchman cuts her off entirely from the world. . . .

"Daland is the personification of avarice. He, the apparently honest sailor, also falls prey to his own egoism. He 'sells' his only child for a cargo of gold and jewels. Wagner described him as 'a portrait of the baseness of life'. In the figure of her own father Senta is contrasted with a character who could have come from a novel by Balzac . . ."

There are some unusual points in Wieland's interpretation, particularly in relation to the Dutchman himself. As traditionally portrayed, he is always the receiver, Senta the giver. Wieland found authority for his apparent divergence in the composer's own writings. In his "Remarks on the Production of the Opera *Der Fliegende Holländer*" (*Bemerkungen zur Aufführung der Oper "Der Fliegende Holländer"*, Collected Writings Volume 5), Wagner wrote: "His love for Senta is expressed in his terrible anxiety for her in the destiny to which she has committed herself in offering him salvation. It comes on him like a dreadful reproach, and in his passionate warning against committing herself to sharing his fate he becomes a completely real human being, whereas up to now he has frequently given the impression of being more a spectre than a man."

Wieland's Dutchman possessed this ambivalence. The spectral side was emphasised by his first appearance, apparently chained to the mast of his ship as if suspended on a cross—an image that conveniently suggested all the prototypes that might be seen in him: Prometheus, Odysseus and the Wandering Jew. His Senta, played in 1959 by Leonie Rysanek, was also close in spirit to Wagner's description in his "Remarks". She was "a robust Nordic girl", naïve rather than sentimental. Daland, on the other hand, with his striped suit and top hat, came dangerously close to being the comic figure against which Wagner in his "Remarks" had spoken a warning. But it was, nevertheless, an interpretation—though a highly coloured one—in line with Wagner's own description: "He is a coarse figure of everyday life, a sailor who for profit defies storms and dangers, and a man to whom the apparent sale of his daughter to a rich man must not be allowed to seem in any way reprehensible. He thinks and acts like hundreds of thousands of others without finding anything at all wrong in it."

Wieland considered his production of *Der Fliegende Holländer*, in contrast to all his other productions, to have been realistic. If he did not, as Wagner demanded, reproduce a ship complete in all details, he certainly managed, by the simple device of allowing the deck of Daland's ship to occupy the whole stage and making his sailors, clustered around the wheel, rock and lurch, to convey a convincing impression of a storm-driven ship. And the Dutchman's ship, appearing suddenly behind it, drenched in a blood-red light, lost none of its electric effect. In the second scene the smoke-darkened beams of Daland's house were certainly as realistic as the buxom, roughly clothed maidens busy at their spinning-wheels below.

As in *Lohengrin*, Wieland's main direction of movement in this production was from back to front, but here it created a remarkably different effect. Where *Lohengrin* had appeared static and contemplative, *Der Fliegende Holländer* gave the impression of brutal, overwhelming force. The effect was achieved partly by the swiftness of the movement and partly by the use of block-like groups instead of gently sinuous lines as in *Lohengrin*. Its most thrilling moment occurred in the third scene, which was laid like the first on the deck of Daland's ship, with the addition of a raised quay to either side of it. When Daland's revelling sailors challenged the Dutchman's crew to appear, a solid mass of wraithlike figures, masked and hairless, flooded down from the ghost ship behind and surged right to the front of the stage, scattering Daland's sailors as they advanced and seeming indeed about to overwhelm the audience.

16

DESIRE FOR CHANGE

1960

UNLIKE HIS PREDECESSORS, Wieland could not find his life's satisfaction in Bayreuth alone. Though accepting his obligations towards the works of his grandfather, he recognised none towards Bayreuth as an institution. In consequence, Wahnfried was no longer the centre of artistic activity that it had been in former times, even when the *Festspielhaus* itself was silent. For long stretches of the year it stood virtually empty. When Wieland and Gertrud were away working on productions in Stuttgart, Hamburg and elsewhere and the children were at boarding-school, only Emma Baer, Wieland's old nanny and now in her old age a devoted motherly housekeeper, came in from her rooms in the chauffeur's annexe to dust and polish.

The children's absence at boarding-school and Wieland's own travels left little opportunity for close contact between them, and during the annual holiday on the island of Sylt they all had to work hard, as Wolf Siegfried told me, to re-establish their family solidarity. All the children were showing definite artistic interests and, though Wieland did not actively encourage them to think of Bayreuth as their ultimate field of activity, he made no deliberate attempt to discourage them. From an early age he had allowed them to attend rehearsals in the *Festspielhaus*, and he listened seriously to their views on his productions. It was no doubt the memory of his own frustrated longings as a child for genuine parental attention that was responsible for his determination to spare his own children that deprivation. Bayreuth was a burden he would willingly give up, he told them, in order to have more time for his family.

Wieland never escaped from the sense of Bayreuth as a burden. It owed its origin, at least in part, to the feeling that a large measure of his success was due to the circumstances of his birth rather than to his own native talent. It was certainly true that the sensation he had caused with his productions in Bayreuth was attributable to some extent to the fact that they had been made there. If, even as a member of the Wagner family, he had made them outside the *Festspielhaus*, the sensation would have been correspondingly less. His one indubitable achievement was to have destroyed the image of Bayreuth as the custodian of an old tradition and to have created a new function for it as an experimental workshop. Yet even in this there was an inhibiting factor. His "new Bayreuth style" was now being copied throughout the world, and he stood in danger of perpetuating, through the authority of his name, a new tradition quite as restrictive as the one he had set out to smash. Only outside Bayreuth would he be free to develop a true identity of his own.

In 1959, having produced the full cycle of Wagner works in the *Festspielhaus*, he could justifiably feel that his obligations to Bayreuth had been met. The opportunity for a loosening of the ties came in 1960 with the impending retirement of Carl Ebert as director of the Berlin *Städtische Oper*. Wieland made it known that he would be interested in taking over the post, and he was encouraged to apply for it. In November 1959, while negotiations were still in progress, Wieland made his debut at the *Städtische Oper* in Berlin with a production of *Tristan und Isolde*. The choice was made by the opera house: Wieland might have preferred in the circumstances to present a non-Wagnerian work. In the previous year he had been allowed in Hamburg to show what he could do with one of the most popular works in the standard operatic repertory.

*

Wieland's *Carmen* contained, to quote Walter Panofsky, "no hint of Spanish folklore and imposed gypsy romanticism. Every corner seemed rather to be permeated with the 'bloody essence of all things Spanish'. Wieland Wagner had discovered it for himself on his travels to the Iberian peninsula. Seville had seemed to him far too beautiful—and far too respectable—to be the town of Carmen (though right for the Barber). Red, the colour of blood, was to be seen in almost every one of the scene settings. Only the smugglers' scene was free of it: Wieland had turned the Pyrenean gorge into a deserted barn. . . . The last act seemed to be drenched in dark, gleaming bull's blood, with a gigantic hoarding covered with bulls' skulls and screaming letters repeating the name Escamillo. The basic scenic plan was uniform in conception, the costumes also. . . . Movements were stylised: all crowd scenes carried out on strict geo-metrical lines, all gestures carefully formalised."

This description suggests the presence of Wieland's usual production hallmarks, yet Wieland himself claimed that his *Carmen*, which he presented in the original version with dialogue, was thoroughly realistic. Realism, as he pointed out to Goléa, does not mean that one must be naturalistic in every detail. "Sensuality—a wild, impulsive, elemental sensuality—domin-ates the work. That is the one salient factor. The other is poverty. The terrible poverty of the half-starved gypsy cigarette girl Carmen provides the key for her identification with the world of smugglers; also for the fact that she fishes for her men in the higher classes of society: among the military, which however is no more than an ordered state of poverty; then among the bullfighters, whose dangerous work is not badly paid. The basic motive of poverty determined the form of my production. The children in the first act are nothing more than half-naked urchins. Lillas Pastia's tavern is no luxuriously fur-nished dance hall, but just the sort of small, smoky, stinking smugglers' den in which three ragged gypsy girls parade their charms."

Behind the realistic story Wieland saw in *Carmen* "exactly those qualities which fascinate me in all the great and valid masterpieces of the music theatre: the basic human situation— that aspect of fate which in some mysterious way brings about a direct connection between love and death." This is Wieland's favourite theme of *Eros thanatos* again, and he was willing to accord Carmen and Don José a place with Tristan and Isolde and with Pelléas and Mélisande in the list of doom-laden lovers—with the difference, in his view, that their love was not mutual. He saw *Carmen* as a story of unrequited love: Micaela loves Don José, Don José loves Carmen, Carmen loves Esca-millo, but in no instance is their love returned.

*

In 1960 the *Städtische Oper* in Berlin announced its decision: Gustav Rudolf Sellner from Darmstadt had been chosen to succeed Ebert as artistic director. Wieland was rejected on the grounds that his commitments in Bayreuth would take up too much of his time. The hope was expressed that he would continue to work in Berlin as a guest producer. It was a severe blow to Wieland, who had been given the impression that his appointment was virtually certain, and his immediate reaction was humanly understandable: he rejected the invitation to undertake guest productions.

He turned his attention back to Bayreuth, to which the Berlin authorities had so demonstratively assigned him. He had no new production on hand—it was the year in which Wolfgang was presenting his first *Ring*—but there was a problem concerning *Der Fliegende Holländer*. Leonie Rysanek, who had sung Senta in the previous year, was not available for the coming festival, and a substitute had to be found. Wolfgang Sawallisch, the conductor both of *Der Fliegende Holländer* and of Wieland's *Carmen* in Hamburg, suggested that Anja Silja should be given a trial in the role. The proposal was based initially on the young singer's striking appearance: her tall slim figure and flowing chestnut hair were natural assets for the role of Senta. But Anja Silja also had a respectable record as a singer. Starting with a permanent engagement in Brunswick at the age of sixteen, she had spent a short time in Stuttgart and was now, at the age of twenty, singing leading roles at the Frankfurt opera.

Wieland knew her by sight: she had for the past few years regularly attended audition sessions in the *Festspielhaus* and had been listened to but politely declined—not surprisingly, since at that time she was singing coloratura, a range for which Wagner offers very little scope. However, Wieland had no other candidate in immediate view for the role of Senta, and he agreed to consider her.

Anja Silja, coached in the role by Sawallisch, arrived in Bayreuth only a few weeks before the festival. She told me of her first meeting with Wieland after the trial run-through. She had known his work and admired him from afar, but had not spoken with him before he summoned her to his office to tell her, not (as she had feared) that she was unsuitable, but that she was engaged. He added that her interpretation so exactly corresponded with his own ideas that she needed no further special rehearsal. She could leave Bayreuth and return for the full final rehearsals a few days before the opening.

Her success as Senta was immediate and striking, though some critics remarked that she owed it to her appearance rather than to her singing, in which they claimed to detect signs of strain towards the end of this taxing role. It was irresponsible, they said, to risk spoiling a voice for the sake of outward appearances, and they predicted that within a few years Anja Silja would be finished as a singer.

They were wrong, of course. In the succeeding years Anja Silja took on, inside and outside Bayreuth, a succession of dramatic roles culminating in the two peaks of Brünnhilde and Isolde. And beside these she occasionally took on parts, such as the Woodbird in *Siegfried*, which are not normally associated with dramatic sopranos. Her voice might have lacked the round beauty of tone that distinguished many of her rivals, yet it was capable of great purity. But above all it was her stage presence and her ever-increasing acting ability which brought her success.

That she was Wieland's creation is a fact that nobody, including Anja Silja herself, feels impelled to deny. But he could not have made her what she became without some contribution from herself. This, leaving aside all question of their personal relations, was a strong constitution, a capacity for hard work and a complete absence of that anxiety neurosis which is behind what is usually described as an artistic temperament. To see her, as I frequently did in Bayreuth, both off stage and at rehearsals, behaving with all the carefree abandon of a mischievous child, bicycling in trousers round the *Festspielhaus*, giggling with the stage assistants, might have led one to doubt the existence in her of any real artistic seriousness. One would be mistaken: under the flippant manner there was a true professional artist, ready to tackle anything she was asked, and always willing to learn.

To a man of Wieland's solitary nature, who had no close

personal friends and was treated with deference outside the family by all the people with whom he came in contact, Anja's complete naturalness of manner, which made no distinction between him and the humblest of his assistants, must have proved at the start rather disconcerting. But he soon discovered that he enjoyed it. Like all socially inhibited individuals, he longed to be treated like a normal human being. This was a freedom that Anja alone, in spite of the great difference in their ages, managed to give him.

Wieland had always been attractive to women. There may have been some affairs in the past—it would be unwise to take account of rumour in so intimate a matter—but certainly none of them had been serious enough to threaten his marriage to Gertrud, which, though based on tension rather than cosy domesticity, had held firm for twenty years. Wieland, however, was now forty-three, an age at which many men begin to experience the feeling of time running out. That feeling, though it might have provided the initial impulse, would not account for the depth and permanence of his attachment to Anja Silja, which lasted until his death. It is clear that she filled a great need in his life. What it was on the personal side we can of course only guess at, but we can be more certain about the artistic aspects of their partnership. It was to a large extent a pupil and teacher relationship. As a singer she came to him completely unspoiled, and she was the willing and intelligent instrument of his artistic experiments. Young and unburdened by the weight of tradition, she could do more than simply follow. Her reactions were spontaneous and revealing, and he heeded them as he heeded the opinions of his own children. And above all, for all her admiration and respect for Wieland, she was not afraid of him.

It was a relationship that brought happiness and profit to them both, though at the cost to Wieland, who was uneasily conscious of the parallels in the life of his grandfather, of great emotional strain. He was not the sort of man who could abandon wife and family without a qualm. The few remaining years of his life were to prove a constant tug-of-war between his inner obligations and inclinations, both in his personal and his artistic life.

17

SIGNS AND SYMBOLS

1961–1962

SINCE THE POST-WAR reopening I had attended the Bayreuth
Festival as a critic for various musical journals. In 1961 I suggested to the British Broadcasting Corporation that a docu-
mentary feature about the "new" Bayreuth might be of
interest. The proposal was accepted and the task of producing
it assigned to Christopher Sykes, with whom I travelled to
Bayreuth a fortnight before the opening of the festival to record
material. Christopher Sykes is a devoted Wagnerian whose
first visit to Bayreuth was made in the last years of Siegfried's
régime, and it was for both of us a fascinating experience to
encounter the festival from the back of the stage. "Bayreuth
Backstage" became the general title for a series of four features
in which, over five years, we examined in increasing detail the
revolution which Wieland and Wolfgang were consolidating in
the *Festspielhaus*.

We were given complete freedom to attend all rehearsals,
and on that first visit even sat through one act of *Siegfried* in the
sunken orchestra pit: "bang in the middle of a thundercloud"
was Christopher's description of the experience. Between
rehearsals we spoke and recorded interviews with singers, conductors, musical coaches, orchestral players, chorus members
and backstage assistants, including Wieland's much older
cousin, Count Gilberto Gravina, whose physical resemblance
to Liszt we found perhaps even greater than Wieland's to
Richard Wagner. We gained an overwhelming impression of
complete devotion to the cause of Wagner, but with it more
than a hint of claustrophobia. Wagner was everywhere—not
only in the *Festspielhaus* itself, looming over the town like Big
Brother (as David Ward, who was singing Fasolt that year,

nicknamed it), but even in the street names (Parsifalstrasse, Rheingoldstrasse, Meistersingerstrasse) and the signed photographs of singers that covered the walls of all the restaurants. We took to eating in a place in the back streets, a modest restaurant which displayed on its main wall, most refreshingly, a portrait of Schubert.

In this year I came for the first time into personal contact with Wieland and his brother. I recorded my impressions in the radio feature: "Wieland looks rather unapproachable—not severe, but as if his thoughts are far away. Wolfgang seems far more conscious of the world around him: he is friendly, informal and full of good humour. We were always coming across his quick, stooping figure in the theatre and outside, while Wieland seemed to be visible only when seated at his producer's desk in the auditorium. But Wieland, when we at last got past his henchmen, proved to be nothing like as forbidding as he looks. . . ."

At that time he was forty-four years old, a thickset figure slightly above middle height. His wavy hair was heavily streaked with white, his complexion highly coloured. His features were inwardly rather than outwardly strong. It was a highly sensitive face, and the eyes behind the spectacles he constantly wore seemed, like the whole man, mild in repose. He spoke quietly and moved almost soundlessly, yet at all times one was mysteriously conscious of his presence. He had only to appear for a hush to fall. It was not a hush of apprehension, but rather of circumspection. One was aware of being in the presence of a keen and searching intelligence that was no less formidable for being so reserved. Wieland did not need emphasis to impose his personality. Even during the strain of rehearsals an outburst of temper was a rare occurrence, and for that reason all the more electrifying when it came.

He could, I am told, be sarcastic and wounding, even violent. He could be cynical and he could be coarse in speech, an unexpected trait which sometimes offended sensitive singers. He was also unforgiving. Reconciliation, after a breach had been made, was rare with him. But to the outside world the main impression was of a man who kept a tight control over his emotions.

Such people often emanate a chilling atmosphere which can

persist even on nearer acquaintance. With Wieland this was not so except, I suppose, with individuals with whom he was completely out of sympathy. As we saw at his more private rehearsals with his singers, he could quickly establish a warm and uninhibited mood. He never imposed a movement or gesture but sought it with the singer together, demonstrating, offering suggestions, but never insisting. He was patient and he was tireless. In 1962 Christopher and I were present throughout fourteen solid hours of rehearsal, spread over a few days, which Wieland devoted to taking two singers new to their roles through the scene between Ortrud and Telramund in *Lohengrin*—a scene taking less than twenty minutes in performance. Exhausting it may have been for Irene Dalis and Ramon Vinay, but they both told us afterwards how valuable the experience had been in giving them a real insight into their roles.

Part of Wieland's skill in handling people was his ability to give—or appear to give—his complete attention to the job in hand, however small. I myself experienced this when, for our first radio feature, he consented to record for us a few words in English, a language which (in view of his British-born mother) he surprisingly could not speak. I translated his German text. We pronounced the words for him, and he wrote them down phonetically, repeated them a few times, looking to us for correction or approval, then carefully spoke them into the microphone. Since they are probably the only sentences in English he ever spoke, and since they have some bearing on the subject of this book, I quote them in full: "Wagner's work is inexhaustible, and there are always new aspects to be revealed. For that reason I think that my method of production is capable of further development. I am certainly working in the direction of even greater simplicity. The basis of all true art is simplicity, not decoration and fussy detail."

*

The 1961 festival opened on 23 July with Wieland's second new production of *Tannhäuser*. Two days later, at a ceremony held in the foyer of the *Festspielhaus*, Wieland and Wolfgang were presented with the ring of honour of the town of Bayreuth

(*Ehrenring der Stadt Bayreuth*). "The joint work of the two brothers," the citation read, "has in the space of ten years made an outstanding contribution to the fame of Richard Wagner and to the honour of the town of Bayreuth." The Bavarian state in the same year gave similar recognition with the award of the *Bayerischer Verdienstorden*.

Wieland's new *Tannhäuser*, a work which, except for a production in Hamburg in 1959, he had not touched since 1954, provided two sizeable sensations. One was the "black Venus" of the coloured singer Grace Bumbry and the other the startling presentation of the Bacchanal by Maurice Béjart's young dancers of the Brussels *Théâtre Royal de la Monnaie*.

Both these innovations were due to Wieland's growing conviction that *Tannhäuser* is, as he told Claus Henning Bachmann (*Opernwelt*, September 1964) "a strict Christian work: the themes of repentance, of representational sacrifice, of redemption and of the insuperable differences of *eros* and *religio* are worked out from the standpoint of Catholic Christianity."

This time Wieland chose to present the conflict between sacred and profane love, not in terms of detached philosophical debate, but in the harsher, more directly emotional light of the historical period in which the action of the opera is set: namely, the Middle Ages. His Venus and Tannhäuser were no longer far apart, as in the first production, but placed close together at the very front of the stage, she enthroned, he sitting at her feet. It was not a reversion to the old-style amorous entanglement. This Venus was no living being, but an all but motionless idol: the erotic goddess herself, and her colour seemed immaterial.

The suffocating effect of sensual enslavement in general— rather than to one woman in particular—was emphasised by the writhing couples in the background, miming their copulations in a glaring red light. In following Wieland's instructions to present eroticism in a repulsive way, Maurice Béjart might certainly be said to have succeeded in his task. It was the conception, rather than the execution, that gave rise to the charges of sensationalism. However logical this conception may have been in relation to Wieland's deliberately moralistic approach to the scene, the disparity between the music and its visual interpretation proved too extreme to carry conviction.

Elisabeth, sensitively portrayed by Victoria de los Angeles, was a woman conscious of sensual feelings towards Tannhäuser yet unable, for reasons of convention as well as of virginal modesty, to reveal them. He, also a slave to convention, could not equate the partner of his sensual lust with the chaste maiden worshipped from afar. As Wieland told Goléa: "He loves Elisabeth in the way one loves a saint. But at the decisive moment in which he is called on to sing the praises of love, his feelings become confused. His erotic desires, which had hitherto been pledged to Venus, suddenly become conscious of a new goal. Elisabeth appears to him all at once in a new light. She becomes a woman to him as he composes, as he sings. He praises the Venusberg—at least it seems that he is praising it. At the same time he is looking at Elisabeth. And she understands him exactly. She is tired of the idealistic Wolfram. She loves Tannhäuser and is ready to unite with him in the flesh. That is why she does what she can to save him. The trouble is that Tannhäuser cannot respond, because in sensual matters Venus has been his downfall. . . . He is unable to touch a woman who is still chaste. He needs Venus and her amorous devices. His reason for going to Rome is that he has failed Elisabeth and wants to try to show himself worthy of her."

Scenically Wieland's second *Tannhäuser* belonged in what Walter Erich Schäfer calls his "period of signs". The first period Schäfer calls geometric and applies it to all Wieland's productions up to about 1955—most obviously to the first *Tannhäuser*. The "period of signs" found its first complete expression in the *Meistersinger* production of 1956, in which an overhanging carved canopy represented the church of the first act, and hanging blobs of lilac the street of the second. Similar realistic fragments characterised the scenery for *Lohengrin* in 1958. In the second *Tannhäuser* production the scenery for the Wartburg valley consisted of a huge cross and a few stylised trees in the background: leafy in the first act, bare in the third. The Wartburg itself was a huge expanse of patterned wall in gold—gold being to Wieland, nurtured on the altar pieces of German churches and the illuminated manuscripts of the *Minnesänger* period, the colour of the Middle Ages.

The third period in Wieland's development is the symbolic, which evolved from the period of "signs" and dominated his work from now on, beginning with his production of *Aida* in Berlin in October 1961.

*

Second thoughts had convinced Wieland that his disappointment over his rejection by the *Städtische Oper* could not allow him to regard Berlin as closed to him for ever. When Sellner invited him to produce two works in the opening season of the *Deutsche Oper*, as the *Städtische Oper* now became on its move to the reconstructed opera house in Charlottenburg, he accepted. *Aida* was followed in December by *Lohengrin*.

As in *Carmen*, Wieland found in *Aida* the basic love-death relationship which allies it with *Tristan und Isolde*. The final scene of the opera, in which Radames and Aida both voluntarily choose to die, is a *Liebestod* that formed the starting point of Wieland's thoughts on the work. He told Panofsky: "I cannot produce a work that ends with a duet of nearly twenty minutes duration either naturalistically or realistically. . . . Death is the path to transcendency. And Radames, by choosing Aida—that is to say, love—attains a higher freedom." This interpretation found symbolic expression in the lighting. Taking his cue (though in reverse order) from *Tristan und Isolde*, in which day and night have symbolic functions, Wieland set the final scene in the dungeon, not in the usual darkness, but in the diffuse light of an other-worldly day. The same symbolic use of lighting was evident in the triumphal scene of the second act, which took place in darkness. Wieland explained his idea to Goléa: "From the moment honour and patriotic duty impel Radames to renounce Aida, there can be only night in his soul. For him now the whole world is covered with this night."

The presence of a huge phallic symbol in Amneris's room could be accepted as a reasonable, if somewhat obvious expression of the nature of her love for Radames. More controversial was the transference of the whole setting of the work from the Egypt of the Pharaohs to a darker Africa of a prehistoric age. His reason for doing this, as Wieland told Panofsky, was that *Aida* is a timeless work, dealing with a number of basic human problems: patriotism, treason, ambition, hate, jealousy.

"What I was trying to do, in regard to the scenery, was to give *Aida* the colourful fragrance that is in it—deriving it not from an Egyptian museum, but from the atmosphere inherent in the work itself. I wanted to get away from false Egyptian artiness and false operatic monumentality, from Hollywoodish historical painting, and return to archaic—which is to say in terms of Egyptology—to pre-dynastic times."

*

Wieland's attempt, which he had resisted with *Carmen*, to press *Aida* into a stern Wagnerian mould was marked by a certain sense of strain, though critics such as H. H. Stuckenschmidt and Heinz Joachim mixed their reproaches with the admission that many scenes were far more than usually effective. Wieland was, however, on much firmer ground with the archetypal work itself, *Tristan und Isolde*, which, ten years after his first production in 1952, he staged in Bayreuth for the second time.

His productions of the work in other places—Stuttgart 1958, Holland and Berlin 1959 and Hamburg 1960—had been basically in line with the first Bayreuth production, though in Stuttgart there were hints of things to come. This production, described by Schäfer himself as unequal, was a transition stage on the way to what was, by general consent, Wieland's most powerful expression in his symbolic style.

The scenic structures dominating each of the acts bore a relationship to each other as well as to the events taking place on the stage. Their resemblance to the sculptures of Henry Moore was not accidental. In conversation with Panofsky Wieland expressed his regret that sculptors of genius like Moore and Lipschitz, who had found the way back to an archetypal form of art, were themselves "out of sympathy with the Wagnerian cosmos". What artists of this sort had neglected to do he consequently set about supplying for himself.

In their rough simplicity his shapes satisfied the historical sense by suggesting the Celtic origins of the legend of Tristan and Isolde. The curved claw-like structure of the first act could be taken literally as a depiction of the prow of a ship, but it also had phallic implications, if one cared to recognise them

Lohengrin at Bayreuth: Act Two (*above*)
Lohengrin at the Metropolitan, New York: Act One;
designs—Wieland Wagner, production—Peter Lehmann (*below*)

*Der Fliegende
Holländer* at
Bayreuth:
Scene One

(Wieland himself certainly did). There were vague erotic implications too in the wide column of the second act, with two round holes in the upper part. Suggestive of eyes, they depicted on a literal level the function of the watch tower they represented. The whole shape hinted at an owl, the bird that lives in the night, like the lovers themselves in Wagner's own textual symbolism. The third act was dominated by a fin-like shape with a single hole in the upper part. Across it ran irregular lines like the marks of a rough stone-cutting instrument, and there were similar marks on the ground. In literal terms this was Tristan's castle, hewn out of the gaunt rocks of Brittany. But the fin-like structure also suggested a sail, the subject and symbol of Tristan's feverish longing in this act.

Apart from these structures the stage was all but bare. A rough screen with a primitive bench before it was set to one side of the stage in the first act to depict Isolde's tent and bed. In the second there was a scarcely visible bench beneath the owl-like watch tower, while in the third there was nothing at all: the wounded Tristan lay on the bare ground.

The importance that Wieland gave to costumes emerged with particular clarity in this production. Not only their shape, but also the material from which they were made were for him significant aspects of their dramatic function. In his search for a material that, like his scenic structures, would be literally as well as symbolically convincing, Wieland came on the idea of leather. Since it is skin, leather seemed to him the nearest thing to nakedness, and he hoped, by using it for his costumes, to achieve a sort of subconscious eroticism.

His insistence in conversation on the erotic qualities of *Tristan und Isolde*, as shown also in his conscious use of phallic symbols, always seemed to me somewhat exaggerated. Eroticism is clearly implicit in the story, but it is only one aspect of Wagner's profoundest essay on his eternal theme of the true nature of love. Whatever Wieland may have said to give the impression that this aspect was of prime importance to him, the programme note he wrote to accompany his production—and above all the production itself—restored the balance. The following excerpts are taken from the English translation, published in the Bayreuth Festival *Tristan* programme of 1968:

F

"Wagner's *Tristan und Isolde* . . . is a mythical work . . . a myth handed down from the realm of age-old Celtic legends, telling of death-dealing Eros, of the breaking of the marriage bond and destructive passion. Such passion, as a sickness unto death, destroys those who succumb to it, body and soul. . . .

"The myth is always contemporary in its significance, no matter whether it deals with a moral code long superseded and the laws of the knightly world, which opposes with all its might that antisocial passion whose desire is for night and whose victory is in death, or whether it concerns the allegedly emancipated society of today. All passion strives against established order and represents a deadly danger to society. Even Richard Wagner remains so objective that through Marke he sets against the dreamers—for whom happiness, society and morality no longer exist, who regard love as their destiny, the ideal and supremely beautiful mystery—the indisputable realities of the world: power, renown, honour, fidelity, chivalry and friendship. . . .

"The story seems to me to possess far deeper significance if Tristan was in fact, as is still to be read on the famous stone in Castle Dor, Marke's son. The eternal strife between father and son . . . which Wagner employed not only dramatically but also musically as the second theme in *Tristan*, appears to me incomparably more tragic (and mythical!) than Tristan's adultery with his uncle's wife. . . .

"What really stands between the lovers? Why is their union in matrimony impossible from the very first bar of the Prelude? What prevents them from finding what society regards as happiness in this life? A situation without a future: when Tristan is first conscious of seeing Isolde he is lying helpless before her as the murderer of her betrothed. . . . Then, at their second meeting, he comes to Isolde as the emissary and vassal of Marke. . . . Tristan himself—this should not be forgotten—like Isolde cannot have been more than sixteen or seventeen years old, and it is no wonder that he feels himself to be far too lowly and insignificant for the renowned daughter of the Irish king. Even after the catastrophe on the ship, Tristan does not for a moment hesitate in the fulfilment of his duty to hand his beloved over to the king. . . .

"Without Marke there would have been nothing left for

Tristan but to marry Isolde—a really unthinkable idea. No one would imagine that Tristan and Isolde could ever be united in marriage: that would be the absolute negation of their passion. Isolde is not a woman one marries, nor is she a *femme inspiratrice* like Eva, but a *femme fatale*. As a wife she—like Senta, Elsa or Elisabeth—would cease to be what she is.

"The innermost hidden motive which dictated all the decisions of both Tristan and Isolde was none other than the death wish, a passion for night. Undoubtedly they loved one another, but each loved the other only from his own standpoint, not the other's . . . (Isolde) allows herself to be led unresisting into Marke's arms, and she greets the breach of her marriage ecstatically, as the triumph not of true love but of death. When Tristan has been mortally wounded by Melot's sword, she does not think of acknowledging him as her lover and following him, but goes on living in Marke's castle—a course of action scarcely credible in any woman other than Isolde. . . .

"(Tristan) too knows at length what Eastern mystics have long recognised . . . 'to yearn and die' is his destiny. Not for him now is the profound forgetfulness into which he fell suicidally in Act Two, offending against Marke no less than against Isolde. Now Isolde is far away, and has evidently betrayed him. He has renounced everything which made up his knightly existence—renown, honour, power and fidelity; he sinks down into the hell of loneliness. . . . His spirit breaks, with his Faustian curse on life. . . . Only then can his spirit be free to behold mystically the 'eternal woman', free for the ecstatic experience of cosmogonic Eros. . . . Panic-stricken fear of meeting Isolde again in this life causes Tristan . . . to tear off his bandages, merely in order to avoid an earthly reunion with Isolde.

"And Isolde? She too dies an earthly death so that her spirit will be free to find fulfilment in a mystical realm. Both of them, Tristan and Isolde, experience in death, as in a final revelation, the totality of passion. . . ."

It is a wider interpretation of *Tristan und Isolde* than Wieland had made in his first Bayreuth production of 1952. In that the outside world was all but eliminated and attention concentrated closely on the love tragedy. His attempt to penetrate further into the work's mysteries may, on the surface, have led

to a sacrifice of sheer romantic beauty, but it did, as it rightly
should, make Marke more than a rather pathetic old man.
The inscription on the stone at Castle Dor in Cornwall to
which Wieland refers in his essay (*Drustans hic jacit Cunomori
filius*) is not perhaps quite conclusive enough to justify positive
acceptance of the historical fact that Tristan was Marke's son
and not his nephew. But in any case Wieland did not tamper
with Wagner's text on the point. He simply used his knowledge
of the inscription to impress on the minds of the singers that
Tristan's tragedy was of the order of Oedipus's. This greatly
raised the dramatic quality of the work.

Tristan's sense of dishonour, which turns his longing for
Isolde into fear, is an essential part of Wagner's dramatic plan,
and to bring out this point Wieland saw the necessity of giving
the outside world and the code of chivalry some sort of visual
form. Thus, in contrast to his first production, he showed the
sailors on the ship and gave Marke a retinue of courtiers. As
with *Lohengrin*, Wieland took account of the composer's preoccupations at the time of writing the work. Wagner had then
been under the spell both of Schopenhauer and of the dramatist
Calderón, whose Spanish conception of honour had made a
deep impression on him.

Wieland's production, though less heavily attacked than
others he had made before, did not entirely escape hostile
criticism. His subjective use of lighting, which caused him to
place the climax of the first act in darkness in defiance of the
text; his decision to allow Tristan and Isolde to fly into each
other's arms immediately they had drunk the love potion; his
introduction of Marke and retinue at the end of the first act—a
hint to the audience presumably (since Tristan and Isolde
did not appear to see them) of the worldly forces against which
the lovers had to contend; and his final scene in which, as the
curtain fell, Isolde was alone visible, standing upright with
outstretched arms: these were seized on as examples of
Wieland's wilful defiance of the composer's stage directions. So,
in a narrow sense, they were. But in an interpretation of the
work which strove to reflect its psychological depths rather
than mere outward appearances, these deviations from the
literal word provided their own justification.

18

HIGH PRESSURE

1962–1965

BEGINNING WITH HIS *Aida* production in Berlin in September 1961, Wieland brought out in the next two years, beside his new productions of *Tristan und Isolde* and *Die Meistersinger* at Bayreuth, no less than fifteen productions in opera houses in Germany, Switzerland, Belgium, Denmark and Italy. The majority were Wagner works, among them the *Ring* at Cologne, in which he tried out ideas for his second production of the cycle at Bayreuth, scheduled for 1965. Among the others were two works by Richard Strauss which he was attempting for the first time: *Elektra* and *Salome*.

Wieland was now at the height of his fame, and it was not surprising that he should be overwhelmed with invitations to produce from opera directors who were well aware of his box office value. Whereas he had previously been careful not to overload himself with work, all at once he appeared to throw caution to the winds.

One can see various motives of a personal nature which might have urged him on: difficulties with his family arising from his association with Anja Silja; her wish to further her own career with his help. But the main motive was financial. Wieland was not a rich man. The capital assets of Bayreuth belonged entirely to his mother, and Wieland's earnings from the festival came only in the form of a relatively modest salary. The money earned with his productions outside Bayreuth was needed to meet the expenses of his family, which were increasing as the children grew older. And at this time he took on a particularly heavy financial commitment. The annual family holiday on the island of Sylt had hitherto been spent in rented houses. In 1963 Wieland bought a little house in the village of

Keitum and set about converting and extending it. The expense involved was enormous, and Wieland, having no capital of his own, was obliged to borrow the money, which amounted to several hundred thousand marks. He was then faced with the need of increasing his earnings steeply in order to pay off the debt.

He was aware that, in accepting so many engagements, he ran the risk of cheapening himself. Yet nevertheless he decided to take the chance. He had sufficient confidence in himself to believe that he could avoid the danger of relaxing his own high standards.

*

Wieland's production of *Elektra* at Stuttgart in January 1962 was built around the personality of Martha Mödl, his early Kundry, Isolde and Brünnhilde. Though she had ceased to appear regularly at Bayreuth, she had continued to sing in opera houses elsewhere, and Wieland's admiration for her was steadfast. One of the last pieces he ever wrote, a contribution to Schäfer's biography *Martha Mödl*, appeared in 1967: "No one has ever demonstrated better than Martha Mödl that complete artistic identification—which is far removed from stage exhibitionism—still exerts a stronger fascination on the public than sheer technical perfection. Singing, acting and personality unite in her to form an absolute indivisible whole, such as Richard Wagner—as we know from his own rapturous descriptions—experienced 130 years ago in the person of Wilhelmine Schröder-Devrient. . . . Martha Mödl possesses a feeling for style of a subtlety which at times is almost frightening. No producer in the world could impose on her or entice from her a movement, a gesture or an expression foreign to the role she is playing. At such moments she jibs like a sensitive horse."

Schäfer has described Martha Mödl's interpretation of the role of Elektra in his book on Wieland Wagner: "The true stature of Elektra was revealed in her unyielding hatred, in her imperious manner when she confronts Clytemnestra, in the moments of stored up, repressed and liberating revenge. . . . Even the contrasts were adapted to this interpretation, as for example in the fine Clytemnestra of Regina Resnik, who was in all respects a woman, scarcely a queen at all. Here Wieland Wagner deliberately changed the balance which has always hitherto existed between these two characters, even in the drama of Sophocles. . . . For the first time a queen flattered and cajoled her relentless daughter."

Wieland's approach to *Salome*, which followed *Elektra* at Stuttgart a few weeks later, was more individual. He found in it evidence of his obsessive theme of *Eros thanatos*, though he admitted it was an extreme border-line case. He wrote in a programme note: "A girl—Lilith and Lulu, virgin and death goddess in one single person—meets the man corresponding to her animus image. This man—an ascetic, a preacher of repentance, prototype of the *homo religiosus*—rejects her love and curses her. He deprives Salome of her function in life, which can now be fulfilled only in death. In a visionary moment Salome realises that the mystery of love is greater than the mystery of death. . . .

"This profoundly tragic encounter between the amoral princess and the priestly man takes place in a decadent world, weakened by lust and perversion, at the turning point of two civilisations. The symbols of decay are Herodias, the Whore of Babylon of Revelations, and Herodes, the Arabian upstart shaken by hallucinations and *Existenzangst*: distorted pictures of humanity, as are the Jewish dogmaticians and the effeminate Syrian who is infatuated with Salome.

"It is remarkable that the eschatological image of the maiden with the severed head of the prophet in her hands, which from the bronze doors of San Zeno in Verona to Picasso has excited the imagination of painters and sculptors, should have found its final poetic and musical expression at the turn of the nineteenth and twentieth centuries. At a time of unbearable pseudo-romanticism, in which love was prettified and cheapened, poets and composers thrust on a sated bourgeois society horrifying images of elemental femininity. Ibsen with his Nora, Wagner with his Kundry, Wedekind with his Lulu and Wilde with his Salome rediscovered the female in the fullness of her existence. Sixty years later these prototypal visions have lost none of their horror—and also none of their greatness."

Probably the feeling that it takes more today than sixty years ago to shock an audience led Wieland to screw *Salome* up to an even higher note of hysteria than usual. It was a production in which realism and stylisation were mixed: sudden and violent movements among the main protagonists and formal patterns among the lesser characters. In front of a silver relief background vaguely reminiscent of a quarry with rock-crystal formations yawned the opening to the great cistern in which Jochanaan was held captive. From this Jochanaan emerged with the desperate leap of an escaping animal: no mild, exalted priest, but a wild-haired fanatic, dressed in a rough skin, nervily wielding a scourge. Herodes was completely bald, an obsessive voluptuary terrified by the force of his own lusts, Herodias a red-haired painted whore with net stockings. Salome had at the beginning the deceptive innocence of a kitten and the sulkiness of a spoiled child. She began the famous dance wrapped in a scarlet veil, which she threw off suddenly to reveal a naked torso, the breasts scantily concealed, the lower part of the body clad to below the knees in black net tights. The dance was more acrobatic than sinuous, the bared figure at the end of it deliberately hermaphroditic, and Herodes retired baffled. The final scene with Jochanaan's head was a horrifying portrait of hysterical sexuality.

It was a brilliant virtuoso display, which owed much to Anja Silja in the title role—and not only to her personality and acting ability, but also to her physical appearance. It is not given to many female opera singers to suggest boyish qualities in the roles that call for it, even when fully clothed.

Ironically perhaps—since fundamentally it was of all his creations the least serious—*Salome* was the most widely successful of Wieland's non-Wagnerian productions. Wherever it was subsequently done—in Berlin in 1962, in Brussels in 1963, in Paris in 1964, in Vienna in 1965 and in Rome in 1966, always with Anja Silja in the title role—it electrified the whole audience and shocked part of it.

Among those who were shocked were Richard Strauss's son, Franz Strauss. He instructed the publishers of his father's operas to inform all opera houses that in future permission to make new productions of them would be granted only if the name of the producer they intended to engage was notified in advance. This unprecedented act led to vehement protest from

Carmen in Hamburg, 1958: final scene

Salome in Stuttgart, 1962

all German opera houses, and Franz Strauss was obliged to admit that he did not intend to play the censor against any producer except one: Wieland Wagner. "It is high time," he declared, "that a warning shot should be fired across this gentleman's bows." However, fire from this quarter could not deter a vessel which (to remain in the metaphor) had silenced far heavier armoury of the same kind in Bayreuth. Dr Strauss's idea, Wieland stated laconically, was very original, but he did not think it was legally valid. He was right, of course, as his continued productions of *Elektra* and *Salome* proved.

*

The charge of sensationalism, levelled against his *Salome* by other critics beside Dr Strauss, were loudly renewed after Wieland's second attempt at *Die Meistersinger* at the Bayreuth Festival of 1963.

The idea of presenting it as a sort of knockabout Elizabethan farce—a German *Shoemaker's Holiday*—came to him, Wieland told me, at the time he was recreating in Berlin, in December 1962, his first Bayreuth production of the work. Very possibly, in the strain of his personal life at the time, he shared something of Wagner's need after the composition of *Tristan und Isolde* for an escape to a lighter, more down-to-earth world. Wieland, always alive to the biographical influences of his grandfather's life, pointed out to me the many places in *Die Meistersinger* in which Wagner had deliberately parodied his own works.

"It goes in *Die Meistersinger* even to the point that the Night Watchman blows an F sharp, the note to which Wagner immediately steers the *Ring* whenever the destruction of the world is being dealt with. It really is curious and interesting to see how after *Tristan* Wagner for once in his life abandoned bitter earnest and became cheerful and lighthearted. There were many cases in the past century of geniuses who went mad, and I believe that *Tristan* was a time when Wagner was on the brink of it, like for instance Hölderlin or Kleist or Schumann. But, healthy Saxon that he was, he sought salvation in Nuremberg, in the key of C major, in Shakespeare and Bach. Wagner himself once said that *Die Meistersinger* is applied Bach."

Equally alive to the facts of the modern world about him,

which he gleaned from reading newspapers and illustrated periodicals in vast quantities, Wieland found another source of inspiration in the accounts of an attack of midsummer madness which occurred in Schwabing, the student quarter of Munich, on 21 June 1962. It was innocently started by three young men playing guitars on the pavement outside a café. The complaints of a neighbouring householder led to a clash between the police and passers-by who were enjoying the music. The clash developed into a near-riot, in which stones were thrown, batons used, the tyres of police cars punctured and traffic brought to a standstill by a sit-down demonstration in the middle of the road.

Out of this proof of the immutability of human nature— Wagner's riot scene in *Die Meistersinger* had itself been inspired by a rather similar scene he had witnessed in Nuremberg as a very young man—grew Wieland's desire to attempt a production based on the quality that distinguishes *Die Meistersinger* from all the other works of Wagner: its contemporary spirit. He set it in its own historical time, the sixteenth century. His costumes were based on the pictures of Breughel and made of hessian, a material commonly used at that period. Gertrud's choreography for the street fight in the second act and the dances in the third reflected the gestures and movements painted by Breughel, and Breughelian satire was also behind the interpretation of the various characters in the play. The mastersingers themselves made their first appearance in the working clothes of their various trades and put on their master-singers' robes—and with it their self-importance—in our sight. Pogner was a self-made man and a snob, content to consider Nuremberg's town clerk a suitable match for his daughter until the chance of wedding her to an aristocrat arose. Beckmesser was a snob too, but an intellectual one, and his interest in Eva was centred more on her father's money than on her personal charms. Eva herself was the spoiled and self-willed daughter of a rich father.

All this, however strange it might seem at first to an audience used to the traditional romantic (that is to say, nineteenth century) approach to the work, can in fact be justified by an unprejudiced reading of the text. I myself felt that Wieland brought out the superb and valid comedy of Wagner's text with a strength never experienced before. I was less convinced by the setting against which he presented the comedy. As he told me, he saw *Die Meistersinger* as a clear expression of Wagner's veneration of Shakespeare, and he therefore felt justified in presenting it on a Shakespearian stage, with a surrounding gallery that remained constant throughout.

Curiously, Wieland did not appear to realise that, in returning to the Shakespearian stage, he was not returning to the spirit of Shakespeare for inspiration, as he had so successfully done with Breughel, but to a theatrical convention which was in its way just as limiting as the nineteenth century Bayreuth convention he had so successfully demolished. Shakespeare transcends the stage conventions of his own time as completely as Wagner had been shown to transcend his, and it is questionable whether either, liberated from his own convention, would show up any better in the conventional setting of the other. Wieland's uncharacteristic flirtation with convention led him in his production of *Die Meistersinger* into unusual errors of judgment in the last two acts: most notably, a Night Watchman stepping over prone bodies at the end of the second act; an overloaded procession of guilds in the meadow scene which was intended to satirise sixteenth century ideas of good taste, yet appeared only to supply evidence of the producer's bad taste; and a final chorus sung by the assembled company directly to the audience, thereby sounding far more nationalistic than in the days of Hitler.

This last device, Wieland told me, he had adopted since it seemed the logical ending for his particular approach to the work as a whole. "I know it will raise a lot of dust," he said, "and I am sure I shall come in for a lot of attacks. But I am used to that."

My conversation with him took place during rehearsals, from which he had rigorously excluded all but the participants and a few privileged people like myself and Christopher Sykes, with whom I was preparing a radio feature on the production. We were all pledged not to talk about what we were seeing until after the first night. Wieland was normally very tolerant about allowing people to watch his rehearsals on the main stage of the *Festspielhaus*, and this veto was a reflection of his awareness that his new *Meistersinger* was in the nature of a bombshell.

He was not mistaken. The first night of the production was noisy, booes alternating with wild applause. The press reaction was more solidly hostile than ever before, and some critics solemnly held up his first production as an example of how *Die Meistersinger* could and should be presented—quite forgetting, apparently, that it too had been attacked and booed in its time. Wieland was widely accused of having deliberately set out to cause a sensation. This, I think, was unjust. There were sufficient revelations in his unusual approach to suggest that it was not only a serious attempt, but also a valid one. The weaknesses of his production were, in my view, the result of a lack of time to prepare it carefully enough. At this time Wieland was certainly pushing himself too hard.

*

Just before *Die Meistersinger* was launched a statement was issued to the press that Wieland had been advised by his doctors to take a prolonged rest, and in fact, after the completion of the *Ring* in Cologne in November 1963, he made no new production until October of the following year. At the Bayreuth Festival of 1964 he confined himself to preparing a revised version of his second *Tannhäuser* production.

Though this is sometimes referred to as a third *Tannhäuser*, the alterations Wieland made scarcely justify the title. They were matters of detail rather than of concept. Venus was still presented as an idol though, in the absence of Grace Bumbry, she had become a white one (Barbro Ericson). The experiment of doubling the roles of Venus and Elisabeth, which Wieland had tried out in Copenhagen the previous September, was not repeated at Bayreuth, though Anja Silja, the Venus-Elisabeth of Copenhagen, eventually sang both roles at different performances in the *Festspielhaus*. Gertrud devised a new Bacchanal to replace Béjart's. It might be described as a sort of ecstatic dance round the golden calf. Among the dancers were Wieland's two younger daughters, Nike and Daphne, who had made their first stage appearance the previous year in *Parsifal* as non-singing Flower Maidens.

After an attempt to engage Carlo Maria Giulini had fallen through, Wieland entrusted *Tannhäuser* to a relatively little-known Austrian conductor, Otmar Suitner. In the following year, however, he persuaded André Cluytens, his favourite conductor for this work, to return. Suitner was put in charge of *Der Fliegende Holländer*.

As this suggests, Wieland's habitual difficulties with his conductors were still continuing. Sawallisch, who had originally been invited to conduct the new *Meistersinger* in 1963, had raised objections to Wieland's decision to give the role of Eva to Anja Silja. Wieland was not prepared to listen to his reasons, and in consequence a valuable relationship ended. Wieland engaged the young American, Thomas Schippers, to take his place, but artistic sympathy proved to be lacking. In the following year Wieland turned, as he had so often done before, to an established conductor of an older generation, Robert Heger, for temporary help.

A much more permanent relationship was established with another distinguished conductor of an older generation, Karl Böhm. Though Wieland owed his abortive invitation to produce the *Ring* in Vienna in 1944 to Böhm, their paths did not again converge until 1959, when they worked together in Berlin on Wieland's production of *Tristan und Isolde*. Böhm, like Clemens Krauss, is an Austrian, and he knew how to avoid in his handling of Wagner's scores that Teutonic ponderousness which Wieland would tolerate from no conductor except Knappertsbusch. Wieland once described Böhm's style as "Wagner via Mozart", though probably he did not intend the remark to be taken too literally. Now that Böhm was free of his previous commitments at the Salzburg Festival, Wieland seized the opportunity to secure him for Bayreuth. Beginning with *Tristan und Isolde* in 1962, he conducted in every festival up to Wieland's death and beyond: not only *Tristan*, but also some performances of *Die Meistersinger* and Wieland's second production of the *Ring*.

Of the seven singers whom Wieland had described in 1955 as "the seed from which the artistic and human community of the new Bayreuth has grown" only two were still appearing there regularly in the early Sixties: Gerhard Stolze, whose long list of roles had included David, Mime and Loge, and Wolfgang Windgassen, who had appeared in every one of the heroic tenor roles, including Rienzi at Stuttgart. Astrid Varnay

had not dropped out entirely, but she had relinquished the
major roles of Brünnhilde and Isolde to Birgit Nilsson, who
first appeared at Bayreuth in 1954 as Elsa in Wolfgang's production of *Lohengrin*. There were other singers still appearing
whose association with Wieland went back even further than
Birgit Nilsson's, notably Leonie Rysanek, George London
(both since 1951), Josef Greindl (his first appearance at
Bayreuth was as Pogner in 1943), Theo Adam, Kurt Böhme,
Hans Hotter and Gustav Neidlinger (all since 1952). Gré
Brouwenstijn, Dietrich Fischer-Dieskau and Ramon Vinay
also worked with Wieland fairly continuously during the
Fifties.

Wieland's loyalty to the singers with whom he had a sympathetic contact, evident from this list, did not prevent him from
seeking promising newcomers for his team. Beside Anja Silja
there was Kerstin Meyer, the Carmen of his Hamburg production, who first came to Bayreuth in 1962 to sing Brangäne and
later took part in his second *Ring*; Jess Thomas who, beginning
with Parsifal in 1961, was able to take some of the weight of
the heroic tenor roles from Wolfgang Windgassen's shoulders;
Thomas Stewart (Amfortas and Gunther); Erwin Wohlfahrt
(David and Mime); Eberhard Wächter (Amfortas, Wolfram,
Kurwenal); and Martti Talvela (Landgraf, Marke, Fasolt,
Hunding). It would be difficult to establish which of the four
qualifications Wieland demanded of his singers—a good voice,
a good figure, an ability to act, a sympathetic relationship—
was the most important in his mind. He looked for—and often
managed to find—all four. But he never regarded sheer beauty
of tone as an end in itself: the voice had to be the servant and
not the master. Carlos Alexander, whose only Bayreuth
appearance was his remarkable Beckmesser of the second
Meistersinger, worked with him in Stuttgart on roles as different
as Jochanaan in *Salome*, Wolfram in *Tannhäuser* (a part he was
enjoined deliberately to desentimentalise), Dr Schön in Berg's
Lulu and Wotan. According to Schäfer, Wieland's verdict on
that performance was: "No vocal giant has moved me so
deeply in Wotan's Farewell as Alexander."

*

Wieland resumed work in October 1964 with a programme fully as onerous as all that had gone before. At the centre of it stood his second production of the *Ring* at Bayreuth, scheduled for July 1965. It was preceded by *Salome* in Paris, *Elektra* in Brussels (with Anja Silja in the title role), *Tristan und Isolde* in Milan and Rome, Verdi's *Otello* in Frankfurt, *Der Fliegende Holländer* in Geneva and *Lohengrin* in Vienna.

Otello was, by general consent, the least successful of all Wieland's productions. He divided Verdi's four acts into ten separate scenes, making use of a revolving stage. Otello (Wolfgang Windgassen) and Desdemona (Anja Silja) sang their love duet in bed. Wieland's reason for this innovation, as explained to Goléa, was, firstly, that they were celebrating their wedding night, and secondly, that the bedroom was the only place in which they could be alone together. They were, after all, on a small and primitive island, not in some fine Venetian palace.

These explanations, though reasonable enough on a mundane level, are clearly below Wieland's usual imaginative standards. So too were the cramped quarters and drab costumes through which he attempted to show Otello, Iago and Cassio as members of an army on active service. The point is of course correct, but it has no relevance to the drama, and Wieland made no attempt to establish any. Beyond describing *Otello* as a drama of jealousy, in which he appeared to find Iago's jealousy more interesting than Otello's, Wieland seemed unable to detect any overriding idea in the work that could set his imagination alight.

19

SECOND PRODUCTION OF THE *RING*

1965

WHEN CHRISTOPHER SYKES and I arrived in Bayreuth three weeks before the opening of the 1965 festival, Wieland greeted us with his customary quiet courtesy and gave us permission to wander where we pleased in recording material for our radio feature. Very soon, however, we became conscious of a change in the atmosphere in the *Festspielhaus*. The old spirit of camera-derie was lacking. Wieland himself seemed withdrawn. The hours we had formerly seen him devote to rehearsals with his singers were now given to his lighting experts, with whom he spent whole days exploring nuances of lighting on the stage. This was boring to watch, and the usual sprinkling of privileged onlookers in the *Festspielhaus* grew smaller and smaller. Even these few appeared to irritate Wieland as never before, and before long he imposed a complete ban on entry to the auditorium. This would not in itself have appeared significant if he had not in previous years been so remarkably tolerant towards intruders. Now it suggested that his nerves were no longer as strong as they once had been. He wanted complete isolation.

The absence of stage rehearsals with his singers was due to some extent to the non-arrival of his Wotan, George London. Less than a week of rehearsal time remained when it became known that he would be unable to appear at all. Theo Adam, who was chosen to replace him, had not sung Wotan under Wieland's direction before. Intense individual rehearsals were necessary—an extra item in Wieland's overloaded schedule. When the *Ring* finally reached the stage, it was not completely ready.

To what extent it fell short of his intentions only Wieland

could fully know, for it was a *Ring* very different in appearance from anything previously seen in Bayreuth. From the very start we were confronted with a *Ring* turned strictly inward. Old familiar perspectives, present if not actually visible in Wieland's earlier production of 1951, had now been banished. The Rhine Maidens were three dimly discerned female shapes spaced widely apart in general darkness. As Alberich groped his way between them, the figure he sought to grasp would be momentarily spotlighted, a provocatively sexual vision that vanished as it came within his reach. The gold gradually took shape above in a form vaguely suggestive of an eye. We were deep in the realm, not of recorded legend, but of obsessive subconscious desire.

In the following scene there was no distant vision of a romantic Valhalla. Wotan and Fricka stood directly before the lower walls of a grim citadel reaching up out of sight. Its rough stones were held together by a dark material which gave the impression of prison bars. The huge scarred tree-trunk hung with skulls that dominated the first act of *Die Walküre*; the vast grid-like structure in the second act of *Siegfried*, through which the immense eyes of the dragon flashed (the only part of that embarrassing monster we were permitted to see); the rough columns of Gunther's palace in *Götterdämmerung*, pitted like a moonscape and suggestive of a human race not yet emerged from primitive animal savagery: all these were reflections of the producer's aim to express the drama in terms of the subconscious mind.

"I think it is impossible to design fully abstract settings for the music of the *Ring*," Wieland told me in a conversation after the dress rehearsal. "My settings abstract essential meanings, not from the stage directions, but from the scenes themselves. In the second scene of *Rheingold* I no longer show the distant vision, the blue sky, the ground covered in flowers, but present the abstraction of Wotan's lust for power in the form of a mysteriously threatening, skyscraper type of building. The citadel is the symbol of Wotan's destructive will for power. But it is not just any castle. The usual sort of romantic castle tells the audience nothing.

"Another example: in the second act of *Siegfried* I provide something between roots, honeycombs, caves—a set which can be anything or everything. The tree in *Die Walküre* is not just any tree, but the tree in which Wotan has plunged the sword. It may be the world ash, or again it might not. I myself have the feeling that it *is* the world ash, or a fragment of it, and now the human race is creeping around it in the figure of Hunding. This is where the fate of the world is decided, or (if you like) where the fate of the world cannot be decided until Siegmund pulls the sword from it. I present a tree that has a sort of totem quality: hence the skulls hanging on it and the mysterious signs carved on it. This tree must impart a sense of awe: it can't be just a nice straightforward ash tree."

The *Ring*, Wieland went on, was not what the whole world usually took it to be—a Germanic heroic epic based on the philosophy of Schopenhauer. "For me it is, firstly, a revival of Greek tragedy; secondly, a return to mythical sources; and thirdly, moralistic drama in the manner both of Schiller and of Brecht. The *Ring* is the mirror which Richard Wagner holds up to humanity. 'This is how you are,' he says, 'and this is what will happen to our world if humanity does not radically change.' As he himself said, he depicted in this work both the beginning and the end of the world."

Wagner's moralistic challenge was addressed to the people of his own time, the society of rationalism and the industrial revolution, which had forgotten its mythical roots. But its message was more than ever applicable to the society of today.

"For me the *Ring* is the most topical and modern of living dramas. Its basic theme is stated with Wotan's very first act—with a wanton practical interference with natural order, symbolised by the carvings on the spear. The work deals with the enslavement of nature and mankind by the political man, by Wotan, and with the adjustment of this political action by Wotan's counterpart, who is Brünnhilde. In my mind Brünnhilde, and not Siegfried, is Wotan's opposite. Her life is based on love, while Wotan's is based on power, with all the negative aspects that Wagner attributes to power, ambition and repression in whatever form they appear throughout the work. We have, God knows, experienced in two world wars all the things of which Wagner warned us. His music may be emotional, beautiful and romantic, but the text shows very clearly and inexorably which paths lead downwards. Brünnhilde sees what the power-intoxicated Wotan prefers not to see: suffering and misery in the world. All her actions, including the death of Siegfried, who has unknowingly betrayed her, are motivated in love, through which she strives to restore order to the world. In the *Ring*, as in every Greek tragedy, order is disturbed and then order is restored. Wotan disturbs it and Brünnhilde restores it. That is the basic theme of the *Ring*."

The whole action was presented on a raised circular platform behind which the scenic designs were erected. This platform was not a repetition of the symbolic *Weltenscheibe* of the 1951 production, but (as Wieland expressed it) "quite simply an acting arena, raised up in order to heighten and sublimate the drama. It is nothing else but the buskin of the ancient Greek theatre, on which human beings were raised up in the literal sense of the word. As far as the *Ring* is concerned, it fulfils the practical function of concentrating the action—which I know from experience can easily fall apart on a stage as large as ours—and reducing the distance between the individual players as far as possible.

"In effect the *Ring* could be called a mythological conversation piece. There are never more than three people on the stage at the same time—leaving aside the Valkyries and the chorus in *Götterdämmerung*—and that over four whole evenings. By keeping my acting area constant, I hold the whole *Ring* together in the same way as musically it is held together by the *Leitmotive*. The whole of the *Ring* is based on only a few basic musical motives, which give it a central unity, however far it may seem at times to stray. And this is exactly what I try to achieve with my smooth, bare platform."

Paul Eberhardt later told me that Wieland had intended to have this circular platform lighted from below to give it the effect of floating. The attempt was abandoned owing to technical difficulties.

Wieland's description of the *Ring* as a mythological conversation piece (his actual word was *Kammerspiel*) is essentially true, even if there are more occasions than those he mentioned during which the number of characters on stage exceeds three. The vital encounters in the drama are all duologues—Wotan-Fricka, Wotan-Erda, Siegmund-Sieglinde, Wotan-Brünnhilde, Siegmund-Brünnhilde, Siegfried-Mime, Siegfried-Wotan, and so on to the end. And in this production these encounters had more than their usual dramatic force. However much the concentration of the action might have helped, it could not alone have achieved the heightened effect. Clearly at some stage of rehearsals, either in Bayreuth or in Cologne, Wieland had worked out with his singers, many of whom had been the same in both productions, clear conceptions of individual character.

Wotan was, if not the most obvious, certainly the main villain of the drama. "Wotan lives in a state of perpetual illusion," Wieland said. "He never experiences ethical or moral enlightenment. He develops in the direction of so-called wisdom, but the character of a Wotan cannot step outside its own limitations: it can only be added to intellectually. In the terms of Wagner's symbolism, he first of all wants the ring for himself. His experiences bring him to the point of wanting it, not for himself, but for the Rhine Maidens. But this is the limit of his apparent self-denial. He remains himself right up to his last appearance in *Siegfried*. He simply becomes wiser or, as I should prefer to put it, cooler, more cunning. He is a political fox."

The character of the music had, in Wieland's opinion, led many producers to present the Wotan of *Siegfried* in a false light. "It sounds like a hymn, and the Wanderer is always portrayed as the wise old St Peter, the distinguished old gentleman with white hair who strides over the stage singing solemn melodies. That is all wrong. He comes to Mime's cave in the first act as a disturber of the peace. He forces Mime into a dangerous game of question and answer because he wants Siegfried at long last to get on with the job of forging the sword. In the second act too all his reasons for action are spurious. His real motive in waking Fafner is to make sure that Fafner is not frightened by the sudden threat of death into giving the ring to Alberich, who has been waiting outside the cave for seventeen or eighteen years. That is one of his aims. Another is to protect Siegfried from Alberich, and so he sets Alberich against Mime. 'Siegfried won't hurt you,' he says. 'It's your brother Mime you want to watch. He's out for world dominion.' Then in the third act he has his last encounter with Erda, whom he has never forgiven for telling him in *Rheingold* that he too is mortal and will meet his end. For of course that is the deep significance of Erda's appearance in *Rheingold*: the gods learn to their dismay that they are subject to the laws of death and decay. And now Wotan comes to tell Erda that she is wrong, and to mock and curse her.

"This scene is perhaps the most interesting interchange in the whole of the *Ring*, though it can hardly be understood without a complete knowledge of the whole text, which is obscured by an overplus of music. It is the last and most basic dispute between the male and female principles, in which the man, Wotan, mocks the Earth Mother and accuses her of knowing nothing. He claims to be able to control fate. He knows better than Erda what is going on. It doesn't take very long for him to discover his mistake. Erda is right and he—as always—is wrong. There is not a single scene throughout the work in which Wotan is shown to be right."

In Wieland's conception the male principle implies political activity, the female a concern for natural order. Wotan's encounters with the female principle are not confined only to Erda, who is Gea, the ancient Greek earth mother, and to Brünnhilde, who starts as Pallas Athene and continues as Prometheus: they include his consort Fricka as well. In her first appearance she is not essentially Wotan's adversary, but rather his companion in guilt. "In the first scene complicity in the building of the citadel—the barracks, the disastrous Valhalla—is attributed to her. So she too is morally guilty, she too is condemned to extinction." In *Die Walküre* there is no emotional contact remaining between her and Wotan. "For that reason I do not treat their scene together as a personal intervention by Fricka. The whole scene is for me simply a soliloquy presented as a dialogue, the struggle in Wotan's heart between his will and his moral self. Fricka is in this scene an embodiment of Wotan's moral self, just as Brünnhilde is the embodiment of his loving self. Fricka represents the principle of deathly morality, and the god Wotan must acknowledge the validity of the moral argument within himself. Everything Fricka says is utterly right. The gods, who created morals, cannot themselves sin against morality."

In production Wieland conveyed the impression of an inner struggle in Wotan's heart rather than a domestic quarrel by placing his Fricka motionless to one side of the acting platform.

She did not once look directly at Wotan, nor did he show
awareness of her actual presence. The positive result in dramatic terms was that his decision to withdraw his protection from
Siegmund appeared less like a weak capitulation than a recognition of stern necessity. And his subsequent punishment of
Brünnhilde for defying him could be seen as more than the
vengeance of outraged authority. It was Wotan's desperate
attempt (accepting Wieland's description of Brünnhilde as the
embodiment of Wotan's loving self) to stifle the emotions that
stood in the way of his ambition.

The difficulty of keeping the end of Wotan's self-imposed
dilemma clearly in sight in *Götterdämmerung*, in which Wotan
does not appear, was solved by an unusual handling of the scene
between Brünnhilde and Waltraute. Wieland told the singer
of Waltraute (Kerstin Meyer) to think of Valhalla as the
Reichskanzlei in Berlin in 1945. Wotan sits like Hitler in the
Bunker, knowing the end is near and resolved to pull the whole
world down with him. Kerstin Meyer told me: "And there is
this girl, and she happens to hear one word from Wotan, which
he says without being aware of saying it. And she thinks, 'I have
the secret of saving the world', and steals out of that Valhalla,
where all are standing still just waiting for the moment when
everything explodes."

Waltraute becomes thus in the singer's mind more than a
formal messenger, merely telling the audience what it ought
to know. She is a girl who, like her sister Brünnhilde, has defied
Wotan in a vain attempt to divert fate. Hers is a smaller rebellion than Brünnhilde's, and one that comes too late and is
made for the wrong reasons. We see how far Wotan has fallen,
when so small and sentimental a character as Waltraute can
defy him and survive without punishment. And we understand
why Brünnhilde sends her away empty-handed: Waltraute's
pitiful account has revealed that Wotan's day is now done, and
the fate of the world rests in Brünnhilde's hands. It is a greater
dramatic yield that we usually receive from the little Waltraute
scene.

In an interpretation of the *Ring* that has the conflict of Wotan
and Brünnhilde at its centre, Siegfried becomes little more than
a subsidiary character. An age that has little taste for Herculean
characters bears the loss cheerfully. But nevertheless Siegfried

has a major part to play on the stage, and Wieland strove in his production to make him as sympathetic as possible. In an interview with Claus Henning Bachmann (*Opernwelt*, September 1964) he said:

"The characterisation of Siegfried depends on the characterisation of the Wanderer and of Mime. If Mime is presented as a comic and helpless old man, then Siegfried will become an unsympathetic boor. But in the framework of the whole cycle Mime is candidate number three for world dominion. . . . He has the fragments of the sword and young Siegfried as his secret weapons. Wotan has his spear and Alberich his moral rights. . . . The negative aspects of Siegfried's character, which are undoubtedly there, must be corrected by clarifying the functions of his partners. . . .

"Above all, any strong-arm tactics towards Mime must be cut out. Only at the height of his dilemma does Siegfried lay a hand on him. The first aspect of Siegfried's character that we see is his love for animals. The second . . . is his longing for a companion, longing for the other person, for a wife, a mother.... The whole second act of *Siegfried* expresses this longing of a person who lives in terrible loneliness, who is constantly searching for his own identity. He hates himself. He seeks commitment, the dethronement of his own ego, and finds it in so-called 'fearing'. . . . His insolence towards the Wanderer arises out of the situation. Siegfried is on his way to find his companion. He is in search of completion. An old man with a spear comes to bar his way—and without any good reason. Young people have a legitimate right to beat down old men's spears."

The problem of presenting Mime in line with Wieland's indisputably correct analysis of his true function in the drama lies in the fact, as he pointed out to Bachmann, that for most of the time he is dissembling. The climax of his role, when he is puzzled by Siegfried's new-found ability to see through his lies, borders in Wagner's presentation of it on the farcical. But Erwin Wohlfahrt, who played the role, succeeded in conveying to the audience the underlying menace of Mime while preserving towards Siegfried the necessary façade of injured innocence. The first act of *Siegfried*, depicting a high-spirited boy completely oblivious of the battle going on before his eyes for the possession of him was a remarkable achievement.

The festival *Rheingold* programme of 1951 contains Wieland's only piece of writing concerning the *Ring*. It is a study of Loge, whom Wieland rather startlingly promotes to a position on the side of the angels. That the character did not in his first production emerge on the stage as clearly as it does in print may have been due to Wieland's lack of experience as a producer at that time, or perhaps to the psychologically less penetrating level of the early production as a whole. In the production of 1965 both producer and singer (Wolfgang Windgassen) succeeded in conveying Wieland's unusual view of Loge in effective stage terms.

"Loge", Wieland wrote, "is neither an idle chatterer nor a crafty intriguer. His statements contain pure truth. . . . Loge in his disinterested wisdom finds Wotan's brooding intelligence, concentrated on the realisation of vast plans, incomprehensible: he is in every respect Wotan's intellectual opposite. Like Erda, he is instinctive. . . . With swift intuition he grasps connections which Wotan, driven by his own daemon, is unable to discern. . . . Ageless and fundamentally sexless, he shares his origins with the Rhine Maidens. . . . He advises when his advice is asked, but refrains from uttering hints or warnings. His essence is that of fire itself, neither good nor bad. . . . In the face of such natural elemental force moral values have no meaning. . . . For the vain struggles of these 'most celestial' gods, for the 'loutish' giants, for Alberich's destructive lust he finds only words of irony, an urge to mock behind which superior wisdom lurks. . . . His musical motives are heard sounding like ironic laughter wherever gods, heroes and dwarfs can be seen hastening to their doom. . . .

"Of course, if we are to believe the scarcely flattering remarks of the gods, dwarfs and giants, then it is true that Loge is nothing but an arch-liar. But that would make him the instigator of the whole tragedy of the *Ring* (and indeed in almost all commentaries on *Rheingold* he is branded as exactly that). And this would lead to a complete reversal of the dramatic premises. . . . Loge's plea on behalf of the Rhine Maidens is quite genuine. He has complete trust in Wotan as the custodian of treaties and the upholder of justice. . . . It is never his aim to destroy the gods. He does not hate them. . . . The gods (and commentators!) are wrong when they suggest

Aida in Berlin, 1961: Amneris's room (*above*)
Otello at Frankfurt, 1965: Act One (*below*)

The grave in the Bayreuth town cemetery

that Loge, by deliberately arousing their greed, is responsible for the disastrous theft of the gold. . . . The desire for the proud citadel was Wotan's, not his, and the contract with the giants was the inevitable consequence of that. Loge may have been the instrument of the contract, but he was not the cause of it. . . . From the very beginning Loge identifies himself with nature's desire for the restoration of its original harmony. He sees that as the highest commandment."

It would need a whole book in itself to do justice to Wieland's attempt to explore the complexities of the *Ring* in the light of modern depth psychology. All I have room for here is a series of impressions, and Wieland's treatment of the giants in the fourth scene of *Rheingold* must serve as a final example of his resource in relating the extraneous stage action to the deeper psychological implications of the drama as a whole. The giants, having agreed to return Freia to the gods in exchange for gold, heap it up in front of her. The pile, as it grows, gradually assumes the rough form of a woman—a shape inspired in Wieland's mind by the Willendorf Venus, a female idol of pre-historic times. It was a moment of revelation, an ironic illustration of the giants' intellectual limitations in their pathetic bid for power. In their attempt to get the best of both worlds, sensual and material, they ended up with an object that gave them neither.

This scene was attacked by some critics on the grounds that it came very close to *Kitsch*. It was perhaps one of those flashes of insight which, if allowed to degenerate into routine, would quickly become cheapened, but its initial impact was unforget-tably rewarding.

Far heavier and more general criticism greeted Wieland's decision to eliminate entirely the little scene in *Götterdämmerung* in which Gutrune anxiously awaits Siegfried's return from the hunt. The cut caused something approaching a sensation both in the *Festspielhaus* itself and in the newspapers, and in the arguments that followed the merits of the production as a whole received insufficient attention. It was not really surprising: though Wieland had meddled with the scores of *Der Fliegende Holländer*, *Tannhäuser* and *Lohengrin*, he had never before dared in Bayreuth to touch any of the mature works. I asked him why he did it.

"Both Karl Böhm and I," he replied, "felt that this scene
does not really come off. It is not strong enough dramatically
to follow the funeral march: only Hagen's reappearance can
do that properly. After the funeral march it really is immaterial
to hear Gutrune asking Brünnhilde if she is awake and then
discovering that she has gone down to the Rhine. By cutting the
scene we achieve a considerable tightening of the whole act. In
Cologne I cut more things than just that."

There are no doubt many things one can do in Cologne that
one cannot do in Bayreuth, and Wieland was well aware of it.
His elimination of so exposed a scene as this one—the only one
in which Gutrune makes an appearance alone and is given
something extended to sing—was clearly an attempt to find out
where the limits lay. The protests gave him a distinct answer:
nobody in Bayreuth, friends or enemies, would tolerate interference with the master's major scores. If Wagner had erred
with this scene—and nobody was prepared to agree with
Wieland that he had—in Bayreuth he must be allowed to make
his own mistakes.

There was no further opportunity for Wieland to show
whether he was prepared to accept this verdict. The *Ring* was
his last production in Bayreuth. If fate had permitted him, he
would certainly have put in further work on it and maybe
restored the cut, which was done by others after his death.
There was, as he knew, room for improvement. In particular
the production needed more light. As one dimly lit scene
followed another—even the mountain top and the forest scenes
were played at most in a half light—it seemed that Wieland,
feeling his way through fascinating subconscious depths, was
still immersed in the process of discovery and was not yet ready
to communicate his findings to the world outside. When, in the
exhilaration of seeing the end in sight, he conjured up with
lighting alone a vision of the final catastrophe—the finest and
most convincing solution of the *Götterdämmerung* denouement I
have ever seen—the potential glory of this *Ring* production
could be glimpsed, as it already had been in some of the earlier
scenes.

20

THE FINAL YEAR

1966

IN NOVEMBER 1965 Wieland went to Brussels to produce *Fidelio*, a work he had not touched since his production of 1954 in Stuttgart. This time he decided to stay closer to Beethoven's final version of the work. As he told Goléa: "I tried to express the rising line of development which leads from the introductory *Singspiel* to the music drama and finally to the religious oratorio of the conclusion. The musical gradation is absolutely clear. In the original version the work begins, not with the duet between Marzelline and Jacquino, but with Marzelline's solo aria. The duet follows that, and then the trio with Rocco, which is usually cut, but which I restored, and then finally the quartet." This leads naturally to a change of level as Leonore emerges from the disguise of Fidelio. "For Beethoven the dramatist it is only logical to portray small people with their small worries in a different musical style from characters on a higher level. Richard Wagner did exactly the same thing with his Daland music."

This almost total reversal of Wieland's previous thoughts on the work led him back both to the *Fidelio* overture and to spoken dialogue, though not to the original text. In collaboration with his singers he worked out passages of speech which played no dramatic role, but merely served to clarify the stage action and separate the musical numbers.

From Brussels Wieland went straight to Vienna to produce *Salome* with Anja Silja in the title role and *Elektra*. Both were essentially repetitions of his former productions in Stuttgart, though *Elektra* was modified to suit the personality of Birgit Nilsson.

The year 1966 brought him two completely new tasks: productions of Alban Berg's operas *Wozzeck* and *Lulu*. Wieland's interest in contemporary music was minimal and, in consenting to produce Berg's works, he was moved primarily by Anja Silja's eagerness to appear in them. Even then he hesitated. Schäfer, who was as keen to present *Lulu* at Stuttgart as Anja Silja was to sing in it, reveals in his book that Wieland returned the score to him three times before finally agreeing to produce it.

Having yielded, Wieland put aside his doubts and set about mastering his subject. He succeeded so thoroughly that *Lulu*, when it emerged at Stuttgart in February 1966, was instantly acclaimed. No other production of his ever received so undividedly favourable a response.

It was totally unlike anything he had done before. The whole action took place within a circle of bars depicting the circus ring in which, in the prologue, the cast is presented to the audience as a group of performing animals. Within this symbolic prison he presented the ensuing drama realistically, using furniture and costumes of the turn of the century, the period in which Frank Wedekind set the satirical comedy on which the opera is based. In this way Wieland held the balance exactly between the overall moral purpose of the play and its working out in terms of actual human relationships. The amoral Lulu in her decadent *fin-de-siècle* world was raised to the stature of the universal *femme fatale*, yet lost nothing of her unique individuality.

A production of *Der Fliegende Holländer* in Hamburg followed in March, and in April Wieland and Anja Silja went to Frankfurt to rehearse the new production of *Wozzeck*. Of Berg's two operas it was the one with which he felt more intellectual sympathy. He saw its theme as the crushing and debilitating effects of poverty, and sought to reflect this in a stage setting that was in general colourless and bare. Marie's surroundings were in detail realistic: a shabby bed, a rickety table, a cot and even (though probably without Samuel Beckett's symbolic intentions) a dustbin or two. In contrast, the objects associated with the people outside Wozzeck's humble domestic world were oversized and formidable. The seat on which the captain sat to be shaved had the opulence of a throne, while the doctor's examination couch looked like some terrible instrument of torture.

In the characters of Wozzeck and Marie, Wieland discovered a sustaining sense of religion. Wozzeck kills Marie out of a sense of respect for the sanctity of love. "This brings us into the realm of metaphysics," Wieland told Goléa. "With the murder of Marie Wozzeck expresses his reverence for God. Wozzeck is the man of prayer. . . . He and Marie are the only two people in the whole drama who possess anything like a soul. . . . It is possible that Marie could not in any case have avoided her fate. But it seems to me the main feature of her character that she does not want to avoid it, that she allows herself deliberately to be led by fate. While Wozzeck is in some way a positive religious figure, Marie represents the negative side. She is the passive, the compulsive believer."

Wozzeck did not altogether please the critics, but it won wholehearted support from its conductor, Pierre Boulez, who wrote penetratingly of it in the Bayreuth Festival *Parsifal* programme of 1967: "In practice Wieland Wagner handled objects like musical themes. He separated them from their usual daily associations in order to give them a significance which they do not normally have. In just the same way, through isolation, through displacement or illogical context, the most banal of words can assume significance in a poetic setting. The arrangement of objects on the stage turned them into archetypes, gave them force and meaning. Scenic interpretations of this kind correspond exactly to the spirit of Berg's musical forms and Büchner's text, in which realism is used basically as the vehicle for imparting timeless truths."

Their coming together proved fruitful to both. Boulez wrote: "In the short time in which I knew him, I never needed to exchange many words with Wieland Wagner. We always understood one another very swiftly, and words would have seemed superfluous to us both. There are certain personalities whose major quality is a sort of magnetism. As far as I am concerned, they are practically the only people with whom I feel naturally in harmony. My work with Wieland Wagner, short as it was, drew my attention above all to the world of opera, the importance and topicality of which I had not previously been prepared to recognise."

Only one of the future projects they discussed together was to be realised—and that only in part. Hans Knappertsbusch had died in 1965, and Wieland, looking for a conductor to succeed him at Bayreuth in 1966, offered *Parsifal* to Boulez, who accepted. This was to be followed by *Don Giovanni* in Stuttgart and *Pélleas et Mélisande* at Covent Garden in London. But there was not, unhappily, to be time for these.

*

In the spring of 1966 Wieland was elected a member of the order *Pour le mérite*. It was a high honour, which Wieland owed to his friends Carl Orff and Wolfgang Schadewaldt, both existing members of the order. Corresponding fairly closely to the British Order of Merit, it is confined to thirty members distinguished in the arts and sciences, who themselves elect new members to fill vacancies caused by death. Though one of Wieland's ancestors, Liszt, had belonged to it, the members of that time had omitted to award the honour to Richard Wagner, and it was partly to repair this omission, as well as to recognise his own achievements, that Wieland was chosen to fill the vacancy caused by the death of Paul Hindemith. Achievement, as the members of the order understand it, implies more than simply eminence in one's chosen field: it involves in addition a definite contribution to knowledge. Wieland's achievement was to have rehabilitated Wagner after the compromising Hitler years and to have restored recognition of the universality of his genius. It was a tribute to his life's work by his artistic colleagues that Wieland valued deeply, all the more so since it came from an order that in Hitler's years of power had been banned.

*

After a production of *Tristan und Isolde* in Paris and *Salome* in Rome, Wieland returned to Bayreuth to prepare for the festival. As well as making some alterations to his *Ring* production, he planned to work with Boulez on *Parsifal*, about which they had already exchanged several letters. "We were in full agreement," Boulez wrote (*Parsifal* programme, 1967), "concerning the need to 'secularise' the work. By that I do not mean that we intended to reduce its mysteries to the level of a purely Freudian narrative, but it was important, for him as for me, to draw a firm dividing line between theatre and religion. The present confusion, which has lasted a long time, has always led to countless misunderstandings."

Boulez arrived in Bayreuth too late to continue the work in person. During rehearsals of the *Ring*, Wieland developed a temperature and suffered spells of dizziness which he at first attributed to overwork, and ignored. But a partial black-out eventually warned him to seek medical advice. He went to see his old friend Helmut Danzer, who was now in charge of the hospital in Kulmbach.

His examination led Danzer to suspect a tumour in the region of the heart, and he told Wieland that there seemed to be a definite cancerous condition, which might or might not be malignant. Wieland proposed that he should present himself for treatment after the festival, but Danzer felt unable to consent. He insisted that Wieland should remain in hospital under observation.

Reluctantly Wieland agreed. He handed over rehearsals of all his productions in the *Festspielhaus* to his assistant Peter Lehmann and then returned to the hospital in Kulmbach—not however, to rest. His secretary moved into the hospital, and from there, with the help of a telephone, a teleprinter and a tape machine, he kept in constant touch with the *Festspielhaus*, listening to rehearsals recorded on tape and passing his comments and instructions back by the same method.

As a result of their observations the doctors decided to send Wieland to the *Universitätsklinik* in Munich for specialised treatment. From there, the festival past and gone without him, Wieland wrote on 28 August to Wolfgang Windgassen: "May I ask you to convey to all your colleagues in this year's performance of *Götterdämmerung* my kindest regards and my special thanks for their fine efforts in this year's festival? I am very sad that I was not able at least to say goodbye to you all personally, after having been forced to leave you so badly in the lurch this year. In particular I want to thank you yourself. I know how great a part your own example played in ensuring that both rehearsals and performances ran so smoothly and in the traditional spirit of Bayreuth."

Further tests conducted at the *Universitätsklinik* raised doubts whether the seat of the cancer was in the heart or the lung. An operation to remove the tumour was considered inadvisable, and Wieland was given treatment, to which he responded so well that he was released from hospital, though still under medical supervision. He moved into Anja Silja's flat in Munich and there, since she was frequently absent fulfilling singing engagements, he spent most of his time alone, with only a cat for permanent and a daily help for occasional company. Gertrud, with whom his contact at that time was all but completely severed, was in Greece. Nobody, apart from the doctors, was aware of the real seriousness of his condition.

In the early autumn Wieland went to the Baltic coast for a short holiday with Anja Silja. It was his last taste of normal life. In October he re-entered the *Universitätsklinik* in Munich. Further tests revealed that the cancer had invaded both lungs.

Gertrud, who had in the meantime returned from Greece, was summoned from Sylt. Anja Silja was in Vienna, rehearsing *The Tales of Hoffmann*. On 16 October, just before the première, Wieland asked Danzer to telephone her to wish her luck and to tell her that he was progressing well.

It was not true, as he himself now knew, and at last he consented to see Gertrud. Though he could scarcely speak, they spent a little while discussing plans of doing a new production of *Tannhäuser* together. Shortly afterwards he lost consciousness, and in the early hours of Monday, 17 October 1966, he died.

The funeral took place in Bayreuth on the following Friday. It began with an official ceremony in the *Festspielhaus*, before which—as throughout Bayreuth—flags flew at half-mast. The coffin was placed in the centre of the stage. The festival orchestra, conducted by Pierre Boulez, played the Prelude to *Parsifal* and the festival chorus, directed by Wilhelm Pitz, sung the concluding chorus from Bach's *St Matthew Passion*. There were speeches by representatives of the Federal Government, the Bavarian Government and the town of Bayreuth, but also by colleagues who had been closer to Wieland, among them Walter Erich Schäfer, Ernst Bloch, Carl Orff and Wolfgang Windgassen.

The burial was private. Only the family and close personal friends were present in the town cemetery when the coffin was placed beside that of Siegfried Wagner in the family grave.

21

CONCLUSION

BEFORE HIS DEATH Wieland had accepted a number of production engagements. *Salome* in Geneva and *Der Fliegende Holländer* in Vienna were taken over by Gertrud; *Der Fliegende Holländer* in Brussels and *Elektra* in Holland by his Bayreuth assistant Renate Ebermann; and *Lohengrin* at the Metropolitan, New York, by his Bayreuth assistant Peter Lehmann. Lehmann was also appointed by Wolfgang Wagner, who now took over sole charge of the Bayreuth Festival, to look after Wieland's productions of *Parsifal* and *Tristan und Isolde*, which continued to be presented in the *Festspielhaus* after his death. The responsibility for Wieland's *Ring* production was given to Hans Hotter.

None of the new productions proved a striking success, and the existing productions at Bayreuth gradually began to lose something of their effectiveness. In no case could the producers who took them over be held to blame. They were simply acting as caretakers. It was not skill that was lacking, but the living touch of the man who had conceived the productions.

The "new Bayreuth style" that Wieland had created was an undoubted fact, and its impact was to be seen, and will certainly continue to be seen, in opera productions throughout the world. But its essence does not lie in its outward forms. The source of Wieland's inspiration lay deeeper within himself.

In an afterword to Victor Gollancz's book *The Ring at Bayreuth*, written in 1966, Wieland came nearest to defining the basis of his outlook: "My generation was taught not to take youthful impressions, from whatever source they come, on trust, but to regard them with a certain degree of scepticism. And this sceptical attitude young people have retained in their thinking ever since. However, it would be unjust to condemn us, the so-called sceptical generation, as simply destructive.

We have seen and experienced things that our fathers and grandfathers were powerless to prevent: acts of destruction which go far beyond human imagining. If one wants to build a new house, one must first dig up the ground in which the foundations are to be laid. My generation has been, and still is concerned not to luxuriate in aesthetic conceptions as if these were defined immutably for all time, but to seek out the inner laws inherent in a work of genius and to interpret it uncompromisingly, as we find it mirrored in our own souls. It seems to me characteristic of the generation to which I belong that no one has yet found a name for its artistic tendencies. That is because its very scepticism demands that it should keep clear of fixed ideas."

Though Wieland chose in this passage to speak of "my generation", it is quite clear that he was speaking more particularly of himself. The representative role was one that was forced on him by circumstances rather than deliberately sought. Fundamentally he was an individualist. There were undoubtedly occasions on which he was consciously provocative, both in his productions and in his replies to criticisms of them: certain aspects of his treatment of *Die Meistersinger* and his first production of *Fidelio*, for example, can be seen as deliberate attempts to shock. That was the negative side of his scepticism, and its artistic value was ephemeral. But there was a positive side which was of much greater importance.

Wieland's horror of the "cliché", as he liked in conversation to describe fixed ideas, was obsessional, and it was directed as much against his own as against those of others. This was the reason why he was constantly seeking new approaches to works which he had already handled successfully, or changing details in current productions. Though his production of *Parsifal*, for instance, was presented yearly at the Bayreuth Festival from 1951 up to his death (and beyond), it never looked exactly the same in two consecutive years. Its final form differed so extensively from its earliest that one could justifiably have considered it a new production. "Successful things," Wieland told Panofsky, "cannot be done better: they can only be done again in a different way. Once a style has been fully developed, it beings to ossify."

Wieland's criticism of Cosima, as he once told me, was not

that she had evolved a "Bayreuth style", but that she insisted on proclaiming it as definitive. His own upbringing in Wahnfried, within its suffocating atmosphere, would have provided incentive enough to rebel against it in later years, but it is not sufficient to explain the explosive nature of his rebellion. There were complicating factors, one of the most significant being that in his youthful years he himself—partly out of ignorance, partly out of a sense of frustration in his relations with his mother and Heinz Tietjen—had been a traditionalist.

This might have provided one reason for self-disgust, and consequently for change. But there was also a much deeper cause, arising out of his relationship with Hitler. The sentence in his afterword to Gollancz's book—"My generation was taught not to take youthful impressions, from whatever source they come, on trust"—is a striking understatement of the effect on his own mind of the discovery that the man whom he had regarded affectionately as a child and from whom he had parted on friendly terms only a few months before the final reckoning, had been responsible for "acts of destruction which go far beyond human imagining". It was this discovery, I think, that turned Wieland's scepticism from a negative to a positive force.

To seek to explain an artist's work by reference to his life might seem a questionable process, yet Wieland himself acknowledged its validity when he spoke of the concern of "my generation" to interpret a work of genius uncompromisingly, "as we find it mirrored in our own souls". In other words, he considered the subjective approach the right one. It was certainly an important element in his own view of his grandfather. "The life and work of an artist form an organic unity", he told Panofsky. "One must not, even in Wagner's case, say yes to his works and no to his life, as seems to be the fashion today. . . .

"He was, as far as I know, the first composer ever to issue programmes and proclamations in his own and in foreign languages. His tremendous urge to communicate his ideas is still regarded as a flaw in his character. His essay on Jews in music, to mention only the darkest chapter in his writings, cannot be justified morally or ethically even from a historical standpoint, but it can be understood as part of Wagner's tendency to attack everything that seemed to him to stand in the way of his work—whether Protestant, Catholic, Saxon, Bavarian, French, Italian or (in this case) Jewish. . . . We can lay his political and philosophical writings aside with an easy conscience. Most of them he wrote during artistically unfruitful periods, and perhaps one should simply regard them as self-communications which opened the way to new artistic deeds."

Wagner offended against public opinion, Wieland went on, by refusing to conform to the popular idea of an artist as a suffering martyr. "All the trouble he caused, all the dressing gowns, all the strong-smelling perfumes and so on would have been ignored, even his demand for a theatre of his own would have been forgiven if he had not been tough enough actually to get his house built against all opposition. . . . One does not as a living person put oneself on the same level as Aeschylus." Wagner did certainly do things to keep up the reputation he had earned as a disturber of the peace. "Think for instance of his sudden infatuation for Gobineau and his dubious racial theories, which started the rot in Wahnfried. . . .

"All the same, it was not so much the person as the work that caused all the annoyance." Wagner appealed to the irrational forces in man. "His is a wild, undomesticated type of theatre, the very opposite of Richard Strauss. He is close in form to Bertolt Brecht, though not in effect. . . . Unlike Brecht, he does not appeal to the intellect, but exclusively to the emotions. . . . Wagner opened up a new and higher dimension in the theatre. He invokes, not the world of make-believe, but the dream image, the subconscious—visually and, above all, musically. . . . Who besides Wagner has ever written music that can persuade an audience to accept without demur as tragic necessities such things as incest, adultery and filicide, to take only three examples from *Die Walküre*? Must not an artist who can achieve such unheard-of things appear suspect in the eyes above all of intellectuals, to whom everything irrational, everything uncontrollable is of its very nature an abomination?"

One cannot pretend that this is very clearly or very logically argued, but it is worth considering both for the light it throws on Wieland's attitude towards his grandfather and his works, and for what it reveals about himself. Obviously what he admired in Richard Wagner and sought to emulate was his individuality, his toughnesss, the vast range of his exploratory spirit and his refusal to accept anything as proved beyond dispute. The attempts of his family and their Bayreuth devotees to confine his speculative, even contradictory genius in one single mould was a betrayal, a reprehensible attempt to yoke a soaring Pegasus to a respectable domestic plough.

"The ideas in Wagner's work," Wieland once wrote, "are valid for all time, because they are eternally human. . . . In realising Wagner's archetypal theatre on a contemporary stage, one must replace the production ideas of a century ago, now grown sterile, by a creative intellectual approach which goes back to the origins of the work itself. Starting from this basic core, the producer must constantly seek new forms for the work by deciphering the codes and hieroglyphs which Wagner bequeathed in his scores to future generations. Every new production is a step on the way to an unknown goal."

These words form the conclusion of Wieland's essay *Denkmalschutz für Wagner?* (Ancient Monument Status for Wagner?) in a paperback entitled *Richard Wagner und das neue Bayreuth*. The book originated in 1962 in an invitation to Wieland to write about the "new" Bayreuth. Time considerations as well as a lack of interest in writing at great length induced Wieland to offer in place of a book of his own a selection of essays by various writers. He chose them from the festival programmes, over the form and content of which he maintained from 1951 to his death a strict direct control. The book reflects the remarkable extension in Wagnerian scholarship that had taken place in the wake of the grandsons' revolution. A number of the contributors were men who, however distinguished in other fields had not previously concerned themselves much with Wagner—among them the philosopher Ernst Bloch, the psychologist Theodor Adorno, the classicist Wolfgang Schadewaldt and the musicologist Hans Mayer. New Wagner specialists of a younger generation, such as Curt von Westernhagen, Walter Panofsky and Siegfried Melchinger also put in an appearance.

It was evidence not only of the fresh wind now blowing in Bayreuth, but also of the fructifying effect which Wieland's productions were exercising on the minds of men (among them a high proportion of Jews) whose appreciation of Wagner had hitherto been stifled by the accumulated prejudices of earlier times. The light these men were then enabled to throw on Wagner's works helped in turn to inspire Wieland to new insights. In his eager search for knowledge there was much he could learn from Adorno, for instance, in the field of psychology. Bloch's researches into Wagner's use of the *Leitmotive* opened up to him new production possibilities. Schadewaldt, with his profound knowledge of the classical era, was able to point out to Wieland significant connections between Wagner's work and the works of Ancient Greece. Both with Bloch and with Schadewaldt he was soon on terms of personal friendship.

It was friendship in Wieland's sense, containing no element of companionship. He was interested in people, not for what they were, but for what they could give him. As Hans Mayer put it in an obituary tribute (Bayreuth Festival *Tannhäuser* programme 1967): "This modern man and insatiably inquisitive artist was bewitchingly adept in the art of listening. In whatever he read or heard he would take note of things that struck his attention. Then he would seize on them or use them as a starting-point for new voyages of discovery. . . .

"When my little book on Wagner appeared (*Richard Wagner in Selbstzeugnissen und Bilddokumenten*), he wrote me a letter. For the first time I saw that rolling, wave-like signature which looked as if it had been conducted by Herbert von Karajan. . . . It was the beginning of a relationship which for me was highly productive. . . . Complete harmony was admittedly never possible. It could not have been achieved, for harmony—even inside himself—was not Wieland Wagner's particular strength. It was part of his insatiable curiosity that he was always trying to see (Wagner's) works from new angles. He lived in a permanent and productive state of contradiction, not least within himself. In talking with him one often felt oneself being forced into the role of a conservative dogmatician, trying to restrain Wieland from wantonly destroying, in his lust for new objective effects, previous obviously valid achievements. He was as polite as he was cunning. He would listen very carefully, would even admit that one was right, but it was all without any guarantee."

Anyone who had anything to do with Wieland will acknowledge the truth of this impression. What Mayer called his "insatiable curiosity" lay behind his disconcerting tendency to seize on any idea thrown up in conversation and to put it through a sort of rapid editorial process in his mind, presenting it back again in his own way, so that one could never be quite sure what was speculation and what was considered opinion. It was a characteristic which, in weaker characters, might have been considered simply evasiveness, but in Wieland it was an aspect of what I mean by his positive scepticism. Any idea that was new to him was worth pursuing to its conclusion in order to test its possible validity. And his method of doing this was to visualise the idea in action. It might in the end prove unworthy or fail to fit in with other parts of the overall conception, but at the moment of consideration it would be given all the force of fact in his mind.

This speculative quality was so integral a part of his work that any attempt to define in exact terms for the benefit of students the revolutionary nature of his ideas on opera production becomes a sheer impossibility. One can note the various technical devices: the bare stage, the ordered movement, the uniformity and relevance of costume, the fluid use of lighting. One can point to the theory of "illuminated space", the archetypal conceptions, the psychological probings as significant aspects. Entering higher regions, one can profitably think about Ernst Bloch's statement in the *Parsifal* programme of 1967: "Quite unlike C. G. Jung, who was the archaic first stimulator of the new style of production, Wieland introduced an element of Not-Yet, of something fermenting, which fitted Wagner's music absolutely in so far as the *Leitmotive* too not only reminds us of what was, but also anticipates in a mysterious and hidden manner what no one yet knows, what is still coming, generating a complex, inter-related time-structure, with advance intimation of a melos which will not be established until much later."

All this is instructive and valuable, but it does not let us fully into the secret. That lies—undiscoverable—in what Wieland called, in a passage already quoted, "a creative intellectual approach which goes back to the origins of the work itself". Creative, by its very nature, implies individual. Wieland's productions—and none more so than his final *Ring* of 1965, with its deep searchings into the subconscious impulses of good and evil—might be seen (to use the phrase of Goethe which Wieland applied to the works of his grandfather) as "fragments of a grand confession"—the confession of a relentlessly introspective character struggling with the implications of his uneasy heritage.

APPENDICES

STAGE SETTINGS AND PRODUCTIONS
BY WIELAND WAGNER

(All stage settings by Wieland Wagner unless otherwise stated.) (Artists shown in brackets took part in performances of the work at the Bayreuth Festival in years following the first production.)

1936
February   *Der Bärenhäuter* (Siegfried Wagner)
LÜBECK   (Scenic designs only)

1937
July   *Parsifal* (Sets only)
BAYREUTH
December   *Schwarzschwanenreich* (Siegfried Wagner)
ANTWERP   (Sets only)

1938
March   *Der Bärenhäuter* (Siegfried Wagner)
COLOGNE   (Sets only)
April   *Sonnenflammen* (Siegfried Wagner)
DÜSSELDORF   (Sets only)

1942
November   *Der Fliegende Holländer*
NUREMBERG   (Sets only)

1943
June   *Die Walküre.* Siegmund: Hendrik Drost.
NUREMBERG   Sieglinde: Eva Hadrabova. Hunding: Otto
               von Rohr. Wotan: John Neergaard.
               Fricka: Grete Pense. Brünnhilde: Ilse Schü-
               ler. Conductor: Alfons Dressel.

July BAYREUTH	*Die Meistersinger* (Sets only)
August NUREMBERG	*Siegfried.* Siegfried: Drost. Mime: Paul Kuën. Wanderer: Neergaard. Alberich: Anton Gruber-Bauer Erda: Pense. Brünnhilde: Elly Doerer. Conductor: Dressel.
September ALTENBURG	*Die Walküre.* Siegmund: Kilian Danner. Sieglinde: Margarete Katz. Hunding: Willy Buhlmann. Wotan: Wolfgang Emil Ritz. Fricka: Helene Oertel. Brünnhilde: Margarete Bäumer. Conductor: Kurt Overhoff.
October ALTENBURG	*Der Freischütz* (Weber). Scenery: Henriette von Schepke. Agathe: Hilma Weiland. Ännchen: Henny Wiemann. Max: Danner. Kaspar: Kurt Jüttner. Conductor: Overhoff.
December ALTENBURG	*Götterdämmerung.* Brünnhilde: Helena Braun. Siegfried: Danner. Hagen: Ferdinand Frantz. Gunther: Ritz. Gutrune: Gertrud Sikorski. Alberich: Buhlmann. Waltraute: Oertel. Conductor: Overhoff.

1944 January ALTENBURG	*Siegfried.* Siegfried: Gotthelf Pistor. Mime: Kuën. Wanderer: Ritz. Alberich: Jüttner. Erda: Oertel. Brünnhilde: Katz. Conductor: Overhoff.
April NUREMBERG	*Götterdämmerung.* Brünnhilde: Schüler. Siegfried: Drost. Hagen: Max Kohl. Gunther: Alexander Fenyves. Gutrune: Erna Balasus. Alberich: Gruber-Bauer. Waltraute: Pense. Conductor: Dressel.
May ALTENBURG	*Rheingold.* Wotan: Ritz. Fricka: Oertel. Loge: Danner. Alberich: Jüttner. Mime: Willy Fröhlich. Fasolt: Friedrich Dalberg. Fafner: Buhlmann. Erda: Margarete Grasnickel. Conductor: Overhoff.
June ALTENBURG	*An allem ist Hütchen schuld* (Siegfried Wagner). Ensemble of Altenburger Landestheater. Conductor: Overhoff.

1951
July   *Parsifal.* Amfortas: George London (Hans
BAYREUTH   Hotter, Dietrich Fischer-Dieskau, Eberhard
            Wächter, Thomas Stewart, Theo Adam).
            Gurnemanz: Ludwig Weber (Josef Greindl,
            Jerome Hines). Parsifal: Wolfgang Wind-
            gassen (Ramon Vinay, Hans Beirer, Jess
            Thomas, Jon Vickers, Sándor Kónya, Hans
            Hopf). Kundry: Martha Mödl (Astrid Var-
            nay, Régine Crespin, Irene Dalis, Barbro
            Ericson). Klingsor: Hermann Uhde (Kurt
            Böhme, Gustav Neidlinger, Toni Blanken-
            heim). Choreography: Gertrud Wagner.
            Conductor: Hans Knappertsbusch (Clemens
            Krauss, André Cluytens, Pierre Boulez).
July   *Der Ring des Nibelungen.* Wotan: Sigurd Björ-
BAYREUTH   ling (Hotter, Uhde). Fricka: Elisabeth
            Höngen, Hanna Ludwig, Ira Malaniuk (Rut
            Siewert, Georgine von Milinkovic, Rita
            Gorr). Loge: Walter Fritz (Erich Witte,
            Rudolf Lustig, Ludwig Suthaus, Fritz Uhl).
            Alberich: Heinrich Pflanzl (Neidlinger, Frans
            Andersson). Mime: Kuën (Gerhard Stolze).
            Fasolt: Weber (Adam, Greindl, Arnold van
            Mill). Fafner: Dalberg (Böhme, Greindl,
            van Mill). Erda: Siewert (Melanie Bugari-
            novic, Maria von Ilosvay, Jean Madeira).
            Siegmund: Günther Treptow (Vinay, Max
            Lorenz, Windgassen, Suthaus, Vickers). Hun-
            ding: van Mill (Greindl). Sieglinde: Leonie
            Rysanek (Inge Borkh, Regina Resnik, Mödl,
            Varnay, Gré Brouwenstijn, Birgit Nilsson).
            Brünnhilde: Varnay (Mödl). Siegfried: Bernd
            Aldenhoff (Lorenz, Windgassen). Gunther:
            Uhde (Hotter, Otto Wiener). Gutrune:
            Mödl (Natalie Hinsch-Gröndahl, Varnay,
            Brouwenstijn, Elisabeth Grümmer). Wal-
            traute: Höngen, Siewert (Malaniuk, Ilosvay,
            Madeira). Conductor: Herbert von Karajan,
            Knappertsbusch (Joseph Keilberth, Krauss).

1952
July   *Tristan und Isolde.* Tristan: Vinay. Isolde:
BAYREUTH   Mödl, Varnay. Marke: Weber. Kurwenal:
                Hotter, Neidlinger. Brangäne: Malaniuk.
                Conductor: Karajan (Eugen Jochum).

1953
March   *Orfeo ed Euridice* (Gluck). Orfeo: Malaniuk.
MUNICH   Euridice: Annelies Kupper. Amor: Antonie
                Fahberg. Conductor: Knappertsbusch.

1954
July   *Tannhäuser.* Landgraf: Greindl. Tannhäuser:
BAYREUTH   Vinay (Wolfgassen). Wolfram: Fischer-Dies-
                kau. Elisabeth: Brouwenstijn. Venus: Her-
                ta Wilfert. Choreography: Gertrud Wagner.
                Conductor: Jochum, Keilberth (Cluytens).
November   *Fidelio* (Beethoven). Leonore: Brouwenstijn.
STUTTGART   Florestan: Windgassen. Marzelline: Lore
                Wissmann. Jacquino: Alfred Pfeifle. Rocco:
                von Rohr. Pizarro: Neidlinger. Fernando:
                Wilhelm Schirp. Conductor: Ferdinand
                Leitner.
                (This production was presented at the Royal
                Festival Hall, London, in September 1955.)

1955
November   *Rheingold.* Wotan: Schirp. Fricka: Grace
STUTTGART   Hoffman. Loge: Windgassen. Alberich:
                Neidlinger. Mime: Pfeifle. Fasolt: von Rohr.
                Fafner: Walter Hagner. Erda: Res Fischer.
                Conductor: Leitner.
December   *Orfeo ed Euridice* (Gluck). Orfeo: Fischer.
STUTTGART   Euridice: Wissman. Amor: Ellinor Junker-
                Giesen. Conductor: Leitner.

1956
March   *Antigonae* (Carl Orff). Antigonae: Mödl.
STUTTGART   Ismene: Hetty Plümacher. Kreon: Uhde.
                Tiresias: Josef Traxel. Eurydice: Hoffman.
                Conductor: Leitner.
July   *Die Meistersinger*. Sachs: Hotter, Neidlinger
BAYREUTH   (Wiener, Greindl). Stolzing: Windgassen
                (Walter Geisler, Traxel, Rudolf Schock, Hans
                Hopf). Pogner: Greindl (Gottlob Frick,
                Hotter, Adam). Eva: Brouwenstijn, Wiss-
                mann (Grümmer, Sena Jurinac). Beck-
                messer: Karl Schmitt-Walter, Blankenheim.
                David: Stolze. Magdalene: Milinkovic
                (Elisabeth Schärtel). Kothner: Fischer-Dies-
                kau, Kurt Rehm (Blankenheim, Wächter,
                Weber). Conductor: Cluytens (Erich Leins-
                dorf, Knappertsbusch, Josef Krips).
October   *Götterdämmerung*. Brünnhilde: Mödl. Siegfried:
STUTTGART   Windgassen. Hagen: von Rohr. Gunther:
                Alfons Herwig. Gutrune: Wissmann. Alber-
                ich: Blankenheim. Waltraute: Hoffman.
                Conductor: Leitner.
November   *Siegfried*. Siegfried: Windgassen. Mime:
STUTTGART   Pfeifle. Wanderer: Neidlinger. Alberich:
                Blankenheim. Erda: Margarethe Bence.
                Brünnhilde: Mödl. Conductor: Leitner.

1957
March   *Die Walküre*. Siegmund: Windgassen. Sieg-
STUTTGART   linde: Rysanek. Hunding: von Rohr. Wotan:
                Neidlinger. Fricka: Hoffman. Brünnhilde:
                Mödl. Conductor: Leitner.
April   *Comoedia de Christi Resurrectione* (Carl Orff).
STUTTGART   World première. Der Teufel: Ernst Gins-
                berg. Singers: Liselotte Rebmann, Sieglinde
                Kahmann, Hans Günter Nöcker. Conductor:
                Heinz Mende.
November   *Rienzi*. Rienzi: Windgassen. Irene: Paula
STUTTGART   Brivkalne. Steffano Colonna: Neidlinger.
                Adriano: Traxel. Paolo Orsini: Nöcker.

Raimondo: von Rohr. Conductor: Lovro von Matacic.

December
HAMBURG

Lohengrin. Lohengrin: Arturo Sergi. Elsa: Grümmer. König Heinrich: van Mill. Telramund: Caspar Broecheler. Ortrud: Helene Werth. Heerrufer: Vladimir Ruzdak. Conductor: Heinz Tietjen. (This production was presented at the Sadler's Wells Theatre, London, in Sept. 1962)

1958
May
STUTTGART

Tristan und Isolde. Tristan: Windgassen. Isolde: Mödl. Marke: von Rohr. Kurwenal: Neidlinger. Brangäne: Hoffman. Conductor: Leitner.

July
BAYREUTH

Lohengrin. Lohengrin: Kónya (Jess Thomas, Windgassen). Elsa: Rysanek (Grümmer, Kupper, Aase Nordmo-Loevberg, Anja Silja). König Heinrich: Kieth Engen (Greindl, Adam, Franz Crass). Telramund: Ernest Blanc (Neidlinger, Vinay). Ortrud: Varnay (Gorr, Dalis). Heerrufer: Erik Saeden, Wächter (Donald Bell, Tom Krause). Conductor: Cluytens (Tietjen, von Matacic, Leitner, Lorin Maazel, Wolfgang Sawallisch).

December
HAMBURG

Carmen (Bizet). Carmen: Kerstin Meyer. Don José: Schock. Micaela: Melitta Muszely. Escamillo: Richard Collett. Choreography: Gertrud Wagner. Conductor: Sawallisch.

1959
February
HAMBURG

Tannhäuser. Landgraf: Greindl. Tannhäuser: Beirer. Wolfram: Hermann Prey. Elisabeth: Grümmer. Venus: Siw Ericsdotter. Choreography: Gertrud Wagner. Conductor: Leopold Ludwig.

June
HOLLAND
FESTIVAL

Tristan und Isolde. Tristan: Vinay. Isolde: Mödl. Marke: Greindl. Kurwenal: Neidlinger. Brangäne: Malaniuk. Conductor: Leitner.

July
BAYREUTH

Der Fliegende Holländer. Holländer: London, Wiener (Crass, Stewart, Hotter). Senta: Rysanek (Silja). Daland: Greindl. Erik: Uhl (Windgassen, William Olvis, Niels Möller). Conductor: Sawallisch (Otmar Suitner).

November
BERLIN

Tristan und Isolde. Tristan: Beirer. Isolde: Mödl. Marke: Greindl. Kurwenal: Tomislav Neralic. Brangäne: Kerstin Meyer. Conductor: Karl Böhm.

1960
January
HAMBURG

Tristan und Isolde. Tristan: Beirer. Isolde: Mödl. Marke: Greindl. Kurwenal: Herbert Fliether. Brangäne: Mimi Aarden. Conductor: Ludwig.

March
STUTTGART

Lohengrin. Lohengrin: Windgassen. Elsa: Ericsdotter. König Heinrich: von Rohr. Telramund: Neidlinger. Ortrud: Varnay. Heerrufer: Raymond Wolansky. Conductor: Leitner.

1961
February
STUTTGART

Der Fliegende Holländer. Holländer: Neidlinger. Senta: Silja. Daland: Fritz Linke. Erik: Eugene Tobin. Conductor: Janos Kulka.

March
COPENHAGEN

Der Fliegende Holländer. Holländer: Andersson. Senta: Anne Lund Christiansen. Daland: Mogens Wedel. Erik: Möller. Conductor: John Frandsen.

July
BAYREUTH

Tannhäuser (second production). Landgraf: Greindl (Martti Talvela). Tannhäuser: Windgassen, Beirer (Hopf, Thomas). Wolfram: Fischer-Dieskau, Wächter (Crass, Prey, Stewart). Elisabeth: Victoria de los Angeles (Rysanek, Brouwenstijn, Silja). Venus: Grace Bumbry (Ericson, Ludmilla Dvorakova, Silja). Choreography: Maurice Béjart (Gertrud Wagner, Birgit Cullberg).

	Conductor: Sawallisch (Suitner, Cluytens, Carl Melles).
September BERLIN	*Aida* (Verdi). Aida: Gloria Davy. Amneris: Christa Ludwig. Radames: Thomas. Amonasro: Walter Berry. Ramphis: Greindl. Conductor: Böhm.
December BERLIN	*Lohengrin.* Lohengrin: Thomas. Elsa: Silja. König Heinrich: Greindl. Telramund: Uhde. Ortrud: Ludwig. Heerrufer: Stewart. Conductor: Heinrich Hollreiser.

1962

January STUTTGART	*Elektra* (R. Strauss). Elektra: Mödl. Chrysothemis: Hildegard Hillebrecht. Klytämnestra: Resnik. Ägisth: Traxel. Orest: Nöcker. Conductor: Leitner.
February STUTTGART	*Salome* (R. Strauss). Salome: Silja. Herodes: Stolze. Herodias: Hoffman. Jochanaan: Carlos Alexander. Narraboth: Thomas. Conductor: Leitner.
March BRUSSELS	*Tristan und Isolde.* Tristan: Windgassen. Isolde: Silja. Marke: Crass. Kurwenal: Neidlinger. Brangäne: Herta Töpper. Conductor: André Vandernoot.
May COLOGNE	*Rheingold.* Wotan: London. Fricka: Schärtel. Loge: Herbert Schachtschneider. Alberich: Zoltan Kelemen. Mime: Erwin Wohlfahrt. Fasolt: Gerd Nienstedt. Fafner: Heiner Horn. Erda: Helen Raab. Conductor: Sawallisch.
July BAYREUTH	*Tristan und Isolde (Second production).* Tristan: Windgassen. Isolde: Nilsson, Mödl (Varnay). Marke: Greindl (Hotter, Talvela). Kurwenal: Wächter (Neidlinger). Brangäne: Meyer (Ludwig, Hoffman). Conductor: Böhm.
October STUTTGART	*Tannhäuser.* Landgraf: von Rohr. Tannhäuser: Windgassen. Wolfram: Alexander. Elisabeth: Jurinac. Venus: Ericsdotter.

Choreography: John Cranko. Conductor: Leitner.

December
BERLIN
Salome (R. Strauss). Salome: Silja. Herodes: Stolze. Herodias: Varnay. Jochanaan: William Dooley. Narraboth: Donald Grobe. Conductor: Bruno Maderna.

December
BERLIN
Die Meistersinger. Sachs: Greindl. Stolzing: Beirer. Pogner: Walter Kreppel. Eva: Pilar Lorengar. Beckmesser: Schmitt-Walter. David: Donald Grobe. Magdalena: Sieglinde Wagner. Kothner: Gerd Feldhoff. Choreography: Erwin Bredow. Conductor: Hollreiser.

1963
January
GENEVA
Tristan und Isolde. Tristan: Windgassen. Isolde: Silja. Marke: Hotter. Kurwenal: Neidlinger. Brangäne: Sona Cervena. Conductor: Alberto Erede.

January
BRUSSELS
Salome (R. Strauss). Salome: Silja. Herodes: Stolze. Herodias: Hoffman. Jochanaan: Alexander. Narraboth: David Thaw. Conductor: Vandernoot.

April
COLOGNE
Die Walküre. Siegmund: Richard Martell. Sieglinde: Hillebrecht. Hunding: Nienstedt. Wotan: London. Fricka: Schärtel. Brünnhilde: Silja. Conductor: Sawallisch.

April
NAPLES
Die Walküre. Siegmund: Windgassen. Sieglinde: Brouwenstijn. Wotan: Hotter. Fricka: Resnik. Brünnhilde: Silja. Conductor: von Matacic.

July
BAYREUTH
Die Meistersinger (*Second production*). Sachs: Wiener, Greindl. Stolzing: Thomas, Windgassen (Kónya). Pogner: Böhme, Adam. Eva: Silja. Beckmesser: Alexander. David: Wohlfahrt. Magdalene: Ruth Hesse. Kothner: Neidlinger. Choreography: Gertrud Wagner. Conductor: Thomas Schippers (Böhm, Robert Heger).

September   *Tannhäuser.* Tannhäuser: Möller. Wolfram: Ib
COPENHAGEN   Hansen. Venus/Elisabeth: Silja. Choreo-
               graphy: Cullberg. Conductor: Frandsen.
October   *Siegfried.* Siegfried: Windgassen. Mime: Wohl-
COLOGNE   fahrt. Wanderer: London. Alberich: Kele-
               men. Erda: Schärtel. Brünnhilde: Silja.
               Conductor: Sawallisch.
November   *Götterdämmerung.* Brünnhilde: Varnay. Sieg-
COLOGNE   fried: Windgassen. Hagen: Nienstedt. Gun-
               ther: Alexander. Gutrune: Isabel Strauss.
               Alberich: Kelemen. Waltraute: Schärtel.
               Conductor: Sawallisch.

1964
October   *Salome* (R. Strauss). Salome: Silja. Herodes:
PARIS   Stolze. Herodias: Varnay. Jochanaan: Stew-
               art. Narraboth: Hermann Winkler. Con-
               ductor: Cluytens.
November   *Elektra* (R. Strauss). Elektra: Silja. Chrysothe-
BRUSSELS   mis: Brouwenstijn. Klytämnestra: Madeira.
               Ägisth: Möller. Orest: Nienstedt. Conduc-
               tor: Vandernoot.
December   *Tristan und Isolde.* Tristan: Windgassen. Isolde:
MILAN   Nilsson. Marke: Crass. Kurwenal: Neid-
               linger. Brangäne: Gort. Conductor: Maazel.

1965
January   *Tristan und Isolde.* Tristan: Beirer. Isolde:
ROME   Silja. Marke: Talvela. Kurwenal: Neid-
               linger. Brangäne: Meyer. Conductor: Cluy-
               tens.
March   *Otello* (Verdi). Otello: Windgassen. Desde-
FRANKFURT   mona: Silja. Iago: Stewart. Cassio: Hermin
               Esser. Lodovico: Crass. Emilia: Rosl Zapf.
               Conductor: Cluytens.
May   *Der Fliegende Holländer.* Holländer: Crass,
GENEVA   Neidlinger. Senta: Silja. Daland: Greindl.
               Erik: Windgassen. Conductor: Georges Seb-
               astian.

May *Lohengrin.* Lohengrin: Thomas. Elsa: Claire
VIENNA Watson. König Heinrich: Talvela. Telra-
mund: Berry. Ortrud: Ludwig. Heerrufer:
Wächter. Conductor: Böhm.

July *Der Ring des Nibelungen (Second production).* Wotan:
BAYREUTH Adam (Hotter). Fricka: Ursula Boese (Anne-
lies Burmeister). Loge: Windgassen. Albe-
rich: Neidlinger. Mime: Wohlfahrt. Fasolt:
Talvela (Greindl). Fafner: Böhme. Freia:
Silja. Erda: Lili Chookasian (Vera Souku-
pova). Siegmund: James King (Claude
Heater, Ticho Parly). Sieglinde: Rysanek
(Gwyneth Jones). Hunding: Talvela
(Greindl). Brünnhilde: Nilsson (Dvorakova,
Varnay). Siegfried: Windgassen. Wanderer:
Greindl. Gunther: Stewart. Gutrune: Dvor-
akova. Hagen: Greindl. Waltraute: Meyer
(Mödl). Conductor: Böhm (Suitner).

October *Fidelio* (Beethoven). Leonore: Silja. Florestan:
BRUSSELS Ernst Kozub, Möller. Marzelline: Rita
Bartos, Ghislaine Morèze. Jacquino: Willy
Hartmann. Rocco: Nienstedt. Pizarro:
Neidlinger. Fernando: Adam, Eduard Wol-
litz. Conductor: Vandernoot.

November *Salome* (R. Strauss). Salome: Silja. Herodes:
VIENNA Stolze. Herodias: Varnay. Jochanaan:
Wächter. Narraboth: Fritz Wunderlich.
Conductor: Zdenek Kosler.

December *Elektra* (R. Strauss). Elektra: Nilsson. Chryso-
VIENNA themis: Rysanek. Klytämnestra: Resnik.
Ägisth: Windgassen. Orest: Wächter. Con-
ductor: Böhm.

1966
February *Lulu* (Alban Berg). Lulu: Silja. Dr Schön:
STUTTGART Alexander. Alwa: Richard Holm. Gräfin
Geschwitz: Cervena. Der Maler: James
Harper. Schigolch: Willy Ferenz. Rodrigo:
William Wildermann. Dr Goll: Engelbert
Czubok. Der Prinz: Stefan Schwer. Der

Theaterdirektor: Heinz Cramer. Ein Tier-
bändiger/Jack the Ripper: Rudolf Knoll.
Conductor: Leitner.
(This production was presented at the Edinburgh Festival of 1966.)

February
PARIS

Tristan und Isolde. Tristan: Windgassen. Isolde:
Nilsson. Marke: Hotter. Kurwenal: Neidlinger. Brangäne: Gorr. Conductor: Sebas-
tian.

March
HAMBURG

Der Fliegende Holländer. Holländer: Adam.
Senta: Silja. Daland: van Mill. Erik:
Ragnar Ulfung. Conductor: Ludwig.

April
FRANKFURT

Wozzeck (Alban Berg). Wozzeck: Nienstedt.
Marie: Silja. Hauptmann: Helmut Mel-
chert. Tambourmajor: Charles O'Neill.
Doktor: Georg Stern. Margaret: Cervena.
Andres: Esser. Conductor: Boulez.

May
ROME

Salome (R. Strauss). Salome: Silja. Herodes:
Möller. Herodias: Varnay. Jochanaan:
Nienstedt. Narraboth: Winkler. Conduc-
tor: Bruno Bartoletti.

BIBLIOGRAPHY

GOLÉA, ANTOINE: *Entretiens avec Wieland Wagner* (Editions Pierre Belfond, Paris, 1967).

GOLLANCZ, VICTOR: *Journey towards Music* (Gollancz, London, 1964).

GOLLANCZ, VICTOR: *The* Ring *at Bayreuth* (Gollancz, London, 1966).

HERZFELD, FRIEDRICH: *Das neue Bayreuth* (Rembrandt Verlag, Berlin, 1960).

KRAFT, ZDENKO VON: *Der Sohn—Siegfried Wagners Leben und Umwelt* (Leopold Stocker Verlag, Graz, 1969).

OVERHOFF, KURT: *Richard Wagners Tristan-Partitur: eine musikalische-philosophische Deutung* (Verlag Julius Steeger & Co, Bayreuth, 1948).

OVERHOFF, KURT: *Richard Wagners Parsifal* (Franz Perneder, Lindau, 1951).

OVERHOFF, KURT: *Die Musikdramen Richard Wagners* (Verlag Anton Pustet, Salzburg, 1967).

PANOFSKY, WALTER: *Wieland Wagner* (Carl Schünemann Verlag, Bremen, 1964).

SCHÄFER, WALTER ERICH: *Martha Mödl* (Friedrich Verlag, Velber, 1967).

SCHÄFER, WALTER ERICH: *Wieland Wagner: Persönlichkeit und Leistung* (Rainer Wunderlich Verlag, Tübingen, 1970).

SKELTON, GEOFFREY: *Wagner at Bayreuth: Experiment and Tradition* (Barrie & Rockliff, London, 1965).

WAGNER, FRIEDELIND (with PAGE COOPER): *The Royal Family of Bayreuth* (Eyre and Spottiswoode, London, 1948).

WAGNER, WIELAND (Editor): *Richard Wagner und das neue Bayreuth* (Paul List Verlag, Munich, 1962).

WAGNER, WIELAND (Editor): *Hundert Jahre Tristan: 19 Essays* (Verlag Lechte, Emsdetten, 1965).

WESSLING, BERNDT W.: *Astrid Varnay* (Carl Schünemann Verlag, Bremen, 1965).

WESSLING, BERNDT W.: *Wolfgang Windgassen* (Carl Schüne-mann Verlag, Bremen, 1967).

Internationale Wagner-Bibliographie 1961–1966 und Wieland Wagner-Bibliographie (Edition Musica, Bayreuth, 1968).

Wieland Wagner inszeniert Richard Wagner: Ein Bildwerk mit einem Geleitwort von K. H. Ruppel (Rosgarten Verlag, Konstanz, 1960).

Bayreuth Festival programmes and programmes of other opera houses as acknowledged in the text.

INDEX

Adam, Theo 174, 176
Adorno, Theodor 197, 198
Aeschylus 12, 40, 140, 196
Aida (Verdi) 159–60, 210
Aldenhoff, Bernd 100
Alexander, Carlos 174
An allem ist Hütchen schuld (S. Wagner) 74–5, 204
Angeles, Victoria de los 158
Antigonae (Orff) 131, 207
Appia, Adolphe 12, 72

Bachmann, Claus Henning 157, 183
Baer, Emma 33, 41, 42, 148
Balzac, Honoré de 40, 146
Banadietrich (S. Wagner) 36
Bärenhäuter, Der (S. Wagner) 36, 47, 49, 57, 203
Baudelaire, Charles 125
Bäumer, Margarethe 73
Beethoven, Ludwig van 11, 127, 128, 187 (see also *Fidelio*)
Beidler, Franz 28
Beidler, Franz Wilhelm 28, 86
Beidler, Isolde (née von Bülow) 28–9
Béjart, Maurice 157, 172
Berg, Alban 11, 187–9 (see also *Lulu*, *Wozzeck*)
Bergfeld, Joachim 16
Bizet, Georges 11 (see also *Carmen*)
Björling, Sigurd 100

Bloch, Ernst 16, 192, 197, 198, 199
Böhm, Karl 74, 173
Böhme, Kurt 174
Braun, Helena 73
Brecht, Bertolt 12, 178, 196
Breughel the Elder, Pieter 170
Brouwenstijn, Gré 127, 174
Bruder Lustig (S. Wagner) 74
Bülow, Blandine von (Countess Gravina) 28, 56
Bülow, Daniela von (Thode, Daniela) 20, 28, 31, 32, 35, 42, 44, 54–6
Bülow, Isolde von (Beidler, Isolde) 28–9
Bumbry, Grace 157, 172

Calderón de la Barca 12, 164
Carmen (Bizet) 85, 149–50, 160, 208
Chamberlain, Eva (née Wagner) 20, 28–9, 31, 42, 44, 56, 62
Chamberlain, Houston Stewart 19–20, 27, 28–9, 37, 40, 72
Cluytens, André 130, 145
Comoedia de Christi Resurrectione (Orff) 133, 207
Craig, Gordon 12, 72

Dalberg, Friedrich 73, 100
Dalis, Irene 156
Danner, Kilian 73

Danzer, Helmut   16, 40, 46, 49, 51, 131, 191, 192
Devrient, Eduard   111–12
Dickens, Charles. 40
Don Giovanni (Mozart)   132, 190
Drexler, Ellen (Wagner, Ellen) 80, 90

Eberhardt, Paul   16, 53, 97, 101–2, 130, 179
Ebermann, Renate   193
Ebert, Carl   149, 151
Elektra (R. Strauss)   132, 165, 166–7, 169, 175, 187, 193, 210, 212, 213
Ericson, Barbro   172

Festspielhaus, Bayreuth (as building)   26–7, 34, 89, 90, 122, 138
Fidelio (Beethoven)   127–9, 139, 187, 194, 206, 213
Fischer-Dieskau, Dietrich   174
Flagstad, Kirsten   99–100
Fliegende Holländer, Der   62–3, 79, 145–7, 175, 188, 193, 203, 209, 212, 214
Frantz, Ferdinand   73
Freischütz, Der (Weber)   62, 68, 72, 204
Freud, Sigmund   89
Furtwängler, Wilhelm   42, 44, 50, 53, 98

Geissmar, Berta   42
Gesellschaft der Freunde von Bayreuth (Society of the Friends of Bayreuth)   93, 136
Gianicelli, Carl   33
Giulini, Carlo Maria   172
Gluck, Christoph Willibald   11, 117 (see also Orfeo ed Euridice)
Goebbels, Joseph   63

Goethe, Johann Wolfgang von 40, 124, 140
Goléa, Antoine   69, 131, 133, 138, 150, 158, 159, 175, 187
Gollancz, Victor   128–9, 193, 195
Golther, Professor   56
Götterdämmerung: see Ring des Nibelungen, Der
Gravina, Blandine, Countess (née von Bülow)   28, 56
Gravina, Count Gilberto   16, 154
Greindl, Josef   174
Gross, Adolf von   37

Haas, Willy   82
Hanke, Willi   63, 65
Hartmann, Rudolf   16, 62, 93, 100, 116–17, 133
Heger, Robert   173
Heilige Linde, Die (S. Wagner) 37
Heyworth, Peter   129
Himmler, Heinrich   36
Hindemith, Paul   115, 190
Hitler, Adolf   14, 32, 34, 42, 44, 74, 182, 190; and Wieland Wagner   14, 21–2, 24, 45, 46–7, 54, 56, 57, 61, 79–80, 81, 195; and Winifred Wagner 20–3, 50; at Bayreuth 19–25, 50–1
Hoesslin, Franz von   23
Homer   89
Höngen, Elisabeth   100
Hopf, Adolf   16, 47
Hotter, Hans   174, 193

Ibsen, Henrik   167

Joachim, Heinz   160
Jochum, Eugen   119, 121, 122
Jung, C. G.   89, 125, 199

Karajan, Herbert von 98–9, 111, 119
Katz, Margarete 73
Keilberth, Joseph 119, 121, 122
Klages, Ludwig 89
Klemperer, Otto 144–5
Klindworth, Karl 29, 30
Klindworth, Senta: see Wagner, Winifred
Knappertsbusch, Hans 98, 102, 118–19, 121, 173, 189–90
Kraft, Zdenko von 30
Krauss, Clemens 62, 119, 121, 173
Kuën, Paul 73, 100, 101

Lafferentz, Bodo 16, 78–9, 80, 84
Lafferentz, Verena (née Wagner) 16, 33, 36, 78, 79, 80, 83
Lauterwasser, Siegfried 16
Legge, Walter 16, 99, 144
Lehmann, Peter 191, 193
Leider, Frida 51
Leinsdorf, Erich 145
Levi, Hermann 23
Liszt, Franz 11, 13, 29, 38, 190
Lohengrin 21, 50, 118, 139–44, 147, 158, 175, 193, 208, 209, 210, 212
London, George 174, 176
Ludwig II, King of Bavaria 20, 26–7, 79, 95, 134
Lulu (Berg) 187–8, 213
Lüsenhop, Ernst 16, 65, 69–70, 71, 73, 74, 86

Mann, Anna 36
Markevitch, Igor 121–2
Maschat, Erich 16, 62
Matacic, Lovro von 145
Mayer, Hans 197, 198–9
Meistersinger von Nürnberg, Die 34, 94, 133–7, 158, 169–72, 173, 194, 204, 207, 211
Melchinger, Siegfried 197
Meyer, Kerstin 174, 182
Mödl, Martha 100, 101, 111, 119, 166–7
Moore, Henry 160
Moses und Aron (Schönberg) 132
Mozart, Wolfgang Amadeus 59, 85, 132
Muck, Karl 42, 44, 56
Mussolini, Benito 34

Neidlinger, Gustav 127, 174
Newman, Ernest 104, 128
Nilsson, Birgit 174, 187

Oertel, Helene 73
Orfeo ed Euridice (Gluck) 117–18, 130, 139, 206
Orff, Carl 11, 16, 58, 130–3, 190, 192
Otello (Verdi) 175, 212
Overhoff, Kurt 16, 59–60, 61–2, 63, 68, 70, 72, 74, 75, 82–3, 85, 86–9, 90, 91, 97, 107, 114–15, 132

Palm, Curt 16, 53
Panofsky, Walter 89, 114, 115, 132, 140, 149, 159, 160, 194, 195, 197
Papen, Franz von 46
Parsifal 23, 27, 34, 45, 50, 52–6, 83, 85, 94, 104–8, 109, 118, 119, 121, 130, 190–1, 193, 194, 203, 205
Pélleas et Mélisande (Debussy) 132, 190
Pellegrini, Alfred 115–16
Pistor, Gotthelf 73
Pitz, Wilhelm 99, 192
Pölzer, Julius 73
Preetorius, Emil 45, 52

Preuss, Friedrich   71

Ravel, Maurice   121
Reinhardt, Richard   67
Reissinger, Gertrud: see Wagner, Gertrud
Resnik, Regina   167
Rheingold: see *Ring des Nibelungen, Der*
Richter, Hans   27
Rienzi   138–9, 207
Ring des Nibelungen, Der   27, 34, 65–74, 83, 108–10, 119, 130, 165, 173, 175, 176–86, 190, 191, 193, 196, 199–200, 203, 204, 205, 206, 207, 210, 211, 212, 213
Ritz, Wolfgang Emil   73
Roller, Alfred   45, 50, 59, 72
Rousseau, Jean Jacques   40
Rysanek, Leonie   100, 146, 151, 174

Salome (R. Strauss)   132, 165, 167–9, 175, 187, 190, 193, 210, 211, 212, 213, 214
Sawallisch, Wolfgang   16, 145, 151, 173
Schadewaldt,   Wolfgang   16, 190, 197, 198
Schäfer, Walter Erich   16, 100, 116, 127, 133, 138, 158, 160, 166, 188, 192
Schippers, Thomas   173
Schmidt, Lieselotte   41–8 passim, 50, 51, 53
Schmolitzky, Arthur   71, 73
Schnorr von Carolsfeld, Ludwig   27
Schopenhauer, Arthur   40, 85, 164
Schröder-Devrient, Wilhelmine   27, 139, 166
Schwarzkopf, Elisabeth   100

Schwarzschwanenreich (S. Wagner)   57, 203
Schweitzer, Albert   110, 115
Sellner, Gustav Rudolf   151, 159
Shakespeare, William   12, 136, 169, 171
Siegfried: see *Ring des Nibelungen, Der*
Sievert, Hildegard   16
Sievert, Ludwig   72–3
Silja, Anja   16, 151–3, 165, 168, 172, 173, 174, 175, 187, 188, 192
Society of the Friends of Bayreuth   93, 136
Sonnenflammen (S. Wagner)   57, 203
Staeger, Ferdinand   58
Stassen, Franz   45–6, 48
Sternengebot (S. Wagner)   36
Stewart, Thomas   174
Stolze, Gerhard   100, 101, 173
Strauss, Franz   168–9
Strauss, Richard   11, 59, 82, 83, 84, 132, 165, 168, 196 (see also *Elektra, Salome*)
Strnad, Oskar   72
Strobel, Gertrud   16
Stuckenschmidt, H. H.   160
Suitner, Otmar   173
Sykes, Christopher   154–5, 156, 171, 176

Tales of Hoffmann (Offenbach)   130, 132, 192
Talvela, Martti   174
Tannhäuser   37–8, 121, 123–7, 130, 140, 157–8, 172, 192, 206, 208, 209, 210, 212
Thode, Daniela (née von Bülow)   20, 28, 31, 32, 35, 42, 44, 54–6
Thode, Henry   28
Thomas, Jess   174

Tietjen, Heinz 43–4, 45, 50, 52, 53, 57, 59, 60–1, 65, 85, 97, 140, 195
Töpper, Hertha 100
Tosca (Puccini) 132
Toscanini, Arturo 43, 44
Treptow, Günther 100
Tristan und Isolde 37, 82, 85, 86–9, 110–12, 119, 130, 144, 145, 149, 160–4, 173, 175, 190, 193, 206, 208, 209, 210, 211, 212, 214

Uhde, Hermann 100, 101, 120

Varnay, Astrid 100, 101, 103, 173–4
Verdi, Giuseppe 11, 175 (see also *Aida*, *Otello*)
Vinay, Ramon 111, 156, 174

Wächter, Eberhard 174
Wagner, Cosima (née Liszt) 20, 27, 33–8 passim, 39, 72, 89; Wieland Wagner's views on 12–13, 55, 67, 194–5
Wagner, Daphne 16, 84, 172
Wagner, Ellen (née Drexler) 80, 90
Wagner, Eva (daughter of Richard Wagner): see Chamberlain, Eva
Wagner, Eva (daughter of Wolfgang Wagner) 90
Wagner, Friedelind 33, 35, 36, 39, 41, 84, 85–6
Wagner, Gertrud (née Reissinger) 16, 47, 52, 53, 58–9, 70, 72, 79, 80, 83–5, 97, 98, 113, 121, 130, 148, 153, 192, 193; first meeting with Wieland Wagner 40; marriage 61; birth of children 62, 78, 81, 84; as choreographer 65,

69, 75, 126, 137, 170, 172
Wagner, Gottfried 90
Wagner, Iris Diana 62, 84, 137
Wagner, Nike 81, 172
Wagner, Richard *passim*; on acting 101; on *Der Fliegende Holländer* 146–7; on *Die Meistersinger von Nürnberg* 134; on *Tristan und Isolde* 111–12; Wieland Wagner's views on 12, 55, 66–7, 94–6, 123–4, 140, 169, 186, 190–1, 195–7
Wagner, Siegfried 19–20, 27–38 *passim*, 43, 57, 72, 74, 192; character 13, 29–30, 35; as composer 36–7, 49, 75; relations with Wieland Wagner 21, 35, 39; terms of will 20, 22, 24, 86, 138. See also under operas: *An allem ist Hütchen schuld; Banadietrich; Bärenhäuter, Der; Bruder Lustig; Heilige Linde, Die; Schwarzschwanenreich; Sonnenflammen; Sternengebot*
Wagner, Verena: see Lafferentz, Verena
Wagner, Wieland: as artist 13, 24, 40, 45–6, 50, 51, 52, 58–9, 61, 83, 84; as conductor 60; as musician 36, 43, 49, 59–60, 83, 85, 88–9; views on costume 72, 161, 170; lighting 70–1, 72, 94, 101–2, 159, 164; music 66–7, 95–6, 128, 131–3, 173; production 94–6, 132, 141–3, 150, 194; scenery 66–7, 69–72, 150, 158, 160, 171, 177–8, 179; singing 99–101, 166, 174; Richard Wagner 12, 55, 66–7, 94–6, 123–4, 140, 169, 186, 190–1, 195–7. **Productions by:** *Aida* 159–

Wagner, Wieland—*cont.*
60, 210; *An allem ist Hütchen schuld* 74–5, 204; *Antigonae* 131, 207; *Carmen* 149–50, 208; *Comoedia de Christi Resurrectione* 133, 207; *Elektra* 166–7, 210, 212, 213; *Fidelio* 127–9, 187, 206, 213; *Fliegende Holländer, Der* 145–7, 151–2, 209, 212, 214; *Lohengrin* 140–4, 208, 209, 210, 212; *Lulu* 188, 213; *Meistersinger von Nürnberg, Die* 133–7, 169–72, 207, 211; *Orfeo ed Euridice* 117–18, 130, 206; *Otello* 175, 212; *Parsifal* 104–8, 118–19, 205; *Rienzi* 138–9, 207; *Ring des Nibelungen, Der* 65–74, 108–10, 176–86, 203–5, 206–7, 210, 211, 212, 213; *Salome* 167–9, 210, 211, 212, 213, 214; *Tannhäuser* 123–7, 157–8, 172, 206, 208, 209, 210, 212; *Tristan und Isolde* 110–12, 160–4, 206, 208, 209, 210, 211, 212, 214; *Wozzeck* 188–9, 214. Sets by: *Bärenhäuter, Der* 47, 49; *Fliegende Holländer, Der* 63; *Parsifal* 50, 52–6. (See also under titles of above operas and *Don Giovanni; Freischütz, Der; Moses und Aron; Pélleas et Mélisande; Sonnenflammen; Schwarzschwanenreich; Tales of Hoffmann; Tosca.*
Wagner, Winifred (née Williams) 16, 29–32, 33, 34, 38, 40–1, 44, 74, 75, 80, 91, 165; character 13–15, 35; as director of Bayreuth Festival 15, 23, 42–3, 50, 60–1, 86; relations with Hitler 19–23, 50–1, 81, 90; relations with Wieland Wagner 35, 47, 49–50, 52, 59, 79, 82, 92–3, 114, 195
Wagner, Wolf Siegfried 16, 78, 84, 148
Wagner, Wolfgang 11, 13, 14, 15, 22, 33, 36, 46, 56, 60–1, 64, 74, 78, 80, 90, 91, 93, 115, 118, 122–3, 145, 155, 156–7, 174, 193
Wahnfried, Villa, Bayreuth: building of 27; damaged by bombs 80; restored 90–2; family grave at 27–8, 35–6, 38, 44; life at 30–32, 34–6, 39–44, 50–51, 65, 79, 89–90, 113–14, 148; Wieland Wagner's attitude to 62, 92, 195
Walküre, Die: see *Ring des Nibelungen, Der*
Ward, David 154
Weber, Ludwig 100, 101
Wedekind, Frank 167, 188
Westernhagen, Curt von 197
Wilde, Oscar 167
Williams, Winifred: see Wagner, Winifred
Windgassen, Wolfgang 100, 101, 127, 173, 174, 175, 184, 191, 192
Wohlfahrt, Erwin 174, 183
Wolzogen, Hans von 19–20, 27, 37, 42
Wozzeck (Berg) 187, 188–9, 214